BELOVED EMMA

BELOVED EMMA

THE ILLUSTRATED LIFE STORY OF

LORI E. WOODLAND
ILLUSTRATED BY LIZ LEMON SWINDLE

DESERET
BOOK

Salt Lake City, Utah

Text © 2008 Lori Echevarria Woodland

Illustrations © Liz Lemon Swindle: *More Than Friends* (page 13); *My Beloved Emma* (page 26); *Elect Lady* (page 41); *Father's Gift* (page 49); *While Emma Sleeps* (page 57); *Emma's Hymns* (page 73); *Thou Shalt Be Comforted* (page 91); *Of One Heart: Emma on the Ice* (page 98); *Day of God's Power* (page 103); *Time to Laugh* (page 111); *Tiny Hands* (page 119); *Fiddle Dance* (page 133); *Going as a Lamb* (page 141); *Forgive Me, Joseph* (page 155)

Library of Congress Cataloging-in-Publication Data

Woodland, Lori E.
    Beloved Emma : the illustrated life story of Emma Smith / Lori E. Woodland ; illustrations by Liz Lemon Swindle.
        p.   cm.
    Includes bibliographical references and index.
    ISBN 978-1-59038-828-0 (hardbound : alk. paper)
    1. Smith, Emma Hale.   2. Mormons—United States—Biography.
I. Swindle, Liz Lemon, 1953–   II. Title.
    BX8695.S515W66 2008
    289.3092—dc22
    [B]   2008023171

Printed in the United States of America
Inland Graphics, Menomonee Falls, WI

10   9   8   7   6   5   4   3   2   1

To my beloved Rich
and for Tina, Kelly, Alicia,
and Christian

Preface

$\mathcal{M}$Y INTEREST IN EMMA HALE SMITH, wife of the Prophet Joseph, was first piqued in the spring of 2000 when I was invited by the coordinator of the Rexburg region seminaries to give a presentation on women of the Restoration at their annual summer in-service meeting. Prior to receiving that invitation, I knew very little about Emma and the role she had played in the restoration of the gospel, but at some time during my preparation for the presentation, my heart turned to her. I was astounded by her willingness to support and sustain her prophet-husband and her gracious and spirited attitude in doing so. Needless to say, most of my teaching that day focused on her.

Soon after giving the presentation, I received invitations to share what I knew about Emma at firesides, workshops, and dinners. One evening after I spoke at a Relief Society anniversary dinner in Idaho Falls, Idaho, an elderly woman asked if I had written down any of the information I had presented. When I responded that I had not, she firmly said, "Well, you need to."

At that time I was employed at Ricks College as the head women's basketball coach as well as a faculty member in the Department of Religious Education, and I had time for little else. Moreover, I was a basketball coach, not a writer. However, on the morning of June 21, 2000, President Gordon B. Hinckley made an announcement regarding the future of Ricks College that has had an everlasting effect upon my life.

President Hinckley's message that day was threefold. He first announced that Ricks College would no longer be a two-year junior college but a four-year university. Second, he declared that the school would no longer be known as Ricks College but would be named Brigham Young University–Idaho. Third, he stated that BYU–Idaho would not sponsor intercollegiate athletics but would cultivate a broad-based activities program to involve most of the student body.

I was stunned! The women's basketball program, which we had worked so hard to build into a recognized and respected regional and national power, was finished. I remember going home that day and praying for understanding and direction. I recall telling the neighbor children and their parents that afternoon, "When the prophet speaks, the debate is over!"

Though the days and weeks that followed were not easy, I continued to pray for understanding and the strength to support President Hinckley in his decision. Soon I was invited to teach full time in the Department of Religious Education, once the intercollegiate basketball program was phased out in 2002. Approximately two weeks before jumping into my new assignment in the religion department, the BYU–Idaho administration asked me to direct the new Physical Activities Program. Little did I know at the time that my willingness to accept this new position would have what I consider eternal consequences.

For the next three years, I had the blessed opportunity to grow into an understanding of what the Lord meant when he commanded the Saints in Kirtland to learn "even by study and also by faith" (D&C 88:118). Because the BYU–Idaho Physical Activities Program was something that had never been tried, we had no blueprint to follow. Our only direction came from the Lord. I soon came to know that when we align our will with the Lord's, nothing is impossible. I learned that through the enabling power of the atonement of our Savior, Jesus Christ, I could do things beyond my own natural ability. After all, if Nephi could build a ship with no ship-building experience, with the Lord's direction I could undertake things I had no experience with.

This book about Emma Hale Smith is the most recent result of my learning-by-faith experiences. I acknowledge, first and foremost, the hand of the Lord in this project. I thank several friends who spent their valuable time reading the manuscript. John and Sherrie Bonner are the best proofreaders on this side of the Grand Canyon, and Lisa Thueson, Michelle Jeppesen, and Marilyn Franz gave me confidence in my writing abilities when I needed it the most. Lisa Thueson also spent hours away from her husband and children to assist in my research. Ron Romig, curator of the Community of Christ Archives in Independence, Missouri, was extremely helpful, as was my editor and friend at Deseret Book, Suzanne Brady.

I gratefully acknowledge my colleagues Kyle Walker, Rob Eaton, and Jerry Glenn, who

~ Descendancy Chart ~

Isaac Hale ——————— Elizabeth Lewis Hale   Joseph Smith Sr. ——— Lucy Mack Smith
March 21, 1763   November 19, 1767   July 12, 1771   July 8, 1775
January 11, 1839   February 16, 1842   September 14, 1840   May 14, 1856

Emma Hale Smith ————————————————— **Joseph Smith Jr.**
July 10, 1804   December 23, 1805
April 30, 1879   June 27, 1844

- Alvin
  June 15, 1828–June 15, 1828

- Thaddeus (twin)
  April 30, 1831–April 30, 1831

- Louisa (twin)
  April 30, 1831–April 30, 1831

- Julia Murdock (twin)
  May 1, 1831–September 10 (or 12), 1880

- Joseph Murdock (twin)
  May 1, 1831–March 29, 1832

- Joseph III
  November 6, 1832–December 10, 1914

- Frederick Granger Williams
  June 20, 1836–April 13, 1862

- Alexander Hale
  June 2, 1838–August 12, 1909

- Don Carlos
  June 13, 1840–August 14 (or 15), 1841

- Baby boy
  December 26, 1842–December 26, 1842

- David Hyrum
  November 17, 1844–August 29, 1904

kept me going in the right direction and assisted in reading the manuscript, and Calvin Stephens, who made me research and write until I got it right.

Finally, I wish to express my love and appreciation to my husband and eternal companion, Rich, who researched, read, and told me at least a thousand times that my writing was great.

Chapter One

GROWING UP ALONG THE NORTHERN BANKS of the Susquehanna River in the township of Harmony, Pennsylvania, was a happy time for young Emma Hale. Those who knew Emma best considered her a tomboy because of her zeal and enthusiasm for the outdoors. The waterways of the Susquehanna served as her canoeing thoroughfare, and the dense forests along the riverbank were her playground.

Born on July 10, 1804, Emma was the seventh of the nine Hale children and "the idol or favorite of the family."[1] She had four older brothers and two older sisters and was often called upon to look after her younger brother and sister. In her youth, Emma was tall and gangly, with strong arms, brown hair, and piercing brown eyes. Her "quick wit" and pleasant personality endeared her to neighbors and friends even as a child.[2]

Playmates were plentiful in Harmony. Besides her eight siblings, Emma had a covey of cousins living nearby. Together they coursed the river in canoes and rode horseback along the riverbanks and throughout the valley. Emma's equestrian prowess and love for horses was admired and noted throughout her lifetime, but "the quality her brothers admired most in Emma was her talent—queer for a girl—of being able to hold her tongue when it was necessary. Like most children who do their thinking in silence, she was sensitive. When her feelings were hurt or the boys adventured beyond the restrictions of Isaac and Elizabeth, she did not tell."[3]

Emma's parents, Isaac and Elizabeth Hale, along with Elizabeth's brother Nathaniel Lewis and his wife, Sara, were among the first to settle in the virtually uninhabited northern Pennsylvania river valley. In or about the year 1790, the two newly wedded couples left their home in Wells, Vermont, with all they owned packed into a cart drawn by a yoke of steers and traveled a distance of about two hundred and twenty miles to their new home near the Susquehanna.[4]

Isaac had set eyes upon their eventual homesite a few years before. He left the security of Vermont to try "the West," where he boarded with a Major Daniel Buck in Ouaquago (now Windsor), New York. While exploring the country south of Ouaquago and hunting for game with which to pay his board, Isaac happened upon the spot along the Susquehanna where he and Elizabeth returned to settle. Nathaniel and Sara settled close by, and later several of Elizabeth's siblings and her parents located near them.

Respected in the community, the Hales lived comfortably on their family farm and "were pioneers of a self-reliant race, brave, honest, of unshaken fidelity and unquestioned integrity."[5] Emma's father, a veteran of the Revolutionary War, provided well for his wife and children. "Father Hale, as he was called, was a pious, an honest, and a shrewd man, who settled in that rough region of country in an early period in order to gratify his propensity for hunting."[6] He was known "as a 'mighty hunter' who 'slaughtered about a hundred deer annually, most of which he sent to the Philadelphia market.'"[7]

Isaac had a unique process for curing and transporting the meat from the wilds and at times bartered for work on the farm with some of the game he took. He was also very generous with his take. Often less-fortunate neighbors would find salt-cured deer or elk meat on their doorstep, left there by Isaac after a successful hunt.

Elizabeth operated an inn—commonly called a tavern—in her home and welcomed travelers moving up and down the Susquehanna and boarders working in the area. Her guests were made comfortable and fed well. While working at the inn Emma learned and began to hone her skills as a gracious hostess and an excellent cook. Travelers "often partook of a good repast of venison, eels, and buckwheat cakes, prepared by her hands."[8]

Education was a priority in Elizabeth's home. All the Hale children could read and write, and Emma enjoyed learning and excelled in the classroom. The Harmony community built a log schoolhouse when she was nine years old and three years later hired the most reputable schoolmaster in the area. Sometime during her late teenage years, Emma left home for a year to attend a girls' school and upon her return to Harmony accepted the post of teacher.

The Hale children were raised in a religious environment in which family prayer and reading from the Bible were common practice. Emma's Uncle Nathaniel, who "was ordained [a] Deacon" in 1807, was known as "a respectable minister of the Methodist Episcopal Church, a man of veracity, and good moral character."[9] "He was rough as a mountain-crag, but deeply pious. . . . He went from house to house inviting the people to come out to meeting. . . . Many were pricked in the heart; [and] a great revival followed."[10]

Emma came by her quick wit honestly. In 1835, a man attending one of Uncle Nat's sermons in South Windsor related the following story: "Provisions often ran scarce in those early days. In such a time, in 1812, Lewis was reading his bible before going to service on one Sunday, when he saw a deer near his house. Taking down his gun, he shot the deer, dressed it and sent portions to his neighbors. Called to account for breaking the Sabbath, he asked his accusers, 'What do you suppose the Lord sent that deer into my field for?' 'Well, I suppose it was to try you.' 'No it wasn't,' he replied, 'for the Lord knows that when He sends me blessings, I don't wait until the next day to take them.'"[11]

Emma's mother, Elizabeth, was also deeply religious and an active member of the Methodist church for fifty years. A friend said, "I never visited her but I thought I had learned something useful."[12]

Emma, who from an early age was religiously inclined, became a member of the Methodist church as well when only seven years old.[13]

Her father, Isaac, however, had strayed from more traditional methods of worship. His belief in God was based on his own reason rather than revelation and communal worship. According to family tradition, Isaac was converted to Christianity when one day he happened upon seven- or eight-year-old Emma praying in the woods and overheard his innocent young daughter's petition for his lost soul. "His proud heart was broken; . . . his soul was melted in tenderness before his God, and he became a convert."[14] Thereafter Isaac became a staunch member of the Methodist church and held many evening prayer meetings in the Hale home.

Emma grew to be an attractive young woman with many close friends and associates. "Her pale skin was clear and her hair dark and straight. Most often she wore it parted in the middle, but when there was a special occasion she wore a cluster of curls which at times were kept in a small box. . . . It was her hands, though, that were particularly beautiful with their long, tapering fingers suggestive of sensitiveness and strength."[15]

Once she reached full maturity, she stood five feet nine inches tall and "was of excellent form, straight and above medium height, features strongly marked, hair and eyes brown, while her general intelligence and fearless integrity, united with her kindness of heart and splendid physical developments commanded both admiration and respect."[16]

Mrs. Mehetable Doolittle, while visiting her grandparents who lived near the Hales, became acquainted with Emma when they were teenagers. Mrs. Doolittle remembered her as "a very pretty and amiable young lady, with fine accomplishments for that period of our inland history."[17] She later recalled that Emma was "a handsome and attractive girl."[18]

When Emma was sixteen, she found the Susquehanna county fair of 1820 especially enjoyable, "for she had a new dress and saw that the young men were interested in her."[19] The following evening suitors began to call. Some attracted her attention, but none turned her head as quickly and as fully as the broad-shouldered, handsome worker who came to board at the inn five years later in November 1825.

Chapter Two

ANOTHER WARM SUMMER HAD COME and gone at the Hale farm, and the onset of unusually cold and wet weather extinguished the blazing New England fall colors earlier than usual in 1825. Emma was busy in her classroom teaching from books used at the time in the area schools. Eager young minds were learning lessons from "Webster's, Crandal's Spelling Books, English readers, Walker's dictionary, Daboll's Arithmetic, Flints Surveying, and Woodridges' & Willett's Geographies."[1]

Elizabeth's inn was in full operation, providing weary travelers and workers hearty meals and a clean, comfortable bed. Isaac and the boys were ever busy on the farm, finishing the last of the grain harvest and looking forward to the fall hunt. Nothing of consequence was happening in the community with the exception of a tale of lost treasure being stirred up by a shirttail relative of Isaac's. William Hale had become enchanted by local folklore that a lost Spanish silver mine was located just northeast of the Hale home, and he was determined to find it. Similar tales of lost treasures and mines rich with ore were common at the time, especially in rural New England.

Motivated by poverty and a lack of physical ambition, William formed a partnership with Josiah Stowell, a farmer living approximately twenty-five miles up the river in South Bainbridge, New York. Stowell—a man of considerable means, who had a solid reputation among his neighbors—had for years heard of the lost mine and was similarly convinced the treasure existed.

In October 1825, when Stowell traveled up the Erie Canal to Manchester, New York, to visit his oldest son, Simpson, he heard talk of a young man in the neighborhood by the name of Joseph Smith who "possessed certain means by which he could discern things invisible to the natural eye."[2] Stories of Joseph's receiving visitations from angels and his testimony of an ancient record written on plates of gold hidden in the earth were being spread throughout the town for anyone who cared to listen.

The Smiths farmed in Manchester and for additional income often hired on for wages with other area farmers or businessmen, who described them as industrious and hard workers. The prospect of hiring someone who could look into the earth and see things buried, coupled with a tough physical work ethic, excited Stowell. He soon paid the Smiths a visit to persuade Joseph to return with him to Pennsylvania to use his unusual powers to help locate the mine.

Joseph initially tried to dissuade him from continuing his digging; however, Stowell was persistent in his pursuit of the treasure and would not consider abandoning it. He offered high wages and a portion of the take from the mine, which eventually convinced Joseph and his father, Joseph Smith Sr., to accompany him to Harmony.

Upon the Smiths' arrival in Pennsylvania, papers of partnership for the mining venture were drawn up, signed, and witnessed by Isaac and Emma's older brother David. Both men initially supported the undertaking and seemed enthralled with the possibility of finding the old mine on their property. The agreement stated that Joseph and his father were to receive two-elevenths of the take from the mine, which was reported possibly to contain "coined money and bars or ingots of Gold or Silver."[3]

When Joseph entered the inn of Isaac and Elizabeth Hale to board on that cold November day, the attraction between him and Emma seemed almost immediate. He was not blind to her good looks and sense of humor, and she enjoyed his thoughtful and kind manner.

Though Emma was somewhat reserved in social settings and sheltered from the harshness of the world, it was evident to him that she was intelligent and had a mind of her own. In turn, Emma, who was nearly a year and a half older than Joseph, was impressed with his innocent self-confidence and maturity. He was bolder and more open in conversation than she, and at gatherings when conversation could have been awkward, Joseph was able to talk easily and openly.

The mining venture didn't last long, nor did Joseph's stay in the inn. After working for less than a month without success, he finally "prevailed with the old gentleman [Stowell] to cease digging."[4] Joseph, however, did not want to cease his relationship with Emma, and quickly found other work in the area, which enabled him to stay close by. He worked for Stowell for a short time, cutting timber on his farm, and then hired on with Joseph Knight, another respected farmer on the Susquehanna.

Although occasion for courting was limited, Joseph made time to call on Emma, and what was at first friendship blossomed into an eternal love. Both possessed and sensed in each other an unusual spiritual maturity, and religion was certainly a topic of their private conversations. Unfortunately, records regarding precisely when Joseph shared with her his experience in the Sacred Grove and his several experiences with the angel Moroni are no longer extant; however, when he did confide in her, she was receptive to his story and recognized his testimony as truth.

Within a few months' time the young couple desired to marry. Joseph knew it was proper to obtain Isaac's blessing on the union and therefore mustered the courage to approach him and ask for Emma's hand. Remembering the occasion, Isaac said, "Young Smith made several visits at my house, and at length asked my consent to his marrying my daughter Emma. This I refused, and gave him my reasons for so doing; some of which were, that he was a stranger, and followed a business that I could not approve [apparently treasure hunting]; he then left the place."[5]

It is impossible to ascertain what actually ignited Isaac's opposition to Joseph. Though he professed that his refusal was based upon Joseph's being a "money digger," he had initially approved of the treasure digging, as evidenced by his witnessing the agreement drawn up by the participating parties. A more likely reason for his disapproval was that on March 20 of that year Joseph had been arrested on charges of "being a disorderly person and imposter."[6] Peter Bridgeman, a nephew of Mrs. Stowell's, felt Joseph was duping his uncle Josiah for money and filed the false charges. Even though Joseph was released after Stowell testified favorably in his behalf, his reputation in the community had been called into question.

Joseph, however, always believed that Isaac's distasteful feelings were fostered by Joseph's sharing his spiritual manifestations and testimony with persons in the community. He later wrote, "Owing to my continuing to assert that I had seen a vision, persecution still followed me, and my wife's father's family were very much opposed to our being married."[7]

There is scant evidence that Emma's mother and sisters disapproved of Joseph, but some of her brothers did join their father in his animosity towards him. "Once, on a fishing trip when the Hale boys teased the usually good-natured Joseph beyond endurance, he threw off his coat and offered to fight them."[8]

Whatever the reason for their disapproval, Emma's father and brothers were among those who partially fulfilled Moroni's prophecy to Joseph when he appeared to him in his bedroom that night in September 1823. On that initial visit, the angel told Joseph that his "name should be had for good and evil among all nations, kindreds, and tongues, or that it should be both good and evil spoken of among all people" (Joseph Smith–History 1:33).

While the Hales and others believed the evil rumors circulating about Joseph, those who took the time to get to know him liked this young man, who testified openly of heavenly messengers having appeared to him. Two of Joseph Knight's sons, Newel and Joseph Jr., developed close ties with the young prophet. In his journal, Newel later wrote: "The business in which my father was engaged often required him to have hired help, and among the many he from time to time employed was a young man by the name of Joseph Smith, Jr., to whom I was particularly attached. His noble deportment, his faithfulness and his kind address, could not fail to win the esteem of those who had the pleasure of his acquaintance. . . . in all his boyish sports and amusements, I never knew any one to gain advantage over him, and yet he was always kind and kept the good will of his playmates. . . .

"During this time, [he] would entertain us with accounts of the wonderful things which had happened to him. It was evident to me that great things were about to be accomplished through him—that the Lord was about to use him as an instrument in His hands to bring to pass the great and mighty work of the last days."[9]

Joseph Knight Jr. said that he and Joseph "worked and slept together," adding "my father said Joseph was the best hand he ever hired."[10] Stowell's youngest son, Josiah Jr., who attended the South Bainbridge school with Joseph when the farm work slowed, described him as "a fine likely young man"[11] and added that Joseph was not profane, never gambled, nor tried to deceive or cheat anyone.

Sometime after the trial and Isaac's refusing him Emma's hand in marriage, Joseph had to return to Manchester for his September 22, 1826, visit to the Hill Cumorah and his annual tutorial appointment with the angel Moroni. After keeping close company for several months and undoubtedly not wanting to separate, Emma and Joseph bade each other good-bye, and Joseph traveled to his home in upstate New York with Josiah Stowell and Joseph Knight.

Joseph's mother, Lucy, said Stowell and Knight made the trip to the Smith farm with her son "for the purpose of procuring a quantity of either wheat or flour; and we . . . made a contract with them in which we agreed to deliver a certain quantity of flour to them the ensuing fall."[12] Apparently a spoken arrangement for Smith's crop, made between Joseph's father and the Susquehanna River farmers, had transpired while Joseph Sr. was searching for the lost mine in Harmony the previous November.

Having his family enter into such a business agreement with his Pennsylvania acquaintances may have been encouraging for Joseph. In his young mind the agreement seemed to erase the blot on his reputation and put him in a more favorable light with Emma's father. It also offered Joseph the opportunity to continue to maintain ties along the Susquehanna and with his sweetheart, Emma.

Chapter Three

RETURNING TO MANCHESTER WAS BITTERSWEET for Joseph. Arriving in time to help with the fall harvest and seeing family and friends once again was delightful. He enjoyed farming, and the several months he had spent working along the Susquehanna was the longest time he had stayed away from home. But returning to the news that his brother Hyrum was engaged to marry Jerusha Barden undoubtedly caused his heart to yearn for Emma.

Additionally, Joseph continued to mourn the death of his oldest brother, Alvin, who had died unexpectedly in November 1823. The brothers had been particularly close, and Alvin "manifested, if such could be the case, greater zeal and anxiety in regard to the Record that had been shown to Joseph, than any of the rest of the family." Alvin had called Joseph to his deathbed and counseled him to be faithful, keep the commandments, "and do everything that lies in your power to obtain the Record."[1] So as the time drew close for Joseph to make his annual trip to the Hill Cumorah the loss of his beloved brother, combined with his missing Emma, weighed heavy on his heart.

On September 22, 1826, as he had done for the previous three years, Joseph climbed the hill approximately three miles from his home to meet Moroni. Again he was taught those things necessary for him to know relative to the coming forth of the Book of Mormon and the restoration of the gospel. Furthermore, according to Joseph Knight Sr., the young prophet on this occasion was given additional instruction regarding his immediate personal affairs. Moroni instructed him that he would receive the plates the following year "if he brought with him the right person."[2] When Joseph asked who the right person might be, it was made manifest that Emma was the one to accompany him.

Now motivated by his attraction to Emma, loneliness, and this revelation, Joseph set out in early November to take Emma as his bride. His choice for a wife was approved by the Lord Himself, and getting to Harmony as soon as possible was Joseph's only ambition.

Before her son left, Lucy remembered that Joseph "called my husband and myself aside and said, 'I have been very lonely ever since Alvin died and I have concluded to get married, and if you have no objections to my uniting myself in marriage with Miss Emma Hale, she would be my choice in preference to any other woman I have ever seen.' We were pleased with his choice and not only consented to his marrying her, but requested him to bring her home with him and live with us."[3]

Joseph again went to work for and boarded with both the Knights and Stowells after his arrival in Bainbridge. How many visits he paid Emma in Harmony is unknown, but he did visit her, and their affection for each other grew. "Family tradition carries a brightly romantic impression of the relationship which developed between the charismatic young prophet—handsome, fair haired, with blue eyes and baby pink coloring—and the tall, slender girl with olive-toned cheeks, warm brown hair and snapping brown eyes."[4]

What neither Emma nor Joseph knew at the time they were courting was that they were distant cousins. Their mothers, Elizabeth Lewis Hale and Lucy Mack Smith, were both descendants of John Howland, one of 102 passengers on the *Mayflower*. During the voyage to the Americas, the eighteen- or nineteen-year-old Howland went on deck during a fierce storm and was thrown into the sea. Miraculously catching hold of "the topsail halyards which hung overboard and ran out at length . . . he held his hold (though he was sundry fathoms under water) till he was hauled up by the same rope to the brim of the water, and then with boat hook and other means got into the ship again and his life saved."[5]

Joseph approached Isaac once again to ask permission to marry his daughter. Quite possibly coached by Emma, on this occasion Joseph made his request with confidence and was outfitted to impress the older man. Instead of Joseph's approaching Isaac dressed like a poor farm boy holding his hat in his hand, Joseph Knight and his family had come to his assistance. This time he arrived in a sleigh pulled by a high-spirited horse and dressed in new clothes. Emma was undoubtedly impressed with Joseph's handsome appearance, but Isaac was not. To the young couple's dismay, he again flatly refused his consent.

Discouraged but undaunted by Isaac's second refusal, Emma and Joseph had little recourse but to wed without her father's approval. On January 18, 1827, after a courtship of fifteen months, they were married by Squire Zechariah Tarbell in South Bainbridge, New York. Emma described her wedding day to her eldest son, Joseph Smith III: "I was visiting at Mr. Stowell's, who lived in Bainbridge, and saw your father there. I had no intention of marrying when I left home; but, during my visit . . . , being importuned by your father, aided by Mr. Stowell, who urged me to marry him, and preferring to marry him [than] to any other man I knew, I consented."[6]

A witness to the wedding party, who at the time lived nearby, saw Emma and Joseph traveling with Josiah Stowell Jr. and his sisters Rhoda and Miriam in their sleigh towards the Susquehanna River. Reaching the water's edge and the ferry, they crossed on the ice and then traveled up "the east side of the river to the home of Squire Tarbell who married them."[7]

As would be expected, Isaac's account of the elopement is very different from Emma's. Practically charging Joseph with abduction, Isaac was quoted as saying, "While I was absent from home, [he] carried off my daughter into the State of New York, where they were married . . . without my approbation or consent."[8] Indeed, the couple did marry against Isaac's will; however, both were of legal age—he being twenty-one and she twenty-two.

Very soon after the wedding and being transported by Josiah Stowell Sr., Emma and Joseph left the Susquehanna area and traveled the 155 miles to Manchester to take up residence with Father and Mother Smith. Welcomed with open arms by Joseph's family, the newlyweds began their life together—a life filled with love, devotion, hardship, sorrow, and great spiritual growth.

Chapter Four

IT WAS LATE JANUARY OR EARLY FEBRUARY 1827 before Emma and Joseph settled in at the Smith home. Joseph resumed working with his father and brothers on the farm, and Emma set up housekeeping with her new extended family.

Lucy in particular was delighted to welcome another daughter-in-law into her home, as Hyrum and his wife, Jerusha, had lived with the Smiths for a short time after their marriage in November 1826, and Lucy treasured the relationship she and Jerusha developed. Lucy wrote that Hyrum had "formed a matrimonial relation with one of the most excellent of women, with whom I had seen much enjoyment, and I hoped for as much happiness with my second daughter-in-law as I had received from the society of the first, and there was no reason why I should expect anything to the contrary."[1]

Nevertheless, a life of normalcy and comfort was not to be enjoyed by the newlyweds, particularly once they left the security of the farm. Previous to the time when Joseph had related to a local minister, whom he trusted, an account of the First Vision, the Smith family had enjoyed the respect of their neighbors and friends. "The hand of friendship was extended on every side, and we blessed God with our whole heart," said Lucy.[2]

As soon as Joseph's confidence was broken by the clergyman and people in the area heard of Joseph's heavenly visitation, persecution continually followed the family. Joseph was from that time forth ridiculed and shunned by his former friends and associates. Being subjected to persecution was new to Emma, but her testimony of Joseph's sacred experiences was growing more firm. Like him, she could not deny the truth of those experiences.

Emma kept in contact with her family and in August wrote her father to ask if she could return home to retrieve her clothing, furniture, cows, and some additional belongings left behind at the elopement. Isaac readily agreed, responding that "her property was safe and at her disposal."[3]

More Than Friends

Soon after this correspondence, Joseph hired a neighbor to transport them to Harmony. During the journey of four to five days, Emma's anxiety must have grown as the time to meet her father drew near. Isaac's initial reaction was about what she had anticipated, for as they pulled into the yard where she had spent years working, playing, and socializing, Isaac approached Joseph in tears, saying, "You have stolen my daughter and married her. I had much rather have followed her to her grave. You spend your time digging for money . . . and thus try to deceive people."[4] But after the tirade and getting his emotions in check, Isaac invited Emma and Joseph to move back to Harmony and live with the family. Furthermore, he offered to assist Joseph in developing a business in the township. They accepted his offer and made the necessary arrangements before returning to the Smith home. Emma's brother Alva was to go to Manchester later to assist the couple in moving their accumulated assets to Harmony.

In Manchester the persecution continued to raise its ugly head. On one occasion, when Joseph was sent to town by his father to do some business and did not return in time for supper, Emma and the family became worried. "We always had a peculiar anxiety about him whenever he was absent, for it seemed as though something was always taking place to jeopardize his life," recalled his mother some years later. Finally arriving very late and "apparently much exhausted" and seeing everyone's anxiety, Joseph smiled and calmly said, "I have taken the severest chastisement that I have ever had in my life. . . . As I passed by the hill of Cumorah, where the plates are, the angel met me and said that I had not been engaged enough in the work of the Lord; that the time had come for the record to be brought forth; and that I must be up and doing and set myself about the things which God had commanded me to do."[5]

Joseph failed to tell his parents that during this same interview, Moroni had informed him that he should again attempt to obtain the plates on September 22.[6] On the other hand, Joseph did make Emma aware of Moroni's command, and she made the preparations necessary to accompany her husband on this sacred errand.

On September 21, Lucy was up late finishing some work when about midnight Joseph walked into the house and asked if she had "a chest with a lock and key." Not having such a chest and knowing why he wanted it, she became alarmed. Consoling her, Joseph said, "Never mind, I can do very well for the present without it—be calm—all is right."[7] Soon afterward, Emma entered the room wearing her riding dress and bonnet, and together she and Joseph left the house.

It would seem more than a coincidence that Josiah Stowell and Joseph Knight had traveled from the Susquehanna to pay the Smith family a visit and had arrived just the day before. Undoubtedly, Joseph had shared with them at a previous time the approximate date on which he was to receive the record, and they could not resist the opportunity of being in Manchester at that time. The men arriving when they did provided the necessary transportation for Emma and Joseph to make the three-mile trip to the Hill Cumorah. Without alerting Knight by asking to borrow his horse and carriage, Joseph harnessed and hitched the horse and readied the carriage for him and Emma to board for their journey.

Arriving at the base of the hill, Joseph left Emma to wait, and he began his ascent to the place where the record written on plates made of gold was buried. Once there he again met Moroni, and the "heavenly messenger delivered them up to me with this charge: that I should be responsible for them; that if I should let them go carelessly, or through any neglect of mine, I should be cut off; but that if I would use all my endeavors to preserve them, until he, the messenger, should call for them, they should be protected."[8]

Additional communication with the angel took the remainder of the night, and it was dawn before Joseph began the descent to meet his wife. Emma's fears were calmed when, after she had spent the whole of the night alone and undoubtedly anxious and worried, her husband appeared from among the trees. Furthermore, she must have felt reassured to see that he carried with him a heavy article covered with his coat. Whether they had previously discussed his plan to secrete the record once he retrieved it from the hill is not known, but after driving a distance down the road toward the farm, Joseph stopped the carriage and left Emma again to hide the plates.

According to Lucy, Joseph entered the woods and "finding an old birch log much decayed, excepting the bark, which was in a measure sound, . . . took his pocket knife and cut the bark with some care, then turned it back and made a hole of sufficient size to receive the plates."[9] Then disguising the place as carefully as possible, he returned to the carriage, and together they rode home.

Lucy was grateful to see the couple drive into the yard, for in their absence she too had had a distressing experience. Father Smith had come to the kitchen table well before their return and had insisted on having Joseph join him for breakfast. Taking several minutes to convince him to eat without his son, she then had to distract Joseph Knight, who entered the house upset because his horse and carriage had been stolen.

Her anxiety rose even higher when Joseph entered the house without the plates. "I trembled so with fear lest all might be lost in consequence of some failure in keeping the commandments of God that I was under the necessity of leaving the room in order to conceal my feelings. Joseph saw this and said, 'Do not be uneasy, mother, all is right—see here, I have got a key.'"[10]

His mother was perplexed by his answer, so Joseph handed her the object he termed a "key" and allowed her to examine it. Describing the event and the Urim and Thummim, which Joseph had given her, Lucy said, "I knew not what he meant, but took the article of which he spoke into my hands and, upon examination, found—with no covering but a silk handkerchief—that it consisted of two smooth three-cornered diamonds set in glass, and the glasses were set in silver bows, which were connected with each other in much the same way as old-fashioned spectacles. He took them again and left me, but said nothing respecting the record."[11]

Emma and Joseph realized quickly why Moroni had given him such a firm charge to keep the plates safe. The months of October and November were filled with chaos and harrowing experiences, which together they endured. Said Joseph of this time, "No sooner was it known that I had them, than the most strenuous exertions were used to get them from me. Every stratagem that could be invented was resorted to for that purpose. . . . The excitement . . . continued, and rumor with her thousand tongues was all the time employed in circulating falsehoods. . . . If I were to relate a thousandth part of them, it would fill up volumes."[12]

The day after Emma and Joseph returned from the hill, Father Smith made a trip to town and heard that a group of ten or twelve men led by Willard Chase, a Methodist class leader, had joined forces in the neighborhood for the purpose of getting the plates from Joseph. Going to the place where the men were gathered, he overheard the details of their plan and returned home to inform Emma and Lucy of their evil designs.

Joseph had been hired to repair a well for an elderly lady living in Macedon, some three or four miles away, and consequently was not at home. Joseph Sr. asked Emma "if she was able to tell where [the plates] were . . . , or whether they were removed from their place."[13] If Emma knew where the record was secreted, she was not at liberty to reveal the location because she answered that she could not tell him. Rather, she suggested that if Father Smith could get a horse, she would ride to Macedon to inform Joseph of his enemies' plan.

Within a few minutes a horse was caught. A hickory withe was put around its neck to signify that the horse was a stray, and Emma was on her way. Joseph, who had had an impression to climb from the well, met her as she rode bareback into the yard. He listened intently while Emma unfolded the plot and then, using the Urim and Thummim, "which he always kept . . . about his person" and by using them "could ascertain, at any time, the approach of danger, either to himself or the [r]ecord,"[14] saw that the plates were not in immediate danger.

He did, however, feel it wise to return home with her to be readily available if trouble continued to brew.

Once home, Joseph decided to retrieve the plates from their hiding place and, if possible, make them more secure. He sent his youngest brother, Don Carlos, to find Hyrum and bring him to the house. When Hyrum arrived, Joseph asked him to make available a chest with a lock and key and then set off to retrieve the hidden record.

Finding the log where the plates were hidden, he removed them and wrapped them in his linen frock. Thinking it safer to stay off the road, Joseph began his walk home through the woods. He wasn't long on his journey when a man hiding behind a log jumped him and struck him in the head with a gun. Joseph turned, knocked the man down, and ran as hard and fast as he could for home. He was similarly attacked two additional times before he finally ran into the yard and fell behind the fence.

After catching his breath, he again sent Don Carlos to Hyrum's home to request that he bring the chest. Hyrum, who had been anxiously waiting to hear the word, responded instantly. When Hyrum arrived, Joseph secured the plates in the wooden box and, exhausted from fatigue and fright, lay down for a brief rest.

Recovering quickly, he recounted his harrowing adventure to Emma and all who had gathered to listen, including Josiah Stowell and Joseph Knight, who had extended their visit. Showing a disjointed thumb to his eager listeners, Joseph turned to his father and said, "I must stop talking, father, and get you to put my thumb in place, for it is very painful."[15]

Soon after carrying the record home, Joseph was warned to better secure both it and the ancient breastplate that had been entrusted to his care. This was done by taking up a portion of the hearth in the house and laying the plates underneath. No sooner had the hearthstones been replaced than a large group of armed men arrived at the house. Not knowing what else to do to combat the mob, Joseph "threw open the doors,"[16] shouted a command, and all the men and boys ran out of the house at once, frightening and running off the intruders.

Warned on another occasion of an approaching mob, Joseph removed the chest from under the hearth, wrapped both the breastplate and the record in some clothes, and moved them across the road to the cooper's shop where Father Smith made barrels and sap buckets. There he hid them in some flax in the shop loft. He then nailed the empty box closed, removed boards from the floor of the shop, and put the box underneath before replacing the boards. That night a mob looking for the treasure tore up the cooper shop floor and smashed the empty box but failed to find the sacred record.

Another circumstance required Joseph's sisters to secure the plates from a group of evil-doers. Being followed by a group of men when he had the plates with him, Joseph ran into the yard, where he saw Katharine watching him from the door of the house. He "thrust a bundle into her arms" and told her to hide it.[17] She quickly took the bundle into the bedroom, put it in the bed next to her older sister, Sophronia, and got into the bed herself. The girls covered themselves and the record and feigned sleep. When the mob entered the room, they saw the apparently sleeping girls and left without bothering them.

Prowlers were seen on the farm during the night, "and it became necessary to keep a night watch-man on duty," but Moroni's promise had certainly held true.[18] Because Joseph did all within his power to keep the record safe, it was protected through the whole of the mob's rummaging and ransacking.

Eventually, however, the harassment and mob activity intensified, and Emma and Joseph knew they had to leave the area. Remembering the earlier arrangement made with her father and brother in Harmony, they contacted Alva Hale and requested that he come to Manchester as soon as possible to transport them and their property to Pennsylvania.

Chapter Five

ALVA ARRIVED SOMETIME IN EARLY DECEMBER to move Emma and Joseph and their belongings to Harmony. While he and Joseph were in the neighboring town of Palmyra doing business, Joseph was approached by an old friend. In his youth Joseph had often hired on with neighbors in order to supplement the family income, and among those for whom he worked was a prosperous farmer by the name of Martin Harris. Harris became particularly attached to young Joseph and the two had kept in contact. "He was only a poor farm boy and had to work hard for his living," said Harris. "He lived close by my farm, and often worked for me hoeing corn for fifty cents a day."[1]

Knowing Martin was one of his few allies, Joseph was pleased to see him but was taken aback when Harris handed him a bag of silver, saying, "Here, Mr. Smith, is fifty dollars; I give this to you to do the Lord's work with; no, I give it to the Lord for his own work."[2] Joseph initially declined the gift and offered to sign a note for the silver, but Harris refused and insisted on giving him the money.

Joseph felt Martin's sincerity but was slightly skeptical because he suspected Martin had breached an earlier confidence. In the fall of 1824, Joseph Sr. and Hyrum had been walling a basement and digging a well for Harris. Each day Martin found an excuse to stop by the worksite to visit, and invariably he steered the conversation towards Joseph's experiences with the angel Moroni and the gold plates. He "would ask many questions, referring frequently to the Bible to prove that heavenly messengers visiting the earth, was not a new doctrine."[3] The family had carefully guarded the story of the 1823 visit Joseph had had with the angel Moroni and of his seeing the hidden gold plates; however, convinced that Martin was a trustworthy friend, Joseph Sr. confided in him the sacred experience. Not long afterward, the story became a common topic of conversation throughout the area, and Joseph felt Martin might have been the source of it.

Nevertheless, the fifty dollars was much needed, particularly in view of Emma and Joseph's move. Joseph related, "In the midst of our afflictions we found a friend in a gentleman by the name of Martin Harris, who came to us and gave me fifty dollars to assist us on our journey. . . . By this timely aid was I enabled to reach the place of my destination in Pennsylvania."[4]

Rumors spread that a mob was forming in Palmyra to tar and feather Joseph. Feeling their lives were in danger, he and Emma made known the appointed time of their departure and then left with Alva in the night a day or two earlier than planned. They were very careful to secure the plates by filling a barrel "about one-third full of beans," placing the record inside, and then filling the barrel to the brim.[5] Alva cut some heavy clubs in the event weapons might be necessary, and after a tearful good-bye on that cold December night, the trio headed down the road.

Emma and Joseph were met with a warm welcome from her family in Harmony. Even Isaac was amiable, and he aided his wife in making the couple comfortable. They enjoyed their meals downstairs with Emma's parents and siblings, and they were given two upstairs rooms in the Hale home for their residency. One of the rooms Emma decorated and prepared for sleeping, and the other she helped her husband set up for the purpose of translating the record.[6]

It had been nearly impossible for Joseph to find a safe time to work on the translation while living in Manchester. Yet, on a rare occasion, "during the quiet hours of the day," he secreted himself in the house by stretching "a curtain enclosing two windows and the fireplace" and experimented at reading the ancient writings. He soon found that developing the gift to translate was not easy and took a good deal of time and effort. The characters on the plates "were on parallel lines, and by experimenting he learned that they had to be translated from right to left."[7]

Now finding peace and security in Harmony, Joseph at once began to copy some of the characters and later translated some of them using the Urim and Thummim.[8] Isaac was initially patient with the work, referring to the record as a "wonderful book of plates."[9] He was allowed to see and heft the chest in which the record was kept, but his patience was short-lived when he was not permitted to see the plates. He angrily told Joseph he did not want anything in his house he was not allowed to see. Out of respect for his father-in-law's edict, Joseph kept the record hidden in the woods until he and Emma were able to relocate.[10]

Emma's oldest brother, Jesse, had built a house on a parcel of land near his parents and left it empty when he moved to Illinois. The house had two rooms on the ground level with floors "of beautiful hardwood maple," one large room upstairs, and a cellar. Just through the front door was a hall and a stairway to the loft. Underneath this stairway was another set of stairs that led to the cellar. On the main floor was a fireplace, where Emma could do her cooking. There was access to "good cold water just under the brow of the hill south of the house" and also a well on the north side of the property.[11]

The couple arranged to purchase from Isaac for two hundred dollars both the home and the thirteen acres of land on which it sat. Although the house was not completely finished, it was theirs, and Emma immediately went about making it comfortable and attractive. They lived primarily on the main floor of the home and in the west side of the upstairs room. The opposite end of the second-story room—which had a window—was made more private with a makeshift wooden partition, and it was here that Joseph did his translation work.

The move, even though it was only a short distance, kept peace in the family and allowed Emma to continue to be near those she dearly loved. Knowing her mother was close by gave Emma a sense of security when she realized she was pregnant with their first child. She and Joseph were thrilled to start a family, and Emma was grateful Elizabeth would be there at the time of her first delivery.

In February Martin Harris and Hyrum Smith traveled from Palmyra to visit Joseph and Emma. Evidently, Joseph had previously arranged for Martin to take copies of the characters Joseph had made from the plates, together with their translation, to linguists in New York for evaluation. During Joseph's initial visit with Moroni in 1823, the angel had explained that the scripture in Isaiah 29:11–12 had to be fulfilled before the record could be translated. Unknowingly, Martin was about to fulfill the scripture. While in New York, he took the material to Charles Anthon, a professor at Columbia University known for his "literary attainments" (Joseph Smith–History 1:64). Professor Anthon authenticated the characters as being ancient hieroglyphics of some unknown language and signed an affidavit to that effect.

As Martin was leaving, however, Anthon asked him how Joseph had known where to find the gold plates that contained the characters. When Martin said that an angel of God had told him, Anthon asked for the certificate he had signed. He tore it up, saying "that there was no such thing now as ministering of angels, and that if [Martin] would bring the plates to him, he would translate them." Martin informed Anthon that a "part of the plates were sealed, and that [he] was forbidden to bring them," to which Anthon replied, "'I cannot read a sealed book.'"[12] Thus was fulfilled Isaiah's prophecy, which reads: "And the vision of all is become unto you as the words of a book that is sealed, which men deliver to one that is learned, saying, Read this, I pray thee: and he saith, I cannot; for it is sealed: And the book is delivered to him that is not learned, saying, Read this, I pray thee: and he saith, I am not learned" (Isaiah 29:11–12).

When Martin returned to his home in Palmyra from his visit to the East, he put his business affairs in order and prepared again to travel to Harmony to further assist Joseph in the translation of the record. His wife, Lucy, who had been one of Emma and Joseph's greatest antagonists while they were living in Manchester and had been left behind against her will on the first trip, was determined this time to accompany her husband. Martin did not oppose her going with him and agreed to return home with her in a couple of weeks.

Emma and Joseph were not at home when the Harrises arrived in Harmony, so Lucy took advantage of their absence, informing Martin that she had come to see the plates. Immediately, she began "ransacking every nook and corner about the house—chests, trunks, cupboards, etc.," looking for the record.[13] Unsuccessful in her search inside the home, she continued searching outside the house the next day. Her hunt was abruptly halted when she asked Emma if it was usual for snakes to be out in the winter. Emma answered that it was not. Lucy related that in her search she had come upon a huge black snake that hissed at her.

As a result of this incident and failing to find the ancient record, she packed her bag and for the remainder of her visit stayed with a neighbor, whom she had befriended during her futile search in the woods. She also "did all that lay in her power to injure Joseph in the estimation of his neighbors—telling them that he was a grand imposter, and, that by his specious pretensions, he had seduced her husband into the belief that he (Joseph Smith) was some great one, merely through a design upon her husband's property."[14] When she returned to her home in Palmyra, she continued spreading her accusations, telling all who would lend her their ear that Joseph had it in his mind to rob her of all her possessions. She also tried mightily to persuade Martin not to return to Harmony once more to further assist Joseph.

Ignoring her plea, Martin left Palmyra and journeyed to Pennsylvania, arriving at the Smiths' home in early April 1828. Emma and her brother Reuben may have begun to assist Joseph with the translation previous to his return, but as soon as she could make him comfortable in her new home, Martin began to act as the prophet's scribe. Their work began on April 12 and continued until June 14. With only a curtain between them, Martin wrote while Joseph, with the Urim and Thummim fastened to the ancient breastplate, "translated the record by the gift and power of God."[15]

Joseph described the ancient record: "[The] records were engraven on plates which had the appearance of gold, each plate was six inches wide and eight inches long, and not quite so thick as common tin. They were filled with engravings, in Egyptian characters, and bound together in a volume as the leaves of a book, with three rings running through the whole. The volume was something near six inches in thickness, a part of which was sealed. The characters on the unsealed part were small, and beautifully engraved."[16]

Months before, and soon after allowing his mother to see the Urim and Thummim, Joseph also allowed Lucy to hold and likewise examine the ancient breastplate. Later Lucy recounted, "It was wrapped in a thin muslin handkerchief, so thin that I could feel its proportions without any difficulty. It was concave on one side and convex on the other, and extended from the neck downwards, as far as the center of the stomach of a man of extraordinary size. It had four straps of the same material, for the purpose of fastening it to the breast, two of which ran back to go over the shoulders, and the other two were designed to fasten to the hips. They were just the width of two of my fingers (for I measured them), and they had holes in the end of them, to be convenient in fastening."[17]

For Emma, the days and weeks during which the translation process progressed were without notable incident. She occasionally had to endure hurtful rumors that were spreading relative to the work and the integrity of her husband, but in comparison to what she had endured while living in Manchester, life was relatively calm. Additionally, a deep bond of trust was developing between her and Joseph. She knew he was a prophet, called by the Lord to perform a "marvelous work and wonder" (2 Nephi 25:17) for the children of men upon the earth, and he in turn trusted her.

Although she was never allowed to see the record, she said, "The plates often lay on the table without any attempt at concealment, wrapped in a small linen table-cloth, which I had given him to fold them in. I once felt of the plates, as they thus lay on the table, tracing their outline and shape. They seemed to be pliable like thick paper, and would rustle with a metallic sound when the edges were moved by the thumb, as one does sometimes thumb the edges of a book." When her son Joseph III asked her if she had ever "uncovered the plates and examined them," she replied, "I did not attempt to handle the plates, other than I have told you (referring to the aforementioned incident), nor uncover them to look at them. I was satisfied that it was the work of God, and therefore did not feel it to be necessary to do so."[18]

Emma found that carrying her first child was more difficult than she had anticipated. She was experiencing a hard pregnancy and was sick much of the time. But on good days she performed the usual tasks of a housewife and spent memorable hours working and visiting with her mother and sisters. What's more, she had occasion to visit with old friends, to whom she would bear testimony of the sacred work Joseph had been called to perform. According to

Eliza Winters Squires, she was often in the Smith home and "much in [Emma's] company." The two were on "very intimate terms," and Emma often told her of Joseph's finding the gold plates.[19]

Though her health was delicate, feeling their unborn child grow within her was surely an exhilarating and sacred experience, one she must have shared with Joseph during those restless and uncomfortable nights. He in turn undoubtedly talked of the translation as that work progressed. Indeed, all seemed right in their lives. Nevertheless, dark days were on the horizon—days that would humble the young couple and shake them to their very core.

Chapter Six

As the time for Emma's delivery neared, Joseph and Martin finished the translation of the book of Lehi, the first book on the plates, and the manuscript was now 116 pages in length. Because the translation process demanded clarity of mind and a great deal of concentration, it is likely Joseph desired to turn his full attention to Emma until the baby was born and she had recovered from the birth. Keeping up with the housework and providing meals for the two men had become increasingly burdensome for her, and she was undoubtedly relieved when Joseph decided to break from the work for a time.

Martin was eager to return home to Palmyra and had been pressing Joseph to allow him to take the 116 pages with him in the hope that physical evidence of the reality of the ancient record might appease his family's narrow-mindedness and his wife's intolerance. Consequently, Joseph sought permission from the Lord through the Urim and Thummim for Martin to take the manuscript, and "the answer was that he must not." When Martin pressured Joseph into inquiring a second time, he reluctantly did so, and again the request was denied. Still not satisfied with the answer, Martin insisted Joseph ask one more time. At this third inquiry, the Lord relented, "and permission was granted him to have the writings on certain conditions: that he show them only to his brother, Preserved Harris, his own wife, his father and mother, and a Mrs. Cobb, a sister to his wife."[1] Still unsettled, Joseph required him to enter into a solemn covenant that he would do only as the Lord instructed. To this Martin readily agreed. The covenant was made, and he left for Palmyra with the only copy of the sacred manuscript.

Shortly after Martin's departure, Emma began to feel the beginning pains of labor, and the local midwife, Rhoda Skinner, was called in to attend her. After a very long and difficult labor, an infant son was born to the young couple on June 15, 1828. Tragically, the baby boy, whom they named Alvin after Joseph's oldest brother, had obvious physical

My Beloved Emma

defects and lived only a few hours. Heartbroken, Emma and Joseph buried him near their home.

The strain of the labor, delivery, and death of the child was almost more than Emma could bear, and for some time Joseph desperately worried that he might lose her as well. For two weeks she lingered between life and death, and he attended to her every need. He "slept not an hour in undisturbed quiet" until Emma gradually began to show improvement, both physically and emotionally.[2]

Encouraged by his wife's beginning recovery, Joseph's thoughts turned to Martin and the manuscript. He had heard nothing from Martin since his departure, and Joseph's anxiety about the 116 pages heightened. Emma, wondering herself why Martin had not returned or sent word, convinced Joseph to go to Palmyra and seek him out. Joseph at first refused to leave but agreed when he saw that she too was worried. So, after arranging for Emma's mother to stay with her, he boarded the first stage for Palmyra.

He reached his parents' farm just outside Palmyra in the small community of Manchester in the early morning hours several days later and immediately sent for Martin. Expecting him to arrive shortly, Lucy prepared breakfast for Joseph and the family, but to their chagrin Martin failed to arrive. They continued to wait for his arrival throughout the morning. Eventually, at half past noon, they saw him slowly walking, head down, up the road towards the house.

When he reached the gate to the yard, he stopped, climbed the fence, and sat atop it with his hat over his eyes. Finally, jumping down, he entered the house and joined in the meal with the Smiths but suddenly dropped his utensils. Hyrum, observing Martin's strange behavior, asked him if he were sick. Martin put his head in his hands and sobbed, "'Oh, I have lost my soul! I have lost my soul!'" Hearing his cry of anguish, Joseph "sprang from the table, exclaiming, 'Martin, have you lost that manuscript? Have you broken your oath, and brought condemnation upon my head as well as your own?'" When Martin replied that he had, Joseph cried, "'Oh, my God!' . . . 'All is lost! all is lost! What shall I do? I have sinned—it is I who tempted the wrath of God. I should have been satisfied with the first answer which I received from the Lord; for he told me that it was not safe to let the writing go out of my possession.' . . . 'And how shall I appear before the Lord? Of what rebuke am I not worthy from the angel of the Most High?'"[3]

Throughout the remainder of the day and into the evening, Joseph continued to lament the loss and was inconsolable as he wept and paced the floor. His thoughts turned to Emma and the effect the loss of the manuscript might have upon her health. He groaned, "Must I . . . return to my wife with such a tale as this? I dare not do it lest I should kill her at once."[4]

When morning came, he left for Harmony to share the distressing news with Emma and accept whatever the Lord might have in store for him. As expected, she too was distraught with the loss of the manuscript, but together they carried the burden. Joseph humbly sought the Lord in continual fervent prayer and a short time later, through the Urim and Thummim, received the revelation now recorded in Doctrine and Covenants 3. In this heavenly communication Joseph was given a severe chastisement but was also shown tender mercy, for the Lord said, "But remember, God is merciful; therefore, repent of that which thou hast done which is contrary to the commandment which I gave you, and thou art still chosen, and art again called to the work" (D&C 3:10).

For two months the plates and the interpreters were taken from the Prophet, and further revelation relative to the work was withheld. Emma continued to recuperate, and together they worked the farm and made improvements around the house. On September 22, the plates and the Urim and Thummim were returned. They were kept at first under their bed and were later moved to "a red morocco trunk [which lay] on Emma's bureau."⁵ The gift of translation was restored, and Joseph was told to be "faithful and continue on unto the finishing of the remainder of the work of translation" and not to "run faster or labor more than [he had] strength and means provided" (D&C 10:3–4). He received additional intelligence from the Lord that because of the evil designs of Satan and the attempts of wicked men to destroy the work, he was not to translate again the portion that had been lost.

Joseph did not recommence translating immediately but continued to farm their land to provide support for Emma and himself. When he did resume the translation, she acted as his scribe and later recounted these sacred experiences: "When my husband was translating the Book of Mormon, I wrote a part of it, as he dictated each sentence, word for word, and when he came to proper names he could not pronounce, or long words, he spelled them out, and while I was writing them, if I made any mistake in spelling, he would stop me and correct my spelling, although it was impossible for him to see how I was writing them down at the time. Even the word *Sarah* he could not pronounce at first, but had to spell it, and I would pronounce it for him. . . .

"One time while he was translating he stopped suddenly, pale as a sheet, and said, 'Emma, did Jerusalem have walls around it?' When I answered, 'Yes,' he replied 'Oh! I was afraid I had been deceived.' He had such a limited knowledge of history at that time that he did not even know that Jerusalem was surrounded by walls."⁶

Years later, when asked by her son about the truthfulness of the Book of Mormon, Emma said, "My belief is that the Book of Mormon is of divine authenticity—I have not the slightest doubt of it. I am satisfied that no man could have dictated the writing of the manuscripts unless he was inspired; for, when acting as his scribe, your father would dictate to me hour after hour; and when returning after meals, or after interruptions, he would at once begin where he had left off, without either seeing the manuscript or having any portion of it read to him. This was a usual thing for him to do. It would have been improbable that a learned man could do this; and for one so . . . unlearned as he was, it was simply impossible."7

In February 1829 Lucy and Joseph Sr. left Manchester for Harmony. They had received no communication from their son since his emotional departure in July, and they were concerned for the work and for the welfare of their son and his wife. Joseph saw their wagon on the road while they were still some distance from the house. He excitedly told Emma that his father and mother were coming and ran to meet them. The reunion was sweet, and as Emma made her in-laws comfortable in their home, Joseph updated them relative to the work. Of this visit Lucy stated later, "We became acquainted with Emma's father, . . . [and] also his family. . . . They were an intelligent and highly respectable family. They were pleasantly situated, and lived in good style. . . . The time of our visit with them, we passed very agreeably, and returned home relieved of a burden which was almost insupportable, and our present joy far overbalanced all our former grief."8

Emma continued to write for Joseph, but her health was still delicate, and when winter set in, she found it increasingly difficult to keep up with the writing as well as to tend to her housework and chores. On April 2, Joseph petitioned the Lord to send him a scribe and was given heavenly assurance that one would arrive shortly.

Several months before Joseph's request, a twenty-two-year-old schoolteacher named Oliver Cowdery had come to board with Joseph's parents in Manchester. The Smiths were at first hesitant to share much with him relative to the sacred work, but within a short time he was made aware of the ancient record and the translation process. Fascinated with the story, he searched for further intelligence and guidance through prayer and received a witness from the Lord regarding the authenticity of the record and the divinity of the work. A few days after receiving this witness, Oliver was ready to make the trip to Pennsylvania to assist the Prophet as his scribe. Accompanied by another of Joseph's younger brothers, Samuel, Oliver reached Harmony on April 5, just three days after Joseph made his prayerful plea.

Two days later the Prophet resumed translating, and Oliver began to write with very few extended breaks. Of this time in the history of the Restoration, Oliver later wrote: "These were days never to be forgotten—to sit under the sound of a voice dictated by the inspiration of heaven, awakened the utmost gratitude of this bosom! Day after day I continued, uninterrupted, to write from his mouth, as he translated with the Urim and Thummim . . . the history or record called 'The Book of Mormon'" (Joseph Smith–History, endnote).

As the men worked, questions arose respecting intelligence received from the ancient writings, and in most cases they inquired of the Lord for answers and guidance. On May 15, 1829, after having found several references to the ordinance of baptism, they entered the woods to pray for further light and knowledge. While Joseph and Oliver were in the attitude of prayer, John called the Baptist "descended in a cloud of light" and conferred upon them "the Priesthood of Aaron, which holds the keys of the ministering of angels, and of the gospel of repentance, and of baptism by immersion for the remission of sins" (Joseph Smith–History 1:68–69). He then instructed Joseph to baptize Oliver, after which Oliver baptized Joseph, also in accordance with John's command.

Even though Emma was not now directly involved in much that transpired regarding the translation, she often cleaned the room in which the men worked, "and she would lift and move [the plates] when she swept and dusted the room and furniture."[9] Though there is no record of what Joseph shared with her regarding the progress of the work, Emma was undoubtedly aware of some of the great spiritual manifestations afforded her husband and Oliver.

Sometime later that month, Samuel returned for another visit, and Hyrum visited shortly thereafter. Emma welcomed the company but was aware that the visitors were rapidly depleting their store of food. Her family was sociable and pleasant to Joseph at this time, but because Isaac continued to assert that the plates and the work he was doing was foolish nonsense, asking her parents for help was not an option.

Miraculously, every time their situation became desperate, Joseph Knight Sr. would arrive from Colesville, New York, with a wagonload of such provisions as potatoes, mackerel, tea, grain, and lined foolscap paper for the transcription. When preparing to make one of these trips to Harmony, Knight's wife, Polly, protested at his going so often and taking so much. To this he replied, "Come go and see." She accompanied him on the nearly thirty-mile journey, and after visiting with Emma and speaking seriously with Joseph regarding the translation and the other revelations he had received, Polly became a stalwart believer in the work.[10]

As the days passed and the translation continued, persecution from groups of unbelieving neighbors began to escalate. "We had been threatened with being mobbed, from time to time, and this, too, by professors of religion," Joseph related. "Their intentions of mobbing us were only counteracted by the influence of my wife's father's family (under Divine providence), who had become very friendly to me, and who were opposed to mobs, and were willing that I should be allowed to continue the work of translation without interruption; and therefore offered and promised us protection from all unlawful proceedings, as far as in them lay" (Joseph Smith–History 1:75).

Though protection afforded by the Hale family was a godsend, it did not extend beyond the immediate area. Threats against Joseph's life became more frequent, and warding off the mobs around the Hale property became more difficult. Emma constantly worried about her husband's life and was always anxious when he left the farm. So in late May or early June of 1829, after prayerful consideration, it was decided that she would stay in Pennsylvania to look after the house and farm and Joseph and Oliver would go to Fayette, New York, to finish the translation of the Book of Mormon.

Chapter Seven

On their journey to Harmony, Pennsylvania, in April 1829, Oliver and Samuel had stopped for a night at the home of Peter Whitmer Sr., a well-situated and respected farmer in Fayette Township, New York. Peter's son David was a friend of Oliver Cowdery, and Oliver enthusiastically told him about Joseph and the ancient record. During their short stay, Samuel bore witness to David of his brother Joseph's divine calling, giving David reason to ponder seriously his own religious beliefs.

Oliver continued to correspond with David once he reached Harmony, telling him he was convinced Joseph had the plates and was translating them by the power of God. So, when the persecution worsened, Oliver wrote him, asking if he would come to move him and Joseph to the Whitmer farm, where they could finish the work in peace. Also in the letter were Oliver's testimony of the Restoration and "a few lines of what they had translated."[1]

David showed the letter to his parents and siblings. His father discouraged him from leaving, reminding him that he had two full days' worth of work to harrow a field of wheat and to spread plaster of paris on another field. Nevertheless, he encouraged David to seek a witness from God regarding the truthfulness of the translation, which through prayer he did.

The next day, when David went out to plow the twenty acres, he "found between five and seven acres of [his] ground had been plowed during the night . . . and the plow was left standing in the furrow."[2] Somewhat perplexed, he hitched his team to the harrow and worked steadily in the grain field, stopping only for dinner, and by evening the full two days' work was finished. When his father saw what David had accomplished in half the usual time, he exclaimed, "There must be an overruling hand in this, and I think you would better go down to Pennsylvania as soon as your plaster of paris is sown."[3]

The following morning, David went to get the fertilizer, which he had left in a pile by his sister's house, but it was gone. "He then ran to his sister, and inquired of her if she knew what had become of it. Being surprised she said, 'Why do you ask me? was it not all sown yesterday?'

"'Not to my knowledge,' answered David.

"'I am astonished at that,' replied his sister, 'for the children came to me in the forenoon, and begged of me to go out and see the men sow plaster in the field, saying, that they never saw anybody sow plaster so fast in their lives. I accordingly went, and saw three men at work in the field, as the children said, but, supposing that you had hired some help, on account of your hurry, I went immediately into the house, and gave the subject no further attention.'"[4]

Accepting these two experiences as a divine witness, David and his father and family were convinced that God's hand was involved, and they encouraged him to leave for Pennsylvania immediately. He made the more than one-hundred-mile journey in two days, and upon his arrival extended his father's invitation for Joseph and Oliver to stay at the Whitmer farm for as long as was necessary to finish the translation. Joseph readily accepted the invitation, and the next day, after bidding Emma good-bye, the three men left for Fayette in David's two-horse wagon.

Before they left, however, Joseph had inquired of the Lord about the transportation of the plates and was told the angel Moroni would take them to the Whitmer farm. As the men journeyed towards Fayette, New York, David related that "when traveling along in a clear open place, a very pleasant, nice-looking old man suddenly appeared by the side of our wagon and saluted us with, 'good morning, it is very warm,' at the same time wiping his face or forehead with his hand. We returned the salutation, and, by a sign from Joseph, I invited him to ride if he was going our way. But he said very pleasantly, 'No, I am going to Cumorah.' . . . We all gazed at him and at each other, and as I looked around enquiringly of Joseph, the old man instantly disappeared. . . . He was, I should think, about five feet eight or nine inches tall and heavy set . . . ; he was dressed in a suit of brown woolen clothes, his hair and beard were white. . . . I also remember that he had on his back a sort of knapsack with something in, shaped like a book. It was the messenger who had the plates, who had taken them from Joseph just prior to our starting from Harmony."[5]

The men arrived at the Whitmer farm sometime in the first week of June 1829 and immediately resumed the translation, with both Oliver and David's older brother John writing for the Prophet. The Whitmer family and many of their neighbors were friendly and supported Joseph, Oliver, and Emma—who, after putting in order her and Joseph's immediate affairs in Harmony—joined her husband. She was greeted graciously by the

Whitmers and made to feel comfortable in their small four-room home, where she and Joseph were given one of the two rooms upstairs.

Joseph soon formed a particular bond with David, who later said of him, "He was a religious and straightforward man. He had to be; for he was illiterate and he could do nothing himself. He had to trust in God. He could not translate unless he was humble and possessed the right feelings towards everyone."[6]

One morning Emma did or said something that agitated Joseph. Upset, he left her and climbed the stairs to the room in which the translation was done. But when he sat down to begin the day's work, he could not translate a "single syllable." Consequently, he left the house and walked into the orchard to ask the Lord for forgiveness. After being gone for about an hour, he entered "the house, and asked Emma's forgiveness." Then he returned to the upstairs room and resumed the work of translation.[7]

The people around Fayette were generally interested in the new gospel message and opened their doors to the brethren. Meetings were held frequently in neighboring homes, where an explanation of the Restoration and instruction regarding the things being revealed were given. Joseph and Oliver received many "inquirers who now began to visit us—some for the sake of finding the truth, others for the purpose of putting hard questions, and trying to confound us."[8] Many were convinced that Joseph had obtained the true and everlasting gospel of Jesus Christ, and Joseph's brother Hyrum and David and Peter Whitmer Jr. entered the waters of baptism. Joseph's brother Samuel, who had been converted on his first visit to Pennsylvania, was the first to be baptized after Joseph and Oliver. Although Emma was not baptized until later, her testimony grew even more sure as she witnessed the miracles that were happening daily.

Near the end of June, Joseph sent word to his parents in Manchester informing them that the translation was nearly completed and requesting they come to Fayette. Even though Martin had caused the Smiths much grief and sorrow, that evening they paid him a visit and shared the good news. Insisting he travel with them to Fayette, the next morning the three "set off together" and reached the Whitmer farm before sunset.[9] The day following, services were held, after which Joseph, Martin, Oliver, and David went into the woods where, after much prayer and supplication, the angel Moroni appeared first to Joseph, Oliver, and David and then to Joseph and Martin. He showed them the plates, the Urim and Thummim, the breastplate, the sword of Laban, and the Liahona.

When the men returned to the house, Joseph, finding his mother and father and Peter's wife, Mary, in a bedroom, threw himself upon the bed and exclaimed, "Father, mother, you do not know how happy I am: the Lord has now caused the plates to be shown to three more besides myself. They have seen an angel . . . now they know for themselves, that I do not go about to deceive people, and I feel as if I was relieved of a burden which was almost too heavy for me to bear, and it rejoices my soul, that I am not any longer to be entirely alone in the world."[10] Soon David, Oliver, and Martin also entered the house and testified of the great and marvelous vision they had experienced.

About this same time, Mary Whitmer was also privileged to have a visitation from the angel Moroni. Feeding, housing, and providing for the needs of the many visitors in her home increased her workload substantially, although Mary uttered not a single complaint. One evening as she walked to the barn to milk the cows, she was met by Moroni, who said to her: "You have been very faithful and diligent in your labors, but you are tired because of the increase of your toil; it is proper, therefore, that you should receive a witness, that your faith may be strengthened."[11] The angel then showed her the plates and left her to finish her day's work.

While in Manchester a few days later, Joseph was permitted to show the plates to eight more witnesses, including his father, Hyrum, Samuel, Hiram Page, and Christian, Jacob, John, and Peter Whitmer Jr. Shortly after the additional witnesses were allowed not just to see but also to handle the ancient gold record, the translation was completed and the plates were returned, as the Prophet had been previously instructed, to the Hill Cumorah.

Oliver accompanied Joseph to the hill to return the record and later told Brigham Young that upon their arrival they had a very unusual experience. President Young related: "Oliver says that when [they] went there, the hill opened, and they walked into a cave, in which there was a large and spacious room. He says he did not think, at the time, whether they had the light of the sun or artificial light; but that it was just as light as day. They laid the plates on a table; it was a large table that stood in the room. Under this table there was a pile of plates as much as two feet high, and there were altogether in this room more plates than probably many wagon loads; they were piled up in the corners and along the walls."[12]

As the Restoration moved forward and great blessings were continually poured out upon the righteous seekers of truth, opposition to the work also escalated. As Joseph prepared to make the relatively short trip from Manchester to Palmyra in order to see about a copyright for the Book of Mormon, word came that a mob of forty men was waiting to jump him on the road. Lucy tried to persuade him to not make the trip, but Joseph comforted her, saying, "Never mind, mother, just put your trust in God, and nothing will hurt me today."[13]

Although he was not harmed or harassed that day, he did meet some of the threatening mob who were sitting on a fence alongside the road. As he approached he removed his hat and greeted each by name and in turn wished them a good morning. Confused by his friendliness and confidence, they all remained on the fence and Joseph passed by without being verbally or physically assaulted.

Once the copyright was secured, Joseph and Oliver sought a reputable publisher and struck an agreement on August 17 with Egbert B. Grandin in Palmyra to print five thousand copies of the Book of Mormon for three thousand dollars. Grandin, reluctant to accept the job of printing the "golden bible," insisted on security for the publishing cost. Once again Martin Harris stepped forward with financial assistance, putting up a portion of his farm for collateral.

Because Emma had previously returned to Harmony and Joseph was anxious to join her, he left Oliver and Hyrum in Palmyra to supervise the printing process. He instructed Oliver to make a second copy of the manuscript for the printer's use and secure the original manuscript at Father and Mother Smith's home, where Lucy put it in a chest and hid it under their bed.

Emma and Joseph were grateful to be together again on their little farm where they spent the winter of 1829 and much of the following spring. Joseph was, however, required to make at least two trips to Palmyra without her during this period: once to protect the copyright from being violated, and again to quiet the fears of Grandin and Martin Harris, who grew anxious after hearing that many of the people in Palmyra planned to boycott the sale of the book after its publication.

During the time that the Book of Mormon was being printed, Joseph related: "We still continued to bear testimony and give information, as far as we had opportunity." "The Lord continue[d] to give us instructions from time to time, concerning the duties which now devolved upon us; . . . [and] also pointed out to us the precise day upon which, according to His will and commandment, we should proceed to organize His Church once more here upon the earth."[14]

On Friday, March 26, the Book of Mormon went on sale at the Palmyra bookstore, and less than two weeks later, on Tuesday, April 6, 1830, The Church of Jesus Christ of Latter-day Saints was organized in Fayette, New York, at the Whitmer farmhouse. "One can envision the horses tied to the fence, their saddles draped over the rails, and the wagons and buggies parked about the yard, with the harnesses thrown on the seats. . . . At least thirty men and women, and perhaps as many as sixty, crowded into the small house."[15] Unfortunately, Emma did not accompany Joseph and Joseph Knight Sr. on this trip and was not present to witness her twenty-four-year-old husband conduct the meeting in which he officially and legally organized the Church.

During this historic gathering, prayers were offered, Joseph and Oliver were respectively sustained as First and Second Elders of the Church, the sacrament was administered, and those who had previously been baptized were given the gift of the Holy Ghost and confirmed members. Near the conclusion of the meeting, Joseph received a revelation which designated him "a seer, a translator, a prophet, [and] an apostle of Jesus Christ" (D&C 21:1) and immediately following, some in attendance were baptized, including Joseph's parents and Martin Harris. With "tears of joy" streaming down his face, Joseph exclaimed after baptizing his father, "Praise to my God! that I lived to see my own father baptized into the true Church of Jesus Christ!"[16]

As President Gordon B. Hinckley observed, "This day of organization was, in effect, a day of commencement, the graduation for Joseph from ten years of remarkable schooling. It had begun with the incomparable vision in the grove in the spring of 1820, when the Father and the Son appeared to the fourteen-year-old boy. It had continued with the tutoring from Moroni, with both warnings and instructions given on multiple occasions. Then there was the translation of the ancient record, and the inspiration, the knowledge, the revelation that came from that experience. There was the bestowal of divine authority, the ancient priesthood again conferred upon men by those who were its rightful possessors—John the Baptist in the case of the Aaronic Priesthood, and Peter, James, and John in the case of the Melchizedek. There were revelations, a number of them, in which the voice of God was heard again, and the channel of communication opened between man and the Creator."[17]

Most of the events that had transpired to this point in the Restoration and the organization of the Church occurred while Joseph was married to his beloved Emma. Although never at the forefront, she stood by her prophet-husband for those first three and a half years without wavering. In her supporting role she accompanied Joseph to the Hill Cumorah to get the plates, even though she was not given an opportunity to see them, and she was the first to act as his scribe and bore solemn witness of the miraculous translation. She did not have the privilege of seeing or speaking with the angel Moroni but delighted when others were afforded that privilege; nor did she enjoy support from her family relative to the work. Indeed, Emma's testimony was built on faith—faith in the Lord Jesus Christ, faith in the reality and divinity of her husband's sacred calling, and faith in the whisperings of the still, small voice which spoke to her heart and mind.

Chapter Eight

*A*FTER THE CHURCH WAS ORGANIZED, Joseph returned to Emma in Harmony, Pennsylvania, but was compelled to travel to New York on several occasions that spring to administer the affairs of the growing religion. Many were receiving the missionaries and believing the message of the Restoration, and converts were being baptized, particularly in the area of Fayette, New York.

On June 9, 1830, the Prophet conducted the first conference of the Church at the Whitmer home in Fayette with about thirty members in attendance. After the meeting, accompanied by Oliver Cowdery and John and David Whitmer, he immediately left for Harmony. They stayed at the farm just long enough for Emma to prepare to travel with them to Colesville to visit the Knight family. There they found many who believed and desired baptism as well.

On Saturday, the brethren erected a makeshift dam across a nearby stream to collect enough water to perform the ordinances after the scheduled Sabbath day meeting. That night, however, their dam was torn down by a group of antagonists. Nevertheless, the small congregation met the next day, and Oliver preached a sermon, after which "others . . . bore testimony to the truth of the Book of Mormon, the doctrine of repentance, baptism for the remission of sins, and laying on of hands for the gift of the Holy Ghost."[1]

Early Monday morning, after the men repaired the dam and before the mob could muster enough in number and strength to cause havoc, Emma walked into the cold creek water and was baptized by Oliver. Twelve others, mostly members of the Knight family, were also baptized but not without being subjected to jeering remarks from the gathering neighbors who pointed at them and asked if they "had been washing sheep."[2] Hoping to escape the verbal abuse, the company moved indoors, but the mob followed, and soon the Newel Knight home was surrounded by about fifty men, who continued to threaten violence.

Around dusk and before Joseph could confirm the newly baptized members, a constable came to the door and arrested him. Emma was frightened and sick at heart as she watched the officer take her husband to jail on a trumped-up charge of "being a disorderly person [and] of setting the country in an uproar by preaching the Book of Mormon."[3] What she did not know was that the constable was Joseph's ally. Within a short distance the officer protected him from the mob that surrounded the wagon in which they rode by giving the horse an unexpected slap with his whip and driving Joseph from the danger. When they reached South Bainbridge, the constable secured a room in a tavern and slept with his feet against the door and his rifle by his side to protect the Prophet while he slept in the bed.

Emma did not spend the night in protected security but rather lay frightened as the mob returned to the Knight farm in a rage. They piled wood against the doors, sunk harness chains in the stream and after overturning their wagons piled wood on some and sunk the others. The mob left the Knight farm in shambles.

Joseph's trial convened the next day, and after his good friend Josiah Stowell and two of Stowell's daughters testified in his behalf, he was released from custody. Within minutes of the acquittal, however, another constable served him with a similar warrant from the neighboring county and took him about fifteen miles to again stand trial. They stayed the night in a tavern where, before retiring, Joseph was fed only a crust of bread and some water and abused and insulted by men who spat on him and shouted, "Prophesy, prophesy!"[4]

After spending the entire next day and evening on trial, the Prophet at about midnight was again acquitted but before being set free was given a severe tongue lashing from members of the court—not because he was guilty of any wrongdoing or because his character or integrity had been compromised but to appease those in the audience who wanted to see him punished for his religious beliefs. Before leaving to find Emma and return home, he was approached by the second constable, who apologized and then asked his forgiveness for mistreating him the night before. He also warned him of a gathering of about three hundred people who planned to tar and feather him once he left the court.

After Joseph's initial arrest, Emma left the Knight farm to stay with her sister Elizabeth, who resided between Colesville and Harmony, and for two days and two nights she worried about her husband's whereabouts and safety. During each day a small group of Mormon women met at Hezekiah Peck's home to pray for the Prophet. After Joseph's first acquittal, John S. Reid, who was not a lawyer but represented Joseph's defense, visited Emma at the Peck home. She went out to meet Reid's wagon, "her very heart strings . . . broken with grief" and with tears "streaming from her eyes."[5] Reid brought her the good news of the acquittal after the first trial and the disappointing news of her husband's second arrest.

Meanwhile, after being acquitted the second time and released from custody, Joseph traveled through the night and early the next morning found Emma "awaiting with much anxiety the issue of those ungodly proceedings."[6] Her emotions were heightened with grief and fright but also with righteous indignation. How, in a country where the Constitution guarantees every man and woman the right and privilege "to worship God according to the dictates of his own conscience," could this be happening?[7] She and Joseph had physically or spiritually abused no one; they were innocent of all the malicious rumors spreading rampantly about the country; and they wanted nothing more than to bring individuals and families to Jesus Christ.

Blessed because of her willingness to suffer persecution and support her prophet-husband, Emma's cries and questions were answered not long after she and Joseph returned to their farm in Harmony. Sometime in July, Joseph received from the Lord a revelation, now recorded in Doctrine and Covenants 25, which was specifically directed to her. In the revelation the Lord called her by name, referred to her as his daughter, and promised that if she were faithful and virtuous, her life would be protected, she need not fear, and she would "receive an inheritance in Zion" (v. 2). She was told that her sins were forgiven and then the Lord said, "Thou art an elect lady, whom I have called" (v. 3). Her calling was to comfort her husband in meekness and to find joy in him "and the glory which shall come upon him" (v. 14). She was to "lay aside the things of this world, and seek for the things of a better" in order to be at his side (v. 10); to be his scribe, teach from the scriptures, and exhort the people whenever necessary (vv. 6–7); and to select a number of hymns for publication to be used by the Church (v. 11). She was admonished to spend time writing and learning, not to murmur, and to beware of pride (vv. 8, 4, 12).

In early August, Emma and Joseph were delighted when Newel Knight, his wife, Sally, and John Whitmer visited them. They enjoyed the companionship of this wonderful couple and friend who had embraced the gospel and throughout their visit spent hours in conversation about the Restoration and all it might mean in their lives. Because the mob in Colesville had made it impossible for Emma and Sally to be confirmed after their baptism, before the company was to leave for home, they planned an intimate sacrament service during which the confirmations could be performed.

Not having any wine on hand for the sacrament, Joseph "set out to procure some . . . but had gone only a short distance when [he] was met by a heavenly messenger"[8] who

Elect Lady

instructed him to not purchase any wine from his enemies and to partake of no wine unless it was made by those belonging to the Church. He was also told: "It mattereth not what ye shall eat or what ye shall drink when ye partake of the sacrament, if it so be that ye do it with an eye single to my glory—remembering unto the Father my body which was laid down for you, and my blood which was shed for the remission of your sins" (D&C 27:2).

When Joseph returned and related this experience to Emma and the others, they prepared their own wine and then held their meeting. After partaking of the sacrament, Joseph and Newel laid their hands upon Emma's head and in the name of Jesus Christ, Joseph confirmed her a member of the Church and invited her to receive the Holy Ghost as her constant companion. The remainder of the evening was spent "in a glorious manner," said Joseph. "The Spirit of the Lord was poured out upon us, we praised the Lord God, and rejoiced exceedingly."[9]

Living in Harmony became increasingly more difficult however, as persecution toward them and the gospel was steadily growing. Most of the maltreatment was heightened due to the persuasions of Emma's uncle Nathaniel Lewis and some of his followers who were spreading fabrications among the people relative to the work and telling Isaac and others of Emma's family "falsehoods . . . of the most shameful nature."[10] The constant talk finally wore Isaac down, and he began to believe the lies and withdrew his earlier promise of protection. As a result Emma and Joseph had to leave their first real home and accept an invitation from the Whitmers to live with them in Fayette.

Emma was distraught at the thought of leaving, probably sensing if she did she might never see nor hear from her family again. She loved her little home, and because she was quite certain she was again pregnant, she wanted desperately to stay near her mother and sisters. So when Newel Knight's wagon rolled into the yard in late August to transport them to New York, she wept and bade a sorrowful good-bye to her parents and siblings. At their parting her father, upset and not wanting to see her go, deepened her distress and caused her heavy heart nearly to break when he said, "No good can ever come of it!"[11]

Chapter Nine

FORTUNATELY, EMMA'S HOMESICKNESS and sadness were greatly remedied when she and Joseph were greeted in Fayette with love and support from the Whitmer family and the growing number of members in the area. The new church was expanding, and there was great excitement in the air caused by the approaching general conference, which had been scheduled to convene on September 26, 1830.

Among the increasing membership in New York was a man by the name of Parley P. Pratt. Around September 1, Pratt came into the country to preach the gospel as it had been taught to him by his friend Sidney Rigdon, a leader of a group of Reformed Baptists living in and around the Kirtland, Ohio, area. As Pratt walked through the countryside, he happened upon the home of a Mr. Hamblin, an old Baptist deacon who had a copy of the Book of Mormon.

After reading from the book for the remainder of the day and into the night, Parley "knew and comprehended that the book was true, as plainly and manifestly as a man comprehends and knows that he exists."[1] Making up his mind "to see the young man who had been the instrument of its discovery and translation,"[2] Parley set out for Manchester to find Joseph Smith. Because the Prophet and Emma were still living in Harmony at the time, he instead met Hyrum. Together they traveled to Fayette where, within a few days, Parley was baptized, given the gift of the Holy Ghost, and ordained an elder in the Church of Jesus Christ.

The September conference assembled as planned and was presided over by the Prophet. Although Emma was again experiencing a difficult pregnancy, she attended the meeting and listened intently as her husband spoke. She must have marveled at his ability to lead a meeting of many people more educated and worldly than her Joseph. She enjoyed partaking of the sacrament, hearing others speak, and witnessing new members' baptisms, confirmations, and ordinations. For three days the membership of a little over sixty souls worshiped together. The Prophet later recorded: "The Holy Ghost came upon us, and filled us with joy unspeakable; and peace, and faith, and hope, and charity abounded in our midst."[3]

Within days of the conference adjournment, Joseph received a revelation calling Parley P. Pratt and another new convert, Ziba Peterson, to accompany Oliver Cowdery and Peter Whitmer Jr. on a mission to the Indian territory at the western edge of the United States. Emma and some of the other women of the Church immediately organized and went to work to prepare clothing for the missionaries. Since cloth was not readily available and expensive, they carded, spun, and sewed until the brethren were outfitted for their new assignment.

Emma worked so hard to prepare the clothing and other necessities for the missionaries that for four weeks afterward she was extremely ill. Lucy recounted later that although Emma's health "was quite delicate . . . she did not favor herself on this account, but whatever her hands found to do, she did with her might, until so far beyond her strength that she brought upon herself a heavy fit of sickness. . . . And, although her strength was exhausted, still her spirits were the same, which, in fact, was always the case with her, even under the most trying circumstances."[4]

In December, as Joseph was addressing a small group of Saints in Waterloo—a town neighboring Fayette—two strange men entered the meeting and listened with interest until the Prophet concluded his message and then invited anyone wishing to speak to do so. One of the strangers was Edward Partridge, a respected and prosperous businessman from Painesville, Ohio. He stood, introduced himself, and after stating he believed all that had been said, asked Joseph to baptize him. Joseph replied, "You are now much fatigued, brother Partridge, and you had better rest to-day, and be baptized tomorrow."[5] Accordingly, Edward was baptized by the Prophet the next day.

The other stranger was Sidney Rigdon, the minister who had converted Parley to the Reformed Baptist faith in Ohio. After traveling west through the Western Reserve, Parley, Oliver, Peter, and Ziba reached the Kirtland area in mid-October, and the first house they visited was Rigdon's, in the nearby town of Mentor. Although he did not accept the missionaries' message immediately, saying, "he had one Bible which he believed was a revelation from God," he did accept a copy of the Book of Mormon from them and promised to read it "to ascertain whether it be a revelation from God or not."[6]

After studying the book for about two weeks, Sidney concluded it was true. He "expressed the utmost amazement that such a man should write a book which seemed to shed a flood of light on all the old scriptures, open all their profoundest mysteries, and give them perfect consistency and complete system. In his fresh enthusiasm he exclaimed that if God ever gave a revelation, surely this must be divine."[7] Within weeks of Sidney's conversion, well over a hundred people were similarly converted and baptized in the Kirtland area—most of them from Rigdon's congregations.

Learning from Edward Partridge and Sidney Rigdon that many were joining the Church in Ohio and realizing that as a result most of the membership was now living in the area of Kirtland, Joseph sought direction from the Lord about how to provide the necessary leadership. Persecution was reaching a crescendo in New York, and it was becoming apparent that the lives of the Prophet and other Church members were in jeopardy. In answer to his prayer, Joseph was told: "I say unto you that the enemy in the secret chambers seeketh your lives. . . . And that ye might escape the power of the enemy, and be gathered unto me a righteous people, . . . ye should go to the Ohio" (D&C 38:28, 31–32; see also 37:1 for the initial command to relocate).

For Emma, the revelation meant another move, which necessitated packing and loading their possessions in Fayette. Some of their household items, including furniture, farm equipment, and livestock, were still in Harmony and had to be retrieved and moved. She was now in her sixth month of pregnancy, and her health continued to be quite frail, making the three-hundred-mile trip that lay ahead an overwhelming undertaking to consider. In addition, the reality of moving west and farther from her family and the gravesite of her firstborn son must have haunted her, for she knew the possibility of returning was slim.

December weather had dropped about four feet of snow, and the freezing rains of January 1831 were leaving a sheet of ice atop it, which produced treacherous conditions for travel. Nonetheless, knowing her husband's life was in danger and that he had been commanded by the Lord to leave New York and go west, Emma had the courage to brave the daunting weather and climb aboard Joseph Knight's sleigh in early January. With as many blankets as they owned covering them, Emma, in company with the Prophet, Edward Partridge, and Sidney Rigdon, began the arduous journey.

One of their first stops was at the home of Joseph's oldest sister, Sophronia, who lived with her husband, Calvin Stoddard, and their baby daughter, Eunice, in Macedon, New York. They stayed briefly but long enough for Joseph and the brethren to teach and baptize several investigators and to afford Emma the blessed opportunity to hold and enjoy her little niece. For the remainder of the trip they found lodging and reprieve from the wind and freezing rain in public houses or with hospitable farmers along the route.

Meanwhile, in Kirtland, a prominent merchant named Newel K. Whitney and his wife,

Elizabeth Ann, received the gospel and were baptized in November 1830. Soon after their baptism, however, the couple was troubled with the many false teachings and misrepresentations entering in among the Saints in the area. Consequently, they prayed faithfully and waited patiently for much needed leadership to arrive and give direction to the struggling members.

On February 1, a sleigh pulled up in front of their store in Kirtland, and a tall, well-built man, who looked to be in his mid-twenties, sprang from the seat, walked through the door, and, as if speaking to an old acquaintance, exclaimed, "Newel K. Whitney, thou art the man." Newel replied, "Stranger, you have the advantage of me; I could not call you by name, as you have me." Answering, the smiling young man said, "I am Joseph, the Prophet. You have prayed me here. Now, what do you want of me?"[8]

Elizabeth Ann Whitney later testified that the arrival of the Prophet was a direct answer to their prayers of faith. Elder Orson F. Whitney, who was Newel's grandson, said of the Prophet's arrival: "By what power did this remarkable man, Joseph Smith, recognize one whom he had never before seen in the flesh? . . . It was because Joseph Smith was a seer, a choice seer; he had actually seen Newel K. Whitney upon his knees, hundreds of miles away, praying for his coming to Kirtland."[9]

Emma and Joseph accepted an invitation to live with Newel Whitney's business partner, Sidney Gilbert, and his family, who resided a short distance down the road. While Joseph rode ahead with Gilbert to his house, Emma stayed at the store to wait while their belongings were transferred from the sleigh to a wagon. Soon she boarded the wagon and with the driver began the downhill trip to the Gilbert residence, but en route and without warning, the wagon slid and tipped, throwing her headlong into the snow. From inside the Gilbert home Joseph heard Emma's screams and ran from the house to help her. Although she was not injured, because of her pregnancy she surely was much shaken.

The Gilberts were living in very crowded conditions, so when Emma realized the imposition she and Joseph would cause, she graciously declined their kind invitation. She and Joseph returned to the Whitney residence, where Elizabeth welcomed them and provided warm and comfortable lodging until Joseph could arrange for more permanent accommodations. Sister Whitney, in particular, showed "every kindness and attention which could be expected."[10] The two women became fast friends and developed a close and trusting relationship that would last well beyond Emma's seven years of residency in the Kirtland area.

Chapter Ten

WITHIN A FEW WEEKS EMMA AND JOSEPH moved into a small one-room cabin built for them about a mile northeast of Kirtland on the Isaac Morley farm. Emma appreciated the privacy the cabin provided and busied herself making it comfortable and homey with what little furniture and housekeeping items she had.

Joseph was quickly inundated with Church business and found that the members "were striving to do the will of God, so far as they knew it, though some strange notions and false spirits had crept in among them."[1] Apparently, about fifty members had formed a communal organization that they referred to as "the family," in which all individual possessions became part of their "family" cooperative. One brother later recalled that while he was in the home of Isaac Morley, another man "came to me and took my watch out of my pocket and walked off as though it was his. I thought he would bring it back soon but was disappointed as he sold it. I asked him what he meant by selling my watch. 'Oh,' said he, 'I thought it was all in the family.'"[2]

Eager to receive guidance and direction regarding the economic well-being of the Saints and the financial needs of the Church, Joseph approached the Lord. The Prophet received a revelation that, among other things, set forth laws governing the consecration of properties. The will of the Lord was that "every man shall be . . . a steward over his own property, or that which he has received by consecration, as much as is sufficient for himself and family." Furthermore, the Lord revealed that if a man had more than was needful for the support of his family, the "residue [was] to be consecrated unto the bishop" to assist those who were in need (D&C 42:32–33; headnote). Not coincidentally, the Prophet had received a revelation less than a week before calling Edward Partridge as the first bishop in the Church.

During much of March and April, Emma enjoyed Joseph's company in the cabin as he and Sidney worked on the revision of the Bible—a task the Prophet had been given by the

Lord while living in Fayette. Because many parts of that ancient record, which were "plain and most precious; and also many covenants of the Lord" (1 Nephi 13:26) had been deleted or otherwise altered, Joseph made "inspired changes, additions, and corrections,"[3] which were either marked in the text of his 1828 H. and E. Phinney Bible or recorded on separate manuscript pages. Although Sidney was Joseph's primary scribe during the revision process, handwriting evidence suggests that on occasion Emma also wrote for the Prophet.

"The hundreds of marks in [the] Bible were written sometimes in pencil and sometimes in ink. Often there is a check . . . or an X-like mark at the beginning and end of a verse in which a correction is to be made. . . . Although no system was used consistently, frequently two dots, vertically aligned like an oversized colon, represented an insertion point. Two dots on either side of a word often signaled the replacement of that word with whatever was recorded on the manuscript. But very often a word was just circled or lined out, either for deletion or for replacement. . . . The new readings were written on the manuscript pages and not in the Bible itself."[4]

As the men worked, Emma awaited the birth of her second child, undoubtedly with growing trepidation. Memories of her last difficult birthing and the loss of baby Alvin were still tender, and this time her family was not close to help with the delivery and provide comfort and support.

On April 30, 1831, in the small cabin and assisted by some neighboring women, Emma gave birth to twins: a boy and a girl, who were named Thaddeus and Louisa. Sadly, the babies lived only three hours, and Emma and Joseph were left to bury them in the Kirtland cemetery and mourn their loss.

The blessings of motherhood were not denied Emma for long, however. Within days the Prophet was approached by John Murdock, whose wife, Julia, had died while giving birth to twins on May 1. Knowing the babies' lives depended on their being nursed and overwhelmed with the reality of having to raise the infants and his three older children alone, Brother Murdock offered Emma and Joseph the opportunity to adopt the infants, whom he had named Julia and Joseph. The twins were soon given to Emma, and her sorrow and heartache were, to some extent, assuaged.

On the very night they received the twins, another enormous worry was dispelled when Mother Smith arrived in Kirtland with a group of eighty members from New York state. The local newspaper had sometime before reported that a company of Saints migrating to Kirtland were drowned in Lake Erie when their boat sank. To learn that the report was false and that Lucy and the others had not suffered tragedy was a great relief to Emma and Joseph.

Father's Gift

A little over a month after Emma and the Prophet reached Kirtland, Lucy and her company had hired a flatboat to transport them from Waterloo to Buffalo on the Erie Canal. Five days later, when they arrived at the dock in Buffalo, they found a group of Saints from Colesville, New York, who had been waiting for passage for nearly a week because twenty feet of ice was blocking the wharf. Lucy was dismayed to learn that she had just missed Father Smith and Hyrum, who had left only a few days earlier to travel overland to reach Kirtland by the first of April. When the waiting Saints counseled her to avoid telling anyone in the harbor who they were and what their purpose for traveling was, Mother Smith stoutly replied that she would "tell the people precisely who [she] was." She added, "'If you are ashamed of Christ, you must not expect to be prospered; and I shall wonder if we do not get to Kirtland before you.'"[5]

Soon thereafter a group of about thirty brethren arrived at the wharf with Thomas B. Marsh among them. He too was opposed to the group's telling others who they were and said that if Lucy's "company persisted in singing and praying, [they] should be mobbed before the next morning." Again Mother Smith, with her usual candor, responded: "'Mob it is, then . . . we shall attend to prayer before sunset, mob or no mob.'"[6]

The next day Lucy addressed her company, "'Now, brethren and sisters, if you will all of you raise your desires to heaven, that the ice may be broken up, and we be set at liberty, as sure as the Lord lives, it will be done.'" No sooner had she finished her appeal and told her company to hurry and get onto the boat than "a noise was heard, like bursting thunder. . . . The ice parted, leaving barely a passage for the boat, and so narrow that as the boat passed through the buckets of the waterwheel were torn off with a crash."[7] The ice closed behind them, leaving the Colesville brethren in Buffalo to resume their wait.

Upon meeting Joseph and Samuel some miles north of Kirtland in Fairport, Ohio, where she and the company eventually landed, Lucy said of her reunion with her sons: "I extended my right hand to Samuel and my left to Joseph. They wept for joy upon seeing me [and took] me from the company"[8] and eventually to the Morley farm. There she had a joyous reunion with Father Smith and Emma and for the first time saw and cradled the infant adopted twins.

Soon hundreds of Saints were pouring into Kirtland, and most were arriving in destitute circumstances. Among those arriving penniless was Brigham Young, who had previously provided well for his family. He later related: "When we arrived in Kirtland [in September 1833], if any man that ever did gather with the Saints was any poorer than I was—it was because he had nothing. . . . I had two children to take care of—that was all. I was a widower. 'Brother Brigham, had you any shoes?' No; not a shoe to my foot, except a pair of borrowed boots. I had no winter clothing, except a homemade coat that I had had three or four years. 'Any pantaloons?' No. 'What did you do? Did you go without?' No; I borrowed a pair to wear till I could get another pair. I had travelled and preached and given away every dollar of my property. . . . but Joseph said: 'come up;' and I went up the best I could."[9]

On June 3, 1831, the fourth general conference of the Church convened at a schoolhouse on the Isaac Morley farm outside Kirtland with approximately two thousand members in attendance. Of the three-day conference Joseph said, "The Lord displayed His power to the most perfect satisfaction of the Saints. . . . It was clearly evident that the Lord gave us power in proportion to the work to be done, and strength according to the race set before us, and grace and help as our needs required. Great harmony prevailed; several were ordained; faith was strengthened; and humility, so necessary for the blessing of God to follow prayer, characterized the Saints."[10]

Although housing in the small community was limited, the members already living there willingly shared their meager means with the many immigrants. Not knowing precisely how to provide for the influx of bedraggled folks, Joseph sought the Lord's direction and the day after the conference adjourned was told to "journey as soon as preparations can be made . . . to the land of Missouri" (D&C 52:3).

Because the Prophet had received revelation from time to time regarding the establishment of Zion, doing so had become a primary objective of the Saints. Many assumed that when the call to relocate in Ohio had come, Kirtland must be the place for the building of Zion and the New Jerusalem. Now, however, it was evident that Zion was to be built elsewhere, most likely somewhere in Missouri. The revelation also called for thirteen pairs of missionaries to leave Kirtland and travel different routes to Jackson County, Missouri, and to proselyte along the way. In addition, the Colesville branch members, including the entire Knight family, were to "journey into the regions westward, unto the land of Missouri, unto the borders of the Lamanites" (D&C 54:8).

Months before, after baptizing Sidney Rigdon and many others of his congregation, Parley and the other missionaries had left the Kirtland area and journeyed westward until they reached Independence, Missouri, a town on the western frontier of the United States. There they lived among the residents and proselyted until Parley was chosen to return to Kirtland to report on their progress. Upon his arrival, he met with the Prophet and reported all he had experienced and learned about the frontier, which Joseph and the others were now commanded to visit.

As all were making preparations to leave for Independence, a talented man named William Wines Phelps arrived in Kirtland, accompanied by his wife and children. Phelps, who was a writer, editor, and printer by trade, had purchased a copy of the Book of Mormon in New York, read it, and subsequently traveled to Kirtland, where within days he was baptized and ordained an elder. In a revelation directed specifically to him, he was told to journey with Joseph and Sidney to Independence, where he would assist Oliver Cowdery in selecting and printing books to be used by children in the Church.

With seven others, including W. W. Phelps, Joseph bade good-bye to Emma and the twins, Julia and Joseph, on June 19 to make the nearly nine-hundred-mile journey to Missouri, where it was promised "the place for the city of the New Jerusalem, should be revealed."[11] They arrived in Jackson County in mid-July after a journey that the Prophet described as "long and tedious."[12]

Jackson County, Missouri, boasted a population of about three thousand, most of whom were farmers. Independence was a small but well-established town with a courthouse, two or three stores, and nearly twenty log homes. Wrote Joseph: "As far as the eye can reach the beautiful rolling prairies lie spread out like a sea of meadows; and are decorated with a growth of flowers so gorgeous and grand as to exceed description." Trees grew in "luxuriant forests" along meandering streams. "The shrubbery is beautiful, and consists in part of plums, grapes, crab apple, and persimmons." The soil was "rich and fertile," yielding "in abundance, wheat, corn, sweet potatoes, cotton and many other common agricultural products. Horses, cattle and hogs . . . are plentiful and seem nearly to raise themselves by grazing in the vast prairie range in summer and feeding upon the bottoms in winter." Numerous "buffalo, elk, deer, bear, wolves, beaver and many smaller animals here roam at pleasure. Turkeys, geese, swans, ducks, yea a variety of the feathered tribe, are among the rich abundance that grace the delightful regions of this goodly land—the heritage of the children of God."[13]

Within days of their arrival and after asking the Lord when and where the city of Zion and the temple should be built, Joseph received revelation that the land upon which they stood was "the land of promise, and the place for the city of Zion" (D&C 57:2). Furthermore, the Prophet learned that Independence was to be the center place of Zion and that the site on which the temple was to be built was just west of the already standing courthouse in the town square.

During the brethren's brief stay, Sidney Rigdon consecrated and dedicated the land for the building up of Zion and the gathering of the Saints, and Joseph dedicated the spot for the temple. He also paid his respects at the funeral of Polly Knight, his and Emma's dear and loyal friend who just two years before, with her good husband, Joseph Knight Sr., had provided desperately needed provisions for the Prophet and Emma in Harmony.

"My mother's health was very poor and had been for a considerable time, yet she would not consent to stop traveling," said Joseph Knight Jr. of Polly's trip to Missouri. "Her only, or her greatest desire, was to set her feet upon the land of Zion, and to have her body interred in that land. I went on shore and bought lumber to make a coffin in case she should die before we arrived at our place of destination—so fast did she fail. But the Lord gave her the desire of her heart, and she lived to stand upon that land."[14]

With most of the immediate affairs of the Church in order and with proper and strong leadership in place in Missouri, Joseph undoubtedly longed to return to Emma, the twins, and the Saints in Kirtland. As a result, just three weeks after his arrival, the Prophet and ten others left Missouri to return to Ohio.

Chapter Eleven

EMMA SPENT THE ENTIRE SUMMER OF 1831 without Joseph, although she enjoyed continued support from Mother and Father Smith. Her in-laws had grown to love and respect her and recognized the trials she was willing to endure for the sake of the gospel. Of Emma, Lucy later penned: "I have never seen a woman in my life, who would endure every species of fatigue and hardship, from month to month, and from year to year, with that unflinching courage, zeal, and patience, which she has ever done; for I know that which she has had to endure—she has been tossed upon the ocean of uncertainty—she has breasted the storms of persecution, and buffeted the rage of men and devils, which would have borne down almost any other woman. It may be, that many may yet have to encounter the same—I pray God, that this may not be the case; but, should it be, may they have grace given them according to their day, even as has been the case with her."[1]

The twins had certainly been a handful throughout the summer; nevertheless, motherhood suited Emma well, and she enjoyed loving them and watching them grow and develop. She understood well the need for her husband's travels and supported and sustained him; nonetheless, she worried for his safety and welfare while he was away. So when he and his party returned from Missouri on August 27, she was relieved to have him home again, safe and sound.

She and the other Saints in Kirtland were to this point unaware of the several revelations received in Missouri and excitedly accepted the news of the revealed location of Zion. Of their hunger for more divine communication, Joseph wrote: "In these infant days of the Church, there was a great anxiety to obtain the word of the Lord upon every subject that in any way concerned our salvation; and as the land of Zion was now the most important temporal object in view, I inquired of the Lord for further information upon the gathering of the Saints . . . and other matters."[2]

On September 12, Joseph moved Emma and the twins from their tiny cabin on the Morley farm to the John Johnson farm, about thirty miles southeast of Kirtland in Hiram, Ohio. John and his wife, Alice, had been converted to the gospel earlier that spring when, out of curiosity regarding the new doctrine being preached, they and some friends paid the Prophet and Emma a visit.

For years, Mrs. Johnson had been suffering from rheumatism in her shoulder and arm that prevented her from lifting her hand as high as her head. During the visit the subject of healing of the sick in ancient days was mentioned, and someone asked, "'Here is Mrs. Johnson with a lame arm: has God given any power to man now on earth to cure her?'"[3] After the conversation turned to another topic several minutes later, the Prophet walked across the room and, "taking Mrs. Johnson by the hand, said in the most solemn and impressive manner; 'Woman, in the name of the Lord Jesus Christ I command thee to be whole.'"[4] Then he left the room. In the presence of those still remaining, Mrs. Johnson easily lifted her arm and was said to have, for the first time in years, hung out her washing the next day without pain.

The Johnsons offered Emma and Joseph two adjoining rooms on the first floor of their large and beautiful New England colonial-style home. The house boasted a great untraditional central fireplace, where Emma cooked for her little family and baked in the brick bustle oven. Baking was an art and required a good deal of work and patience. She first shoveled hot coals into the oven, stoked them to a flame, and when proper baking temperature was attained, removed the coals and put in her bread or pastries. The customary procedure for testing the temperature was for a woman to put her hand in the oven. If the heat was unbearable in twelve seconds, the oven was "hot." If she could endure eighteen seconds, the temperature was said to be "quick"; twenty-four seconds, "moderate"; and thirty seconds or more, "warm."[5]

Joseph and Sidney resumed their work on the translation of the Bible in an upstairs room on the southeast side of the house. In consequence of their effort, they often turned to the Lord for understanding and were given several revelations introducing faith-altering new doctrine. After receiving one of the most poignant of these revelations, the Prophet wrote: "It was apparent that many important points touching the salvation of man, had been taken from the Bible, or lost before it was compiled. It appeared self-evident from what truths were left, that if God rewarded every one according to the deeds done in the body the term 'Heaven,' as intended for the Saints' eternal home must include more kingdoms than one."[6]

The revelation, which was received in a vision in mid-February 1832, detailed the three degrees of glory that exist in the eternal world and outlined the doctrine that all men will live after death and be assigned to the degree that they inherit through their faith and good works. Philo Dibble, a Church member who witnessed most of the reception of the vision, explained: "Joseph would, at intervals, say: 'What do I see?' as one might say while looking out the window and beholding what all in the room could not see. Then he would relate what he had seen or what he was looking at. Then Sidney replied, 'I see the same.' Presently Sidney would say, 'What do I see?' and would repeat what he had seen or was seeing, and Joseph would reply, 'I see the same.'

"This manner of conversation was repeated at short intervals to the end of the vision, and during the whole time not a word was spoken by any other person. Not a sound nor motion made by anyone but Joseph and Sidney, and it seemed to me that they never moved a joint or limb during the time I was there, which I think was over an hour, and to the end of the vision.

"Joseph sat firmly and calmly all the time in the midst of a magnificent glory, but Sidney sat limp and pale, apparently as limber as a rag, observing which, Joseph remarked, smilingly, 'Sidney is not used to it as I am.'"[7]

Although Joseph later observed, "Nothing could be more pleasing to the Saints upon the order of the kingdom of the Lord, than the light which burst upon the world through the . . . vision," the new doctrine was diametrically different from the Church members' former belief in heaven and hell and was for many difficult to fathom.[8] Brigham Young later confessed: "My traditions were such, that when the Vision came first to me, it was directly contrary and opposed to my former education. I said, Wait a little. I did not reject it; but I could not understand it. I then could feel what incorrect tradition had done for me. . . . I used to think and pray, to read and think, until I knew and fully understood it for myself, by the visions of the Holy Spirit."[9]

At this time in the Kirtland area, the number of members of the Church was quickly overtaking the number of others in the population, and the Saints were gaining control of civic affairs in the community. This change caused no small stir. Persecution began and then escalated when disgruntled members apostatized and joined the antagonistic nonmember forces. Indeed, Mormon was inspired when he wrote in the Book of Mormon: "And thus we can plainly discern, that after a people have been once enlightened by the Spirit of God, and have had great knowledge of things pertaining to righteousness, and then have fallen away into sin and transgression, they become more hardened, and thus their state becomes worse than though they had never known these things" (Alma 24:30). Many of these offended apostates would from this time forward cause great havoc and sorrow in the lives of Emma and Joseph.

On the night of March 24, 1832, Emma and Joseph were up late with the twins, who were both suffering from the measles. Emma soon took Julia to bed and Joseph stayed up rocking little Joseph, who was the sicker of the two. During the night Emma awoke and persuaded Joseph to bring the baby to bed. Soon afterward, she was awakened by soft tapping on the windows but paid little attention. Moments later she was startled when, with a burst of fury, about a dozen drunken marauders broke through the door, surrounded the bed, and amid Emma's terrified screams, dragged Joseph by his hair and limbs from the house into the night.

"I made a desperate struggle, as I was forced out, to extricate myself, but only cleared one leg, with which I made a pass at one man, and he fell on the door steps," wrote Joseph. "I was immediately overpowered again; and they swore . . . they would kill me if I did not be still, which quieted me. As they passed around the house with me, the fellow that I kicked came to me and thrust his hand, all covered with blood, into my face and with an exulting hoarse laugh, muttered: 'Gee, gee . . . I'll fix ye.'

"They then seized me by the throat and held on till I lost my breath. After I came to, as they passed along with me, about thirty rods from the house, I saw Elder Rigdon stretched out on the ground, whither they had dragged him by his heels. I supposed he was dead. I began to plead with them . . . [to] 'spare my life' . . . to which they replied, 'G—d—ye, call on yer God for help, we'll show ye no mercy.'"[10]

After the mob, which had grown to fifty or sixty men, dragged the Prophet a considerable distance from the Johnson home, some discussion ensued, and the decision was made to spare his life. Instead, they tore off his remaining clothes and ruthlessly beat and scratched him. Someone called for Simonds Ryder, who was one of the more hardened and vocal apostates, to bring a bucket of tar. Another cried with an oath, "Let us tar up his mouth."[11] Knowing the tar, if inhaled, could choke and kill him, Joseph turned his head and clenched his teeth to prevent them from forcing the sticky paddle into his mouth. Another man had a vial of poison, which he broke against Joseph's teeth when he tried to force him to drink from it.

Plans to castrate the Prophet had also been made; however, when the physician who was to perform the mutilation saw the pitiful state in which Joseph lay, his heart softened, and the gruesome plan was frustrated. The final assault came when a man jumped on him and

While Emma Sleeps

after scratching his body with his fingernails "like a mad cat" said, "G—d—ye, that's the way the Holy Ghost falls on folks!"[12]

Finally left alone, Joseph lay naked in the field, pulling tar from his lips to allow himself to "breathe more freely."[13] At length, he recovered enough to have sufficient strength to stand, and when he saw light coming from the Johnson home in the distance, he walked toward it. Emma met him at the front door and, thinking the tar was blood and that he had been beaten to a pulp, fainted. Because some neighboring sisters had gathered in her bedroom upon hearing the fracas, Joseph called for a blanket, which he wrapped around himself before entering the house.

While Emma recovered from the shock and then tended the feverish twins, the Johnsons, who had been barricaded in their bedroom by the mob before the Prophet's abduction, spent the remainder of the night scraping tar from Joseph's body and washing him. When morning dawned, Emma helped him clothe and ready himself to conduct and speak at their usual Sunday meeting. Later, from a short distance, she must have admired her husband's strength and fortitude as he stood on the front step of the Johnson home and taught the gospel of Jesus Christ. While listening, she may have detected an audible whistle in his speech, the result of a front tooth having been chipped by the mob.

As the Prophet looked out into the gathered faces, he recognized several men who had participated in the horrific events of the previous night. Said Joseph of that Sunday service, "With my flesh all scarified and defaced, I preached to the congregation as usual, and in the afternoon of the same day baptized three individuals."[14]

Within hours of the assault, Emma noticed that little Joseph, who had been more exposed than Julia to the cold and humid night air when the mob broke into their room, was showing symptoms of a serious cold. Already weakened by measles, his health worsened until five days later, on Friday, March 29, he died. Emma was overcome with grief at the loss of her fourth infant. As she watched her son's lifeless body lowered into the cold ground, she did not yet know the doctrine, which would later be revealed, that in the hereafter mothers could one day have the opportunity of raising their deceased children.

Chapter Twelve

THREE DAYS AFTER THE DEATH of little Joseph, the Prophet left with Newel K. Whitney and others for Missouri. With them they carried hymns Emma had selected and copied for W. W. Phelps to proof and print in Independence. Because violence continued to threaten the Johnson farm, before departing, Joseph and Newel advised Emma to take Julia to Kirtland and stay with Elizabeth. Because the men wished to avoid further trouble, they did not return to Kirtland before leaving for Missouri and therefore Elizabeth was unaware of Newel's insistent invitation.

When Emma arrived at the Whitney home, the door was answered by Elizabeth's aunt Sarah, who was antagonistic towards the Church and not fond of the influence Emma and Joseph were having on her family. Elizabeth was sick in bed in a back bedroom and did not hear the brief conversation Emma had with the older woman, so she had no knowledge that her aunt had denied the Prophet's wife and daughter a place to stay.

Humiliated at being turned away and to avoid causing hard feelings, Emma told no one of the embarrassing incident, including Elizabeth, and instead drifted from one home to another until Joseph and his party returned from Missouri sometime in June. Many years later Emma confided to her mother-in-law, Lucy, that she still felt mortified by the memory of that day. Elizabeth, who did not find out about her aunt's insult until much later, remarked, "I would have shared the last morsel with either of them, and was grieved beyond comparison when I found what she [Aunt Sarah] had done."[1]

Joseph and Newel stayed only a few weeks in Jackson County and would have arrived in Kirtland before the middle of June, but an accident delayed their return. Both men had to jump from the coach in which they were riding when the horses spooked and stampeded. The Prophet was uninjured; however, Newel failed to clear the coach completely, and his leg was broken when it caught in the spoke of the wheel. Rather than leave him alone at an inn in Greenville, Indiana, Joseph stayed with his friend for four weeks until his leg was healed sufficiently for travel.

Joseph's time at the inn was nearly as uncomfortable as Newel's. One evening after dinner, he became ill and vomited "large quantities of blood and poisonous matter," heaving so violently that he dislocated his jaw.[2] He also became very homesick and, unaware of Emma and Julia's indigent circumstances, was disheartened when a letter from Elizabeth was delivered by Martin Harris to Newel and he received no word from Emma. In consequence he penned the following:

> Dear Wife:
>
> I would inform you that Brother Martin has arrived here and brought the pleasing news that our families were well when he left there which greatly cheered our hearts and revived our spirits. . . . My situation is a very unpleasant one although I will endeavor to be contented, the Lord assisting me. . . . Sister Whitney wrote a letter to her husband which was very cheering and being unwell at that time and filled with much anxiety it would have been very consoling to me to have received a few lines from you but as you did not take the trouble, I will try to be contented with my lot knowing that God is my friend. In him I shall find comfort. . . . I should like [to] see little Julia and once more take her on my knee and converse with you on all the subjects which concern us. . . . I subscribe myself your husband. The Lord bless you and peace be with [you]. So farewell until I return.[3]

Emma undoubtedly felt somewhat hurt because of the unwarranted chastisement she received in the communication, but she also realized Joseph had no way of knowing she was reduced to nearly vagabond status. Even though she too was experiencing times of nausea and ill health because of her third pregnancy, she remained upbeat and busy. Lucy Smith later gave an account of Emma's attitude at the time: "She was then young and, being naturally ambitious, her whole heart was occupied in the work of the Lord, and she felt no interest except for the church and the cause of truth. Whatever her hands found to do she did with her might and did not ask the selfish question, 'Shall I be benefitted more than anyone else?' If elders were sent away to preach, she was the first to volunteer her service, to assist in clothing them for their journey. And, let her own privations be what they might, . . . she scorned to complain. . . . During Joseph's absence she was not idle, for she labored faithfully for the interest of those with whom she stayed, cheering them by her lively and spirited conversation."4

Emma was grateful to see Joseph again when he and Newel returned to Kirtland and was relieved to know she would not have to return to the Johnson farm, where mischief towards the members was still being perpetrated. Instead, the Whitneys invited them to take up residence above their store, where three good-sized upstairs rooms, previously used for storage, were made available to them, as well as a ground-level kitchen, of which Emma enjoyed full use.

Joseph and Emma's living quarters soon became the headquarters of the Church, and Emma welcomed into her home many visitors, curiosity seekers, and numbers of new converts who continued to gather to Ohio. Indeed, "they came, men, women, and children, in every conceivable manner, some with horses, oxen, and vehicles rough and rude, while others had walked all or part of the distance. The future 'City of the Saints' appeared like one besieged. Every available house, shop, hut, or barn was filled to its utmost capacity. Even boxes were roughly extemporized and used for shelter until something more permanent could be secured."5

In early October, Joseph left Emma again and headed east with Newel for New York and Massachusetts. The purpose of the trip was to purchase goods for the Whitney mercantile and proselyte along the way. Knowing how difficult his last trip from home had been for Emma and the anxiety and fear she was feeling as the birth of another child was drawing near, he asked Hyrum to watch over her and Julia in his absence.

In a letter written to Emma upon returning to his room in lower Manhattan after a day in New York City, Joseph expressed his affection and concern to "my dear wife" and Julia: "This day I have been walking through the most splendid part of the City of New Y[ork]. The buildings are truly great and wonderful to the astonishing of every beholder. . . . I returned to my room to meditate and calm my mind and behold the thoughts of home, of Emma and Julia rushes . . . upon my mind like a flood and I could wish for a moment to be with them. My breast is filled with feelings and tenderness of a parent and a husband. . . . I feel as if I wanted to say something to you to comfort you in your peculiar trial and present affliction. I hope God will give you strength that you may not faint. I pray God to soften the hearts of those around you to be kind to you and take the burden off your shoulders as much as possible and not afflict you. I feel for you for I know your state and that others do not but you must comfort yourself knowing that God is your friend in heaven and that you have one true and living friend on earth, your husband."6

Less than a month later, when the Prophet arrived in Kirtland in the early morning of November 6, someone shouted to him that he had a son! About two o'clock that morning, Emma once again felt the hard pains of labor and delivered a baby boy into the world. As she lay exhausted, the reassurance that the baby lived was encouraging, and her spirits were further bolstered when Joseph excitedly entered their room. Their reunion was tender as they rejoiced together at the birth of this healthy son, whom they named Joseph Smith the Third.

Chapter Thirteen

As THE LITTLE FAMILY OF FOUR WELCOMED in the new year of 1833, Joseph received revelation about the education of the Saints. Said the Lord: "And I give unto you a commandment that you shall teach one another the doctrine of the kingdom. Teach ye diligently and my grace shall attend you, that you may be instructed more perfectly. . . . Teach one another words of wisdom; yea, seek ye out of the best books words of wisdom; seek learning, even by study and also by faith. . . . Appoint among yourselves a teacher, and let not all be spokesmen at once; but let one speak at a time and let all listen unto his sayings, that when all have spoken that all may be edified of all, and that every man may have an equal privilege" (D&C 88:77–78, 118, 122).

In consequence of the revelation, Joseph organized the School of the Prophets in late January, and meetings were held in the room directly above Emma's kitchen. The school met frequently during that winter to discuss the affairs of the Church and to be instructed in the doctrines of the kingdom as well as in grammar and other secular subjects. Most of the brethren who attended the meetings either smoked or chewed tobacco, and within a month's time Emma had had about all she could stand of the smoke filling her home and the chewing tobacco residue staining her hardwood floor. She commented to her husband that "it would be a good thing if a revelation could be a hand declaring the use of tobacco a sin, and commanding its suppression."[1]

Joseph, who was also bothered at having to teach the brethren "in a cloud of tobacco smoke," took the problem to the Lord and received the revelation now called the Word of Wisdom.[2] Included in the communication were several principles and promises, including abstinence from alcoholic beverages, tea, coffee, and tobacco; dietary guidelines; and the assurance that if the teachings were observed, one would enjoy greater physical, mental, and emotional health and protection from the adversary.

In the same revelation in which Joseph was given instruction concerning the schooling of the Saints, he also received the command to build a temple, for the Lord said, "Establish a house, even a house of prayer, a house of fasting, a house of faith, a house of learning, a house of glory, a house of order, a house of God" (D&C 88:119). Because the Saints failed to act upon the revelation, on June 1 they were rebuked and again commanded to "build a house, in the which house I design to endow those whom I have chosen with power from on high" (D&C 95:8). Without further delay, ground was broken for a temple, and on July 23, 1833, the cornerstones were laid.

Regarding the plan for the construction of the temple, Joseph initially counseled with the brethren and, according to his mother, received various opinions: "Some were in favor of building a frame house, but others were of a mind to put up a log house. Joseph reminded them that they were not building a house for a man, but for God; 'and shall we, brethren,' said he, 'build a house for our God, of logs? No, I have a better plan than that. I have a plan of the house of the Lord, given by himself; and you will soon see by this, the difference between our calculations and his idea of things.'"[3]

Nearly every member of the Church in Kirtland was engaged in one way or another in building the temple for the next two and a half years, and many were beginning to learn that this was the reason for their gathering to Ohio. According to the Prophet, "The main object [of gathering] was to build unto the Lord a house whereby He could reveal unto His people the ordinances of His house and the glories of His kingdom, and teach the people the way of salvation; for there are certain ordinances and principles that, when they are taught and practiced, must be done in a place or house built for that purpose."[4]

Joseph labored alongside the brethren when possible, cutting and hauling stone from a quarry two miles away for the outside walls; and cutting, drying, and seasoning the lumber for the finish work and inside furnishings. Emma was asked to coordinate the sisters' efforts, for they were no less engaged than the men. They worked at spinning, weaving, and knitting clothes for the workers to wear, and as the construction neared completion, they wove the carpets and sewed the veil of the temple. The Prophet expressed his gratitude for their labors: "Well, sisters, . . . you are always on hand. The sisters are always first and foremost in all good works. Mary was first at the resurrection; and the sisters now are the first to work on the inside of the temple."[5]

The construction served to fuel the fires of persecution in Kirtland toward the Saints, and they were forced to place guards around the temple site. The Prophet received constant threats against his life, and "it was found necessary to keep continual guard to prevent his being murdered by his enemies."[6] Emma's concern for her husband's welfare intensified as she too endured constant harassment.

Meanwhile, nearly one thousand miles away in Missouri, the Saints found the early months of 1833 pleasant and prosperous. Parley P. Pratt declared that "there has seldom, if ever, been a happier people upon the earth than the Church of the Saints now were."[7] Spring welcomed the migration of numbers of Saints into Jackson County from Kirtland and other areas, and these new arrivals purchased property, built homes, and cultivated their fields. W. W. Phelps was busy in his shop editing and printing the Saints' local newspaper, *The Evening and the Morning Star,* and the Book of Commandments, which contained the revelations received by the Prophet to date.

In July the original settlers in Jackson County became anxious as they watched the membership of the Church grow and heard rumors that thousands more were coming. The local talk was unsettling to the Protestant ministers, who feared losing some of their flock to this "fanatical" religion. One minister wrote, "The 'Mormons' are the common enemies of mankind and ought to be destroyed"; another went "from house to house, seeking to destroy The Church by spreading slanderous falsehoods, to incite the people to acts of violence against the saints."[8] In addition, Missouri was a slave state, so the citizens of Jackson County became nervous when they learned that sentiments among some of the Saints leaned toward abolition. There were economic concerns as well. The original settlers believed Mormon merchants were monopolizing the Saints' business because most of them had no money and bartered for goods and supplies.

The conflict finally came to a head on July 20, when four to five hundred anti-Mormon citizens demanded that the Saints leave the area and that W. W. Phelps cease printing the *The Evening and the Morning Star.* After some conversation between the antagonists and Church leaders, members were given fifteen minutes to pack up and leave all they owned and had worked for.

When the Saints refused to do so, the mob became violent, seriously damaging the Phelps print shop and residence and destroying most of the printed sheets of the Book of Commandments. Some of the pages containing the sacred revelations were saved by Mary Elizabeth and Caroline Rollins—sisters aged fourteen and twelve, who grabbed as many sheets as they could carry from a pile of rubble in front of the shop and hid in a cornfield until the mobbers left.

The hymns Emma had compiled were likely among the papers destroyed, and the press that had been transported at great cost from Cincinnati was thrown from a second-story window. Later that day Bishop Partridge was tarred and feathered in the public square, but when he bore the humiliation and pain of the attack with "so much resignation and meekness," the mob allowed him "to retire in silence, many looking very solemn, their sympathies having been touched."[9]

On July 23, the very day on which the cornerstones were laid for the Kirtland Temple in Ohio, the mob again attacked the Saints in Missouri, setting fire to haystacks and grain fields and destroying several homes, barns, and businesses. The violence continued throughout the fall. Members' houses were unroofed, some of the brethren were beaten nearly to death, and two Missourians and one member of the Church were killed.

Finally, in November, the Saints in Jackson County surrendered their homes and properties and agreed to leave Jackson County. Two sisters died when a group of about 130 women and children, whose husbands and fathers had left them to find wagons, were driven from their homes. Elder Parley P. Pratt described the horrific scene: "Hundreds of people were seen in every direction, some in tents and some in the open air around their fires, while the rain descended in torrents. Husbands were inquiring for their wives, wives for their husbands; parents for children, and children for parents."[10]

Lyman Wight, who likewise witnessed the expulsion, said: "Mobs went from house to house, thrusting poles and rails in at the windows and doors of the houses of the Saints. . . . I saw one hundred and ninety women and children driven thirty miles across the prairie, with three decrepit men only in their company, . . . the ground thinly crusted with sleet; and I could easily follow on their trail by the blood that flowed from their lacerated feet on the stubble of the burnt prairie!"[11]

Most of the Saints sought refuge in Clay County, where they were offered food, shelter, and opportunities for work by the local citizens. A conference was held there on January 1, 1834, in which their plight was discussed, and the members thought it best to send someone to Kirtland to counsel with the Prophet. Elders Parley Pratt and Lyman Wight volunteered to make the trip and soon thereafter set out on horseback for Ohio.

Joseph had been kept apprised of the seriousness of the situation and continually sought the Lord's guidance for providing comfort to the Missouri Saints. In a letter following the July attacks he wrote, "Brethren if I were with you I should take an active part in your sufferings, and although nature shrinks, yet my spirit would not let me forsake you unto death God helping me."[12] When Elders Pratt and Wight reached Kirtland near the end of February 1834, they met with the Prophet and the high council in his and Emma's home. After hearing the men's report and the discussion which followed, Joseph announced that he was going to Missouri to aid in the redemption of Zion.

While preparations were being made for the trip, a young man named Wilford Woodruff arrived in town looking for the Prophet. Of his first meeting with Joseph and his stay in the Smith home, Wilford wrote: "I found him and his brother Hyrum out shooting at a mark with a brace of pistols. When they stopped shooting, I was introduced to Brother Joseph, and he shook hands with me most heartily. He invited me to make his habitation my home while I tarried in Kirtland. . . . I . . . was greatly edified and blest during my stay." Wilford Woodruff recorded that during his visit the Prophet invited him to help tan a wolf hide, which they did after stretching it over the back of one of Emma's chairs.[13]

When Emma heard of her husband's intention to redeem Zion, she knew she would be left to spend another summer without him. She must also have wondered what redeeming Zion would entail. Would Joseph and the others engage in actual combat, or could the conflict be otherwise resolved? All the same, she kissed him and waved good-bye on May 5 and watched as he and one hundred other men, including Wilford Woodruff and Brigham Young, rode west. En route, Joseph and his company met with Hyrum and a group of Saints from Michigan. Together they made up Zion's Camp—as the small army was called—which consisted of two hundred and seven men, eleven women, eleven children, and twenty-five wagons loaded with supplies and provisions.[14]

Zion's Camp reached Clay County by mid-June, and though they learned that nearly four hundred men had gathered to come up against them, they were ready and willing to do whatever was necessary to regain the Missouri Saints' properties. Nevertheless, after kneeling in prayer, the Prophet Joseph stayed their hand before any fighting ensued and promised the camp protection from on high. He commanded the army: "Stand still and see the salvation of God."[15] The camp was disbanded on July 3 without entering into any physical conflict with the Missourians.

Although Emma wrote and sent several letters to Joseph throughout the summer, the only correspondence she received in return were two letters, both written well before the camp had reached Missouri. In them Joseph sent his love, a little money, and his concern for her welfare. Notwithstanding her lack of personal correspondence from him, she did have access to horrifying reports printed in the Ohio newspapers during the late summer months, which stated that Joseph had been shot in the leg, that the limb had been amputated, and that he had died three days after the surgery. Whether she received word that Joseph was alive and well before he arrived in Kirtland is not known, but to finally see and hold him again when he arrived in early August was a comfort and blessing.

Though Zion's Camp did nothing to regain the property of the Saints in Missouri, it did try the mettle and serve as a test of the faith and sacrifice of those who served. When the Quorum of the Twelve Apostles and the First Quorum of the Seventy were organized the following year, in 1835, all but three of the original members of the Quorum of the Twelve Apostles and every member of the original Quorum of the Seventy had made the march of nearly one thousand miles to Missouri with Zion's Camp.

Chapter Fourteen

THE TWO YEARS FOLLOWING ZION'S CAMP were a glorious time for the Kirtland Saints. Although persecution—particularly from apostates—abounded, great spiritual manifestations were had, the membership continued to grow, and the leadership was strengthened. Before the Missouri march, the Prophet told a group of priesthood leaders: "You know no more concerning the destinies of this Church and kingdom than a babe upon its mother's lap. You don't comprehend it. . . . It is only a little handful of Priesthood you see here tonight, but this Church will fill North and South America. It will fill the world. . . . It will fill the Rocky Mountains."[1]

Sometime during the summer of 1834, Emma and Joseph moved into a house built for them on the hill near the temple site, and Joseph moved his office to the newly built combination schoolhouse and printing office in November.[2] Nevertheless, their home continued to be the hub of Church activity, and the demands on Emma steadily increased. When Joseph was at home, much of his time was spent studying, in meetings, or greeting the "multitude of visitors . . . who came to inquire after the work of the Lord."[3]

Emma's dinner table was always surrounded by guests, and often many were invited to stay overnight. As the pace of the temple construction quickened, she provided room and board for several of the workers and others who needed care and provisions. One evening a brother with a badly infected and swollen arm visited, and though she did not know the man, Emma prepared an herb poultice for his arm and provided him a warm bed for the night.

More than once, Saints in need bypassed the Prophet and showed up on her doorstep seeking assistance. One sister recorded that although her family went to bed hungry, they were comforted by knowing that in the morning they could go see Sister Emma and be provided for. Caroline Crosby, whose husband was hired by a builder to do some finish work on Emma and Joseph's home, noted that as her husband was working alone on the house

"Sister Emma . . . came in one day, and inquired of him whether or where he got his provision. He told her he was entirely without, and knew not where to look, as he had no money, and the boss who employed him had no means in his hands. She then went into her chamber, and brought him a nice ham [weighing] 20 lbs. Telling him that it was a present for his faithfulness, and that he should bring a sack, and get as much flour as he could to take home. Accordingly he came home rejoicing, considering it a perfect Godsend. It was a beautiful white flour, and the ham was very sweet. I thought nothing ever tasted half as good."[4]

Though busy, Emma always made time for her children. One day when young Joseph wanted to go fishing with some of the older neighborhood boys, Emma helped him prepare. "My mother, to gratify me, procured a little pole and attached a thread thereto, with a bent pin for a hook, and away I marched to the creek. I threw my hook without bait into the water and the little fishes gathered to it as it fell. By some strange chance one became fastened to it and was drawn to the shore. In great excitement I dropped the pole and gathering the fish in my hands rushed to the house with it, shouting, 'I've got one! I've got one!'"[5]

Life in Kirtland became ever more social, with the members meeting often in singing schools, prayer meetings, and church services. Before the temple was completed, meetings were held in the schoolhouse, and members would arrive early to get a seat. "It was quite a curiosity to see them coming so early, almost as soon as light in order to get a seat. And finally they decided on taking their turns in staying away, as the weather was so cold,"[6] wrote Sister Crosby.

The friendship enjoyed by Emma with Elizabeth Whitney flourished as the two women prepared large dinners of simple food for the steady flow of new arrivals in the community and for those with special needs already living in Kirtland. Said the Prophet, "The lame, the halt, and the blind were invited, according to the instructions of the Savior."[7]

Often Emma accompanied Joseph to check on the welfare of the Saints and visit them in their homes. Together with the children, they attended meetings, weddings, funerals, and various other social events. On occasion Emma was invited to sit in council with the brethren and was not reserved in expressing her opinions. Emma, whether directly or indirectly, was as much a part of the Saints' day-to-day lives as was Joseph.

In December 1834 she received her patriarchal blessing from Father Smith, who had been set apart as the first Patriarch of the Church. As the Lord's mouthpiece, the Patriarch said: "Emma, my daughter-in-law, thou art blessed of the Lord, for thy faithfulness and truth: thou shalt be blessed with thy husband and rejoice in the glory which will come upon him: thy soul has been afflicted because of the wickedness of men in seeking the destruction of thy companion, and thy whole soul has been drawn out in prayer for his deliverance, rejoice, for the Lord thy God has heard thy supplication. Thou hast grieved for the hardness of the hearts of thy father's house, and thou hast longed for their salvation. The Lord will have respect to thy cries, and by his judgments he will cause some of them to see their folly and repent of their sins; but it will be by affliction that they will be saved. Thou shalt see many days; yea, the Lord will spare thee till thou art satisfied, for thou shalt see thy redeemer. Thy heart shalt rejoice in the great work of the Lord, and no one shall take thy rejoicing from thee. Thou shalt ever remember the great condescension of thy God in permitting thee to accompany my son when the angel delivered the record of the Nephites to his care. Thou hast seen much sorrow because the Lord has taken from thee three of thy children: in this thou art not to be blamed, for he knows thy pure desires to raise up a family, that the name of my son might be blessed. And now, behold, I say unto thee, that thus saith the Lord, if thou will believe, thou shalt yet be blessed in this thing and thou shalt bring forth other children, to the joy and satisfaction of thy soul, and to the rejoicing of thy friends. Thou shalt be blessed with understanding, and have power to instruct thy sex. Teach thy family righteousness, and thy little ones the way of life, and the holy angels shall watch over thee and thou shalt be saved in the kingdom of God, even so, Amen."[8]

Emma's estrangement from her family and her inability to convince them of the truthfulness of the gospel caused her much sorrow. Although she considered Joseph's family her own, it had been five long years since she had seen her parents or any of her siblings, so it was a delightful blessing when in 1835 she met an old acquaintance, William R. Hine, from Harmony. Said Hine of the reunion: "When I first saw Emma on the streets in Kirtland, she threw her arms around me and I think kissed me, and inquired all about her father's family. I brought her letters and took some later to Mr. [Isaac] Hale from her."[9]

On July 3, 1835, an interesting character named Michael H. Chandler arrived in Kirtland looking for the Prophet. With him he brought four Egyptian mummies and some papyrus scrolls he had inherited from an uncle who had discovered them in Egypt. Previously, he had allowed several scholars in the East to examine the characters on the scrolls, but when he was told of Joseph and his ability to read ancient writings, Chandler sought him out. According to Orson Pratt, "The prophet took them and repaired to his room and inquired of the Lord concerning them. The Lord told him they were sacred records" and enabled Joseph to translate some of the characters.[10] When he gave Chandler his translation, the collector signed a certificate testifying that it corresponded "in the most minute matters" with those of the eastern scholars.[11]

Chandler agreed to sell the ancient scrolls and the mummies to the Church. Because they were kept in her home, Emma's workload was increased by the number of visitors who came to view the artifacts. She obliged the curiosity seekers by showing them the mummies and explaining what she had learned from Joseph about the characters on the scrolls.

Joseph's immediate concern was more with the papyri than the mummies. Without delay he began to translate the ancient characters and soon realized they were the writings of Abraham and Joseph, who was betrayed by his brothers and sold into Egypt. The Prophet described the record as "beautifully written on papyrus, with black, and a small part red, ink or paint, in perfect preservation. The characters are such as you find upon the coffins of mummies—hieroglyphics . . . with many characters of letters like the present . . . form of the Hebrew without points."[12]

In September Emma was given an additional responsibility, one she surely enjoyed, when in a meeting of the high council "it was . . . decided that Sister Emma Smith proceed to make [another] selection of Sacred Hymns . . . and that President W. W. Phelps be appointed to revise and arrange them for printing."[13] Though the first attempt at printing the book in Independence had been frustrated, the hymnbook Emma had been compiling since before leaving New York in 1830 was finally to be printed.

The hymnal was printed in the Church's printing office by the Church-owned Literary Firm. The pocket-sized, leather-bound book, which contained no musical scores, measured three by four inches and presented the words to ninety hymns to be sung to various well-known religious tunes, including lyrics by W. W. Phelps, Eliza R. Snow, Parley P. Pratt, and Edward Partridge. Although the date printed on the hymnal was 1835, it did not come off the press until February 1836, just in time for use during the dedication of the temple.

Though Emma and Joseph's relationship was close, they occasionally experienced misunderstandings in their marriage. Joseph recorded in November 1835 that one Sunday he chastised her "for leaving the meeting before Sacrament," and as Emma gave no apparent reason for her early departure, the Prophet assumed she was ashamed or sorry, for he continued his account saying, "she made no reply, but manifested contrition by weeping."[14] Likewise, misunderstandings within the Smith family circle were not common but did occasionally occur. Joseph's brother William did not always see eye to eye with the Prophet. On one occasion William became angry when Joseph expressed an opinion different from his regarding debates in the School of the Prophets "and at length became much enraged . . . and used violence"[15] toward Joseph and others present. Because Father and Mother Smith

Emma's Hymns

were at the time living with William and were dismayed at his behavior, Joseph invited his parents to move into Emma's already crowded home.

Lucy later provided a colorful depiction of their living conditions: "How often I have, with my . . . daughters-in-law, parted every bed in the house for the accommodation of the brethren, and then laid a single blanket on the floor for my husband and myself, while Joseph slept upon the same hard floor, with nothing but a cloak for both bed and bedding, Emma placing herself by his side to share his comfort—and this was our rest for two weeks together, while we labored hard every day. But those who were accommodated by our privations did not know how we fared, for neither Emma nor I suffered them to know that we took unwearied pains for them."[16]

About this same time, Emma suspected she was again pregnant, and although she seemed to enjoy better health with this pregnancy than earlier ones, she undoubtedly experienced problems relative to carrying the child. The Prophet's schedule was very busy, but he helped her around the house as much as occasion permitted and wrote of the contentment he enjoyed while spending time near the fireside reading, studying, and teaching the children grammar. Christmas of 1835 was particularly special, as they spent the entire day together. In his journal Joseph recorded, "Enjoyed myself at home with my family, all day, it being Christmas, the only time I have had this privilege so satisfactorily for a long period."[17]

Chapter Fifteen

THE TEMPLE WAS COMPLETED IN MARCH 1836, less than three years from the beginning of construction but not without many sacrifices, many miracles, and much persecution. Because the building was over one hundred feet high to the top of the steeple, men worked under dangerous circumstances on the scaffolding and not without accident. Moreover, the kiln in which green wood was dried and cured caught fire several times, burning thousands of board feet of lumber.

Brigham Young remembered that he and the Prophet "worked on that building day after day; also, many others did so. They did not have molasses to eat with their johnny cake. Sometimes they had shoes, and sometimes not; sometimes they would have tolerable pants, and, sometimes, very ragged ones."[1] Heber C. Kimball recorded: "While we were building the Temple, in Kirtland . . . we were persecuted and were under the necessity of laying upon the floor with our firelocks by our sides to sustain ourselves, as there were mobs gathering all around us to destroy us, and prevent us from building the Temple."[2]

The temple was dedicated on Sunday, March 27, and was attended by more than one thousand people. Many others who were denied a place inside gathered in the nearby school-house or outside the temple windows, which were left open in order for them to hear. The meeting began at nine o'clock with a scripture and opening hymn, after which Sidney Rigdon spoke for two and a half hours. Emma, now about five months pregnant, then raised her right arm to the square with hundreds of others to sustain her Joseph as the prophet and seer of the dispensation of the fulness of times. The morning meeting then was ended with song and prayer.

After an intermission of fifteen to twenty minutes, the afternoon service continued with hymns, the sustaining of other officers of the Church, and a short address by the Prophet. Then he read the dedicatory prayer, which was revealed to him previously. After the prayer,

W. W. Phelps's hymn "The Spirit of God like a Fire Is Burning" was sung, the sacrament was administered, and several brethren bore their testimonies. The entire congregation then participated in the Hosanna Shout, "shouting three times, 'Hosanna, hosanna, hosanna to God and the Lamb,'"3 followed by three amens. The service, which lasted about seven hours, ended with the Prophet pronouncing a blessing on all in attendance.

That evening the Prophet met with the brethren in a priesthood meeting "and gave them instructions in relation to the spirit of prophecy." He exhorted the brethren, "Do not quench the Spirit, for the first one that opens his mouth shall receive the Spirit of prophecy."4 When Joseph's cousin George A. Smith stood and began to speak, Joseph recorded that "a noise was heard like the sound of a rushing mighty wind, which filled the Temple, and all the congregation simultaneously arose, being moved upon by an invisible power. . . . I beheld the Temple was filled with angels, which fact I declared to the congregation. The people in the neighborhood came running together (hearing an unusual sound within, and seeing a bright light like a pillar of fire resting upon the Temple), and were astonished at what was taking place."5

As wonderful and miraculous as these spiritual experiences were, the climax of this Pentecostal period came the following Sunday, when the Savior appeared to the Prophet and Oliver Cowdery and approved the temple, saying, "I have accepted this house, and my name shall be here; and I will manifest myself to my people in mercy in this house" (D&C 110:7). At the close of that vision, Moses appeared and committed to them "the keys of the gathering of Israel" (D&C 110:11). Then Elias appeared and brought back "the great Abrahamic covenant whereby the faithful receive promises of eternal increase, promises that through celestial marriage their eternal posterity shall be as numerous as the sands upon the seashore."6

In a third visitation, Elijah appeared and "restored to this Church and, if they would receive it, to the world, the keys of the sealing power; and that sealing power puts the stamp of approval upon every ordinance that is done in this Church and more particularly those that are performed in the temples of the Lord. Through that restoration," wrote President Joseph Fielding Smith, "each of you . . . has the privilege . . . to have your wife sealed to you for time and for all eternity, and your children sealed to you also."7 Joseph later taught the Saints that the word *turn* in Malachi's prophecy that Elijah would come "to turn the hearts of the fathers to the children, and the children to the fathers" (D&C 110:15) should be translated as "bind, or seal"8 and that the Saints could become saviors on Mount Zion by "going forth and receiving all the ordinances, baptisms, confirmations, washings, anointings, ordinations and sealing powers upon their heads, in behalf of all their progenitors who are dead, and redeem them that they may come forth in the first resurrection."[9]

For Emma, the Melchizedek Priesthood keys restored by the ancient prophets and the marvelous truths being revealed through her prophet-husband brought great comfort. In combination with the revelation Joseph received in the Kirtland Temple in January 1836 that "all children who die before they arrive at the years of accountability, are saved in the celestial kingdom of heaven,"[10] she now had greater hope and a deeper understanding of the salvation of her lost children.

Three days after the restoration of the Melchizedek Priesthood keys, a grand meeting was held in the temple in which more than four hundred worthy priesthood holders who had been previously washed and anointed were "endowed with power from on high" (D&C 38:32). The endowment that was bestowed upon them was not the full endowment, which was received later in Nauvoo, but a preparatory one.

Chapter Sixteen

EMMA AND JOSEPH'S HOME WAS FILLED with the cries of a newborn on June 20, 1836, when Emma gave birth to a baby boy, named Frederick Granger Williams Smith for Joseph's counselor in the First Presidency. The joy this healthy child and second living son brought into their home was indeed a tender mercy.

To Emma's dismay, however, it was necessary for Joseph to leave with his brother Hyrum, Oliver Cowdery, and Sidney Rigdon for Salem, Massachusetts, just three weeks after Frederick's birth. Heavy debt had been incurred from the building of the temple and other construction projects as well as from aid given to the Missouri Saints and immigrants arriving daily in Kirtland. The brethren were going east in hopes of securing funds that would bring solvency to the Church.

Joseph was gone nearly three months, but Emma was not left alone to care for the children, the house, and the visitors. Two years before, in April 1835, Eliza R. Snow had joined the Church and less than a year later had come to Kirtland to participate in the temple dedication. Afterward Emma and Joseph invited her to live with them and to teach Julia and young Joseph. Eliza, who was single and Emma's age, was well educated and had written and published poetry for some years. She was slender, above medium height, with dark red hair, striking brown eyes, and a radiant, dignified countenance. Not long after moving into Emma's home, she also established a school for young ladies, which was soon well attended.

Nonetheless, even with Eliza's help and friendship, Emma was of course relieved and delighted when Joseph and his companions returned to Kirtland in September. Her feelings of relief were short-lived, though, when the following day the Prophet addressed the brethren in a meeting: "Brethren, I am rejoiced to see you. . . . We are now nearly as happy as we can be on earth. We have accomplished more than we had any reason to expect when we began. . . . Furthermore, we have everything that is necessary to our comfort and convenience, and, judging from appearances, one would not suppose that anything could occur which would break up our friendship for each other. . . . But, brethren, beware; for I tell you in the name of the Lord, that there is an evil in this very congregation, which, if not repented of, will result in setting many of you . . . so much at enmity against me, that you will have a desire to take my life."[1]

When those last words reached Emma's ears, they must have instilled within her a deep fear for her husband's welfare. His life had been threatened many times before, but for Joseph to prophesy openly that the enemy was among his supposed friends and confidants was beyond distressing. Speculation about who the traitors might be spread quickly through Kirtland and surely gripped Emma's heart and mind as well. Who could she trust, confide in, and rely on? Her fears were justified, as the strength of the Church and its leaders began to erode quickly.

One contributor to the deterioration was the failure of the Kirtland Safety Society. The heavy debt incurred by the Church had not been alleviated by the trip to Massachusetts, so the brethren decided to attract investors and establish a banking society similar to others being created throughout the state. The Kirtland Safety Society, which was formed to provide revenue to the Church by offering loans, currency, and a safe place for individuals to deposit money, opened its doors for business on January 2, 1837.

It met immediate opposition when anti-Mormon businessmen refused to accept the currency and local newspapers declared the notes useless. When enemies of the Church secured a good deal of the currency and made a run on the bank by demanding gold or silver in exchange, the Society was unable to make good on all the notes because the bank's primary capital was in land. Larger economic factors were involved also, as a banking scare later referred to as the Panic of 1837 had started that spring in New York and spread quickly west until it hit Kirtland. Nonetheless, the most hurtful blow for Emma and Joseph was the discovery that money had been embezzled by one or more of the brethren employed by the Society.

The Kirtland Safety Society was forced to close its doors in November 1837, and the two hundred shareholders lost nearly all of their invested capital. Joseph and Emma took the heaviest loss in the venture because, although they had sufficient assets in property and goods to cover their debt, they had little cash and were unable to liquidate their assets immediately to pay their creditors. In consequence, Joseph was hit with seventeen lawsuits for debts amounting to more than thirty thousand dollars.

Even before the bank failure, faultfinding and evil-speaking against Joseph were spreading among the members, particularly when he was away preaching the gospel or on business trips. Eliza R. Snow recognized the wickedness creeping in among the people soon after the dedication of the temple. She reflected that "a spirit of speculation had crept into the hearts of some of the Twelve, and nearly, if not every quorum was more or less infected. . . . many who had been humble and faithful . . . were getting haughty in their spirits, and lifted up in the pride of their hearts. As the Saints drank in the love and spirit of the world, the Spirit of the Lord withdrew from their hearts, and they were filled with pride and hatred toward those who maintained their integrity."[2]

While men in high leadership positions declared Joseph a fallen prophet, spiritually stronger men, such as Brigham Young and Heber C. Kimball, put their very lives on the line and spoke out publicly in his behalf. At a meeting in the temple, both men listened while complaints were spoken against their beloved leader. Finally hearing enough, Brigham Young stood and declared that Joseph was a prophet and that the murmurers "could not destroy the appointment of the Prophet of God, they could only destroy their own authority, cut the thread that bound them to the Prophet and to God, and sink themselves to hell."[3] Of these dark days Caroline Crosby recorded: "Many of our most intimate associates were among the apostates. . . . These were some of our nighest neighbors and friends. We had taken sweet counsel together, and walked to the house of God as friends. They came out boldly against the prophet, and signed an instrument . . . renouncing all their alliance with the church."[4]

Meanwhile, amidst the turmoil Emma continued to live her life with some appearance of normalcy. She received help in November 1836, when she and Joseph agreed to provide food, housing, and an education for young Hervey Cowdery, a nephew of Oliver. In return Hervey helped in and around the house and before long found a place in Emma's heart. In a letter to her husband, Emma expressed her affection for the young man when she asked Joseph if he would "write some words of encouragement to Hervey, for he is very faithful not only in business, but in taking up his cross in the family."[5]

In an effort to escape the negative forces against him in Kirtland, Joseph was gone much of the time but not without purpose. In all his travels he was proclaiming the gospel and strengthening the Church. Emma stayed in Kirtland to care for the children, run the household, attend to visitors, and protect their property and other possessions. In a letter dated April 25, 1837, Emma wrote to Joseph: "We were glad enough to hear that you are well. . . . We are all well as usual. . . . I cannot tell you my feelings when I found I could not see you before you left, yet I expect you can realize them, the children feel very anxious about you because they don't know where you have gone; . . . I verily feel that if I had no more confidence in God than some I could name, I should be in a sad case indeed but I still believe that if we humble ourselves, and are as faithful as we can be we shall be delivered from every snare that may be laid for our feet, and our lives and property will be saved. . . . My time is out, I pray that God will keep you in . . . safety till we all meet again."[6]

A week later she expressed concern for their finances when she wrote: "The situation of your business is such as is very difficult for me to do anything . . . partnership matters give everybody such an unaccountable right to every particle of property or money that they can lay their hands on. . . . I have been so treated that I have come to the determination not to let any man or woman have anything whatever without being well assured, that it goes to your advantage."[7]

Emma articulated in this same letter great concern for a young man she was caring for who was sick with measles. Certainly thoughts of her little Joseph Murdock, who had been weakened by the disease before he died of pneumonia in 1832, flooded her memory as she shared her worry that young Joseph or Frederick might fall ill: "There was a young man came with Brother Baldwin . . . and he is here yet and is very sick with the measles which makes much confusion and trouble for me, and is also a subject of much fear and anxiety unto me, as you know that neither of your little boys have ever had them. I wish it could be possible for you to be home . . . You must remember them for they all remember you, and I could hardly pacify Julia and Joseph when they found out you were not coming home soon."[8]

When the Prophet did return to Kirtland in early June, he fell extremely ill and was confined to his room for several days. Mary Fielding, a convert and a schoolteacher from Canada, related that our "beloved Brother Joseph Smith appeared to be so far gone that Brother Rigdon told us that he should not . . . live till night."[9] Aware of the seriousness of his condition, Joseph asked Emma to pray for him and later observed: "My afflictions continued to increase, and were very severe, insomuch that I was unable to raise my head from my pillow." With Emma offering prayers in his behalf and a local doctor administering "herbs and mild food," the Prophet regained his strength within a few days and "was able to resume [his] usual labors."[10]

That fall another heart-wrenching crisis hit the Smith family when Hyrum's wife, Jerusha, became gravely ill after giving birth to their sixth child. Hyrum was in Missouri on Church business, and Emma and Lucy ministered to her every need. Despite their care, however, her health failed rapidly. Emma must have been distraught at Jerusha's death. For ten years—since they were both newly married and living on the Smith farm in Manchester—they had shared countless joys and heartaches.

When Hyrum returned to Kirtland soon after his beloved wife's death, he took Joseph's counsel and married Mary Fielding on 24 December 1837. Regarding the short time that elapsed between Jerusha's death and his remarriage, Hyrum explained, "It was not because I had less love or regard for Jerusha, that I married so soon, but it was for the sake of my children."[11]

As if the weight of their personal tragedies was not heavy enough, the conspiracies and persecution against the Prophet, his family, and his faithful associates reached a crescendo by the end of 1837. Joseph's counselor in the First Presidency, Frederick G. Williams, four of the Quorum of the Twelve Apostles, and Martin Harris had turned against him; when the final tally was taken, it is estimated that up to three hundred members in Kirtland alone apostatized. Of the confusion and turmoil, Mary Fielding Smith later recorded: "For altho here is a great number of faithful precious souls, yea the Salt of the Earth is here, yet it may be truely called a place where Satan has his seat."[12]

Emma and the children had firsthand experience with anti-Mormon abuse. On one occasion while riding with Joseph to nearby Painesville, the family came upon a horse-drawn sleigh. When Joseph politely asked the two men in the sleigh to let him and his family pass, they did so and then "bawled out, 'Do you get any revelations lately?'"and then cursed the Prophet and his family with foul language.[13]

Elder Brigham Young was forced to flee Kirtland on December 22 when a mob of apostates "had threatened to destroy him because he would proclaim publicly and privately that he knew by the power of the Holy Ghost that [Joseph] was a Prophet . . . [and] had not transgressed and fallen as the apostates declared."[14] Elder Heber C. Kimball gave a vivid description of these horrifying times: "A man's life was in danger the moment he spoke in defense of the Prophet of God . . . for those who apostatized sought every means and opportunity to draw others after them. They also entered into combinations to obtain wealth by fraud and every means that was evil."[15]

On January 12, 1838, Joseph was warned by a sympathetic apostate of a plot to assassinate him and Sidney. In consequence, about ten o'clock that night—after bidding Emma good-bye and accompanied by Sidney—he left home on horseback for the relative safety of Norton, Ohio, a town sixty miles from Kirtland. The following day, Emma helped load a few provisions into a wagon driven by Joseph's brother Don Carlos and with her Julia, young Joseph, and Frederick, in company with Sidney Rigdon's wife and children, departed from Kirtland. She left behind many friends, her home, the beautiful temple on the hill, and almost all the temporal possessions she and Joseph had worked for and accumulated. The future was uncertain, and undoubtedly Emma feared for the welfare of her three small children and the unborn child she had been carrying for at least four months.

Chapter Seventeen

On the morning of March 29, 1836, just two days after the temple dedication in Kirtland, Joseph, Oliver, Hyrum, and the Prophet's counselors "met in the most holy place in the Lord's House, and sought for a revelation from Him concerning the authorities of the Church going to Zion."[1]

Emma too had expressed her desire to move to Missouri a few months before when the subject was broached one evening while she and Joseph were hosting a dinner party. Bishop Newel K. Whitney mentioned to Bishop Edward Partridge, who had come from Missouri to update the Prophet on the plight of the Saints there, that perhaps within a year they would enjoy dinner together in the land of Zion. With her thoughts never far from the redemption and habitation of Zion as well, Emma observed that "she hoped it might be the case, that not only they, but the rest of the company present, might be seated around her table on that land of promise."[2] Nevertheless, Emma obviously envisioned her departure from Kirtland to the land of Zion to be under much more favorable circumstances than it actually was.

Joseph had to wait only thirty-six hours in Norton before she and the children arrived safe and well. They tarried with Church members there until January 16, and then the two families set out on their nearly one-thousand-mile journey in covered wagons and in freezing conditions for Far West. Although only five years old at the time and admitting that his memories were somewhat confused about that journey, Joseph III recounted: "I can remember that across the center of the covered wagon in which we rode there was a division made by fastening up blankets, and that Father and someone else occupied the back part of the wagon by turns. I remember we reached a river, which I now suppose was the Wabash in Indiana, and that the roads running through the low lands were of the kind known as corduroy. Some who had been riding in the wagons walked over these roads, and I also did so, for a ways, stepping carefully over the rigid poles holding to the hand of my mother."[3]

Not far into their journey the small party realized they were being pursued by an armed group of enemies from Kirtland. Several times Joseph and Sidney were forced to secrete themselves in the back of the wagon to avoid being caught by the mob that often crossed their route. Twice they stayed in the same boardinghouse with their pursuers, and on one of those occasions, only a slight partition separated Emma, her children, and her husband from the armed men. As she lay listening she heard their enemies swear out threats and oaths of what they would do to Joseph if they caught him and later that night bore the fear and humiliation of their invading the family's quarters to examine Joseph and Sidney. Miraculously, they did not recognize the Prophet or Sidney that night, nor did they know them on other occasions when they met them on the streets of towns through which they passed.

En route they were helped by a family in Knox County, Ohio, and allowed to stay in a vacant house on their property. The family later recorded that "the Prophet and his family remained in the building for a few days and that when they left, the building had been neatly cleaned."[4] Two of the boys in the family were so touched by the message left with them by the Prophet that they later moved to Nauvoo, Illinois, where they joined the Church.

Desperate for money and rest, the worn and tired company stopped for nine days in Dublin, Indiana, where Joseph sought unsuccessfully to find work cutting cordwood. Once again the Lord showed his hand in their journey, when a member gave the Prophet three hundred dollars after selling a piece of property. Before their departure from Dublin, the Rigdons decided to travel a different route; however, Emma and Joseph continued to have the companionship of Brigham Young and his family, who had met them on the trail before they arrived in Dublin.

Sometime in February and well before the ice on the Mississippi had fully thawed, the company reached Quincy, Illinois. Brigham Young related, "Joseph and I went down to the river and examined the ice. We soon learned that by going through the flat boat which lay the end to the shore, and placing a few planks from the outer end on the ice, we could reach the heavy ice which had floated down the river a few days previous, sufficient to bear up our teams. We hauled our wagons through the boat and on to the ice by hand, then led our horses on to the solid ice, and drove across the river by attaching a rope to the wagon and to the team, so that they would be some distance apart. The last horse which was led on to the ice was Joseph's favorite, Charlie. He broke the ice at every step for several rods."[5]

About a week later they made their way through Missouri to the Salt River, where they found the ice broken up, but the ferry they had hoped to hire for their crossing had sunk. During a search of the shoreline, Joseph and Brigham discovered a pool of still water upon which "the old ice had sunk, and . . . had another foot of ice frozen over; and by plunging our wagons 2½ or 3 feet into the water, we could gain the solid ice on the pond; at the other shores we found the same."[6]

Once the wagons and teams were across, Emma—now six months pregnant—and the children crossed the open water by balancing themselves and walking across an abandoned canoe that had been placed from the shore to the ice. Pulling the canoe behind them, they walked over the ice to the other bank and by using the canoe again as a bridge made it to shore. "In this way we crossed the families and landed directly in the woods, on a very steep sideling hill," said Brigham Young. "We managed to get our wagons along the cleft of the bank; six or eight men held them up, and thus we worked our way to the road."[7]

Tired, wet, and cold, the bedraggled caravan pressed forward until they were met by teams driven by the brethren some one hundred and twenty miles from their destination. Another escort led by Thomas B. Marsh met them "with open arms" when they were within eight miles of Far West, and after staying the night in a member's home outside the city, Emma, Joseph, and the children were met by even more Saints "who came to make us welcome to their little Zion."[8]

On March 14, two months and one day from the time they left Kirtland, Church members at Far West excitedly left their homes and their work to meet the Prophet and his family as they rode into town in a borrowed carriage. The reunion with their dear Missouri friends was sweet as Emma and the children were heartily received with hugs and kisses. Many of the brethren and sisters whom they met were from the Colesville Branch in New York, whom Emma had known since her baptism at the Knight farm in 1830 and had not seen since they left Ohio in 1831.

Far West was a community of about five thousand on the vast western Missouri prairie of Caldwell County. Since their expulsion from Jackson County in 1833 and their departure from Clay County about eighteen months later, the Saints had settled the less desirable flatlands of Caldwell County. They had erected about one hundred buildings surrounding a public square and a site for the temple. Approximately two thousand farms had been surveyed, plowed, and planted, and though the members lived in log cabins or shanties, they were happy and the city was flourishing with "four dry goods stores, three family grocery stores, several blacksmith shops, two hotels, a printing shop, and a large schoolhouse that doubled as a church and courthouse."[9]

With no home to go to and nothing with which to set up housekeeping, Emma, Joseph, and the children were welcomed into the home of George W. Harris, where they were "treated . . . with all possible kindness, . . . the brethren bringing in such things as we had need of for our comfort and convenience."[10] Expressing his satisfaction about the state of the Church in a letter sent to Kirtland about two weeks after their arrival in Far West, Joseph observed that "the saints at this time are in union & peace & love prevails throughout, in a word, Heaven smiles upon the saints in Caldwell. . . . We have no uneasiness about the power of our enemies in this place to do us harm."[11]

Soon, however, the Prophet's contentment was overridden with the reality that some of the leaders in Far West were as evil and as apostate as those they had escaped from in Kirtland. Before the Prophet's arrival in March, several prominent leaders had left the Church. In April, two of the Three Witnesses—Oliver Cowdery and David Whitmer—were excommunicated, as was Lyman Johnson of the Quorum of the Twelve Apostles. Joseph quickly became engulfed in administering the business of the Church and ministering to the members. He also spent a good deal of time "writing a history of the Church from the earliest period of its existence."[12] On the other hand, Emma worked to make the small cabin eventually built for them near the town square as homey as possible with borrowed furnishings, linens, and cooking utensils. One day, while Joseph helped her plant their garden, he reflected on the relative easiness of their life in Ohio: "All we had to do back in Kirtland was put out the fire and call the dog, but settling is a different thing." Emma loyally replied that she preferred settling.[13]

Chapter Eighteen

ACCOMPANIED BY SOME OF THE BRETHREN, the Prophet left Far West in mid-May to explore the country north of Caldwell County. Traveling horseback some twenty-five miles, the company reached the base of Tower Hill, "a name [Joseph] gave the place in consequence of the remains of an old Nephite altar or tower that stood there."[1]

Later that same day and about half a mile up the river, Joseph and a few of the brethren visited another beautiful spot, "which the brethren called 'Spring Hill,' but by the mouth of the Lord it was named Adam-ondi-Ahman, because, said He, it is the place where Adam shall come to visit his people, or the Ancient of Days shall sit, as spoken of by Daniel the Prophet." The Prophet described this sacred area as being "situated on an elevated spot of ground, which renders the place as healthful as any part of the United States, and overlooking the river and the country round about, it is certainly a beautiful location."[2]

After exploring more of the country north and east of Far West, Joseph returned home on June 1, and none too soon, because the very next day, June 2, 1838, Emma gave birth to a son, whom they named Alexander Hale Smith after General Alexander Doniphan, Joseph's Missouri ally. Doniphan, who was not a member of the Church, had taken the side of the Saints at the time of Zion's Camp in 1834 and supported their taking up arms in defense of their properties. He said, "I love to hear that they have brethren coming to their assistance. Greater love can no man show, than he who lays down his life for his brethren."[3]

Two days after Alexander's birth, Joseph left again for Adam-ondi-Ahman and stayed well over a week, helping the brethren survey, clear land, and build houses. Because the women of the Church spent much of their time washing, sewing, and cooking together, and with Emma having a newborn and three active older children to care for, it would be expected that many of the sisters stepped in to offer her assistance during Joseph's absence.

On the Fourth of July, Far West was alive with people celebrating not only the independence

of the United States but also their "'Declaration of Independence' from all mobs and persecutions which [had] been inflicted upon them."[3] A parade made up of the infantry or militia, the First Presidency, the Quorum of the Twelve Apostles, and other mounted men and
women was enjoyed by all. It is doubtful Emma was horseback that day due to the recent
birth of Alexander, but surely she enjoyed the music, food, and fanfare. After the parade, the
four cornerstones were laid for the Far West Temple, and the congregation together gave the
Hosanna Shout.

During much of August, Emma took pleasure in having Joseph at home for several days
on end. He did little but help her with the children and house with occasional breaks for
studying, to walk or ride about the city, or to visit his parents, who had arrived in Far West a
few weeks before.

Adding to their contentment, a large company of Saints from Ohio, known as the Kirtland Camp, arrived in Far West on October 2 and two days later began to settle at Adam-
ondi-Ahman. Because Joseph regretted having to leave Ohio before discharging his debts, he
sent Oliver Granger from Far West to Kirtland to dispose of Church properties and resolve
every debt incurred there. Granger's faithful efforts were recognized by the Lord when he
said: "I remember my servant Oliver Granger; behold, verily I say unto him that his name
shall be had in sacred remembrance from generation to generation, forever and ever" (D&C
117:12).

Nonetheless, that fall the peace and tranquility Emma and her family had enjoyed for a
short time was interrupted. Copies of an inflammatory speech given on the Fourth of July
by Sidney Rigdon fell into the hands of several Missouri officials and before long anti-
Mormon mobs were gathering to run the Saints from the country. Elder Parley P. Pratt
described the tension that existed between the Missourians and the Saints at this time: "War
clouds began again to lower with dark and threatening aspect. Those who had combined
against the laws in the adjoining counties, had long watched our increasing power and pros-
perity with jealousy, and with greedy and avaricious eyes. It was a common boast that, as
soon as we had completed our extensive improvements, and made a plentiful crop, they
would drive us from the State, and once more enrich themselves with the spoils."[4]

The tension described by Parley manifested itself in the neighboring town of Gallatin
when a group of Missourians denied some of the Mormons the right to vote, and a fight with
rocks and clubs ensued. A rumor spread that Joseph had organized more than five hundred
men and was riding throughout the country threatening area settlers with death; in truth, he
rode to Gallatin with about twenty-five men to assess the conflict. The tension was increased

by affidavits endorsed by apostates that smeared Joseph's character and spread lies about his intentions.

A few days after the Gallatin incident, Joseph sat writing a letter in his parents' cabin when a group of armed men approached the door. Lucy wrote of the visit that followed: "Thinking they had come for some refreshment, I offered them chairs, . . . but they replied, 'We do not choose to sit down; we have come here to kill Joe Smith and all the Mormons.'" When she asked why they sought Joseph Smith's life, they replied that it had been reported that he had killed seven men and they intended to carry out their orders to kill him. Lucy then asked if they intended to kill her as well, and they answered yes. To this Lucy said, "Very well, . . . I want you to act the gentleman about it, and do the job quick. Just shoot me down at once, then I shall be at rest; but I should not like to be murdered by inches."[5]

Seeing that Joseph had finished his letter, his mother then said, "Gentlemen, suffer me to make you acquainted with Joseph Smith, the Prophet." Joseph stepped forward, shook their hands, seated himself again, and taught them some of the basic views of the Church and proclaimed his innocence. When finished he said, "Mother, I believe I will go home now—Emma will be expecting me."[6] Immediately, two of the men jumped up and offered to escort and protect him on his way, and together they left. Lucy overheard the others as they were leaving speak of the power they felt when they shook the Prophet's hand and express their resolve never again to seek to harm him.

Soon small skirmishes were taking place throughout the country, which escalated into a full-fledged war. In what has since become known as the Battle of Crooked River, several of the brethren were wounded and three men were killed. Two of the dead were Church members, Gideon Carter and David W. Patten, a member of the Quorum of the Twelve. Also dead was Patrick O'Bannion, who was not a member of the Church. Young Joseph remembered his mother caring for a young man wounded in the battle. Arthur Millikin, the drummer in the Mormon militia, had been shot in both legs. He was carried to Emma's front door, where he was taken upstairs, doctored, and hidden until he recovered.

Joseph and others had petitioned the heads of the Missouri government for protection, but their appeals fell on deaf ears. Moreover, the Battle of Crooked River provided Governor Lilburn W. Boggs with the fuel necessary to wage war against the Mormons. On October 27 he wrote: "The Mormons must be treated as enemies and *must be exterminated* or driven from the state, if necessary for the public good."[7]

Two days after the issuance of the extermination order, Emma heard the heartrending news that the Saints at Haun's Mill—a small settlement about sixteen miles east of Far

West—had been attacked. Seventeen men and boys were killed. Additional reports poured in, revealing that in every part of the surrounding country Emma's friends were being driven from their homes and left with no possessions, food, or the means to procure such necessities. In Far West, where Joseph had previously counseled the members to gather for their safety, Emma shared all she possessed with those who rode or walked into the settlement. When Lyman Wight came to the house, Emma offered him a piece of bread. He thanked her, saying, "Why, Sister Emma, with a chunk of cornbread like this in my hand, I could go out of doors and stand at the corner of the house in the northwest wind and eat myself into a sweat."[8]

Emma and Mother Smith were soon caring for extended family members as well. In an attempt to follow the Prophet's admonition to gather to Far West and because her husband, Samuel, was already there on an errand, Mary Bailey Smith left home with her three-week-old baby and her other children to make the thirty-mile trip to Far West. She began her journey through a driving rainstorm in a borrowed lumber wagon driven by an eleven-year-old boy. When Samuel met her and the children about ten miles from the city, Mary "was entirely speechless and stiff with the cold."[9] After Mary received a priesthood blessing, Emma and Lucy attended to her every need until she regained her health.

As the Missourians surrounded Far West, the brethren stacked timber, wagons, and furniture to build a barricade while the sisters packed a few provisions in case they were driven from their homes. Some of the women, afraid of being molested, dressed in men's clothing to disguise their gender "and stood, gun in hand, guarding their homes."[10] Though the militia, which outnumbered the Mormons five to one, held back from engaging in battle, Colonel George Hinkle, one of the highest ranking officers among the Saints, deceitfully betrayed the Prophet, persuading him and several others to ride out of Far West to negotiate for peace. As soon as the men rode out, "instead of being treated with that respect which is due from one citizen to another,"[11] they were surrounded by the Missourians, "many of whom were dressed and painted like Indian warriors."[12] They were immediately arrested "and treated with the utmost contempt."[13] Later that night, in an illegal court martial, the prisoners were sentenced to be executed the next morning in the public square of Far West.

Meanwhile, Emma listened and wept through the night as members of the militia shot their weapons into the air and "set up a constant yell, like so many bloodhounds let loose upon their prey."[14] She, along with Mother and Father Smith, who also heard the awful screaming and gunshots, believed the wild men were killing Joseph.

Parley reported that through the night they lay in the rain while the guards mocked and

Thou Shalt Be Comforted

taunted the Prophet. When General Alexander Doniphan received the command to execute the brethren at nine o'clock in the morning, he indignantly replied: "It is cold-blooded murder. I will not obey your order . . . and if you execute these men, I will hold you responsible before an earthly tribunal, so help me God."[15]

On November 1, the Missouri militia entered Far West, found and arrested Hyrum, and vandalized the city. Emma and her children were driven from their home, and they watched while their few possessions were ransacked and ruined. Other homes were wrecked, anything of value was stolen, and women were raped. The following day, before being taken to Independence and understanding they still might be executed, the Prophet and the other prisoners persuaded their guards to allow them to see their families. Joseph said, "I found my wife and children in tears, who feared we had been shot by those who had sworn to take our lives, and that they would see me no more. When I entered my house, they clung to my garments, their eyes streaming with tears, while mingled emotions of joy and sorrow were manifested in their countenances. I requested to have a private interview with them a few minutes, but this privilege was denied me by the guard. . . . My partner wept, my children clung to me, until they were thrust from me by the swords of the guards."[16]

Joseph III vividly recalled that day: "When he was brought to the house by an armed guard I ran out of the gate to greet him, but was roughly pushed away from his side by a sword in the hand of the guard and not allowed to go near him. My mother, also, was not permitted to approach him and had to receive his farewell by word of lip only."[17] It was reported that young Joseph, who refused to let go of his father's leg and asked, "Father, is the mob going to kill you?" was slapped away by the flat of the guard's sword and told, "You little brat, go back; you will see your father no more."[18]

When Lucy heard Joseph and Hyrum were inside the city, she ran to the town square. There she fought her way through the crowd for about one hundred yards to the wagon in which her sons were held captive. She was unable to see them because a canvas cover had been nailed tightly to the wagon to hide them, but she held Hyrum's hand, which he extended under the cloth. Going then to the back of the wagon, she gripped Joseph's hand and said, "Joseph, do speak to your poor mother once more—I cannot bear to go till I hear your voice." In reply and just before the horses pulling the wagon tore his hand from hers, Joseph sobbed, "God bless you mother!"[19]

Chapter Nineteen

AFTER THE PROPHET AND HIS FELLOW PRISONERS were taken from Far West, the Saints in the city were told by General John B. Clark, the commanding officer for the "Mormon War," to stay put through the remainder of the winter. Food was in short supply, and many survived on parched corn. Joseph III recalled: "Times were hard and we had little to eat except that which was raised directly from the soil or gathered from the hunt. One day all we had to eat for dinner was corn bread made from meal with only the addition of salt and water, and seasoned as we ate with New Orleans molasses."[1]

Initially, the only information Emma had regarding Joseph and his fate was Clark's opinion, which he openly shared with the Saints: "As for your leaders, do not once think—do not imagine for a moment—do not let it enter your mind that they will be delivered, or that you will see their faces again, for their fate is fixed—their die is cast—their doom is sealed."[2]

The brethren were taken first to Independence, where hundreds came to gawk at them as they were put on public display. Later that day Joseph wrote to Emma: "My dear and beloved companion, of my bosom, in tribulation and affliction, I would inform you that I am well, and that we are all of us in good spirits. . . . I have great anxiety about you, and my lovely children . . . Those little children are subjects of my meditation continually. Tell them that Father is yet alive. . . . Oh, Emma, for God sake, do not forsake me nor the truth but remember me. If I do not meet you again in this life may God grant that we may meet in heaven. I cannot express my feelings. My heart is full. Farewell, oh my kind and affectionate Emma. I am yours forever, your husband and your friend."[3]

To learn that Joseph was well and in good spirits must have relieved to some extent the emotional torment Emma was experiencing. She felt additional comfort when Lucy shared with the family an experience she had soon after her sons were taken from Far West: "I was filled with the Spirit of God, and received the following by the gift of prophecy: 'Let your heart be comforted concerning your children, they shall not be harmed by their enemies; and, in less than four years, Joseph shall speak before the judges and great men of the land, for his voice shall be heard in their councils. And in five years from this time he will have power over all his enemies.'"[4]

After spending four days in Independence, the prisoners were transported to Richmond, where they were charged with "treason, murder, arson, burglary, larceny, and stealing." They were thrown into an old log house, chained together, and guarded by some "of the most noisy, foul-mouthed, vulgar, disgraceful rabble that ever defiled the earth."[5] Parley, who lay next to the Prophet one night, recalled that they listened to the guard's filthy language and boasts "as they recounted to each other their deeds of rapine, murder, robbery, etc., which they had committed among the *'Mormons'* while at Far West and vicinity. They even boasted of defiling by force wives, daughters and virgins, and of shooting or dashing out the brains of men, women and children." After listening for some time and knowing that Joseph was awake and also hearing the vile tales, Parley, who had said nothing to him, watched as the Prophet suddenly rose "to his feet, and spoke in a voice of thunder, or as the roaring lion, uttering," as closely as Parley could remember, the following:

"*'SILENCE, ye fiends of the infernal pit. In the name of Jesus Christ I rebuke you, and command you to be still; I will not live another minute and hear such language. Cease such talk, or you or I die THIS INSTANT!'*

"He ceased to speak. He stood erect in terrible majesty. Chained, and without a weapon; calm, unruffled and dignified as an angel, he looked upon the quailing guards, whose weapons were lowered or dropped to the ground; whose knees smote together, and who, shrinking into a corner, or crouching at his feet, begged his pardon, and remained quiet till a change of guards.

"I have seen the ministers of justice, clothed in magisterial robes, and criminals arraigned before them, while life was suspended on a breath, in the Courts of England; I have witnessed a Congress in solemn session to give laws to nations; I have tried to conceive of kings, of royal courts, of thrones and crowns; and of emperors assembled to decide the fate of kingdoms; but dignity and majesty have I seen but *once,* as it stood in chains, at midnight, in a dungeon in an obscure village of Missouri."[6]

After receiving Joseph's letter from Independence, Emma penned a hasty reply and sent it with Jeremiah Willey, who had stopped by her home to offer her and the children comfort. Though her letter is no longer in existence, Joseph received it with great satisfaction and, on the opening day of his trial, responded to "My Dear Emma": "We are prisoners in chains, and under strong guards, for Christ's sake and for no other cause . . . I have this consolation that I am an innocent man. . . . I received your letter which I read over and over again. It was a sweet morsel to me. Oh God, grant that I may have the privilege of seeing once more my lovely Family, . . . to press them to my bosom and kiss their lovely cheeks would fill my heart with unspeakable gratitude. Tell the children that I am alive and trust I shall come and see them before long. Comfort their hearts all you can, and try to be comforted yourself. . . . Oh my affectionate Emma, I want you to remember that I am [a] true and faithful friend, to you and the children, forever. My heart is entwined around yours forever and ever. Oh, may God bless you all. Amen."[7]

In a postscript, he encouraged Emma to write often and, if possible, to bring the children to Richmond to see him. Although she did not have the opportunity to visit him there, she did visit on several occasions after he and five of his fellow captives were moved on December 1, 1838, to Liberty Jail in Daviess County.

Because Liberty Jail was nothing more than a small, two-storied stone dungeon, Emma must have been mortified to see the conditions in which her husband was held. The ceiling of the bottom floor where the brethren were held was not sufficiently high for them to stand erect, and the place was cold, damp, and smoke filled with filthy straw covering the dirt floor. The only natural light they had filtered through small, narrow, barred windows on the second floor and found its way through a hole in the floor, which also served as the only access to the bottom level.

Emma carried a permit to visit Joseph in the jail and on at least two occasions took young Joseph with her. On their first visit, Phoebe Rigdon and her eleven-year-old son, John, accompanied them; together they rode the forty miles "in a 2-seated carriage, drawn by a beautiful span of cream horses."[8] Because they got off to a late start in the morning and did not arrive at the jail until after dark, they were not allowed to see the prisoners until the next morning. During their three-day stay, John and young Joseph grew restless. On occasion, the jailer would allow them to leave and walk around the town. John related that young Joseph would stay close to him, "as he was a little afraid to stay out alone thinking there might be danger."[9] Regarding the same trip, Joseph III remembered Emma's leaving him to spend the night with his father in the jail and a man, whom he thought was a visitor, singing "two ditties or ballads"[10] for the prisoners.

On December 20, Emma left the children in Far West, and accompanied by the wives of Caleb Baldwin and Reynolds Cahoon, was driven to Liberty to stay with her husband for two days. She returned to find her home had been burglarized and her remaining possessions thrown about. Gone were most of her treasured possessions, including "one roll of linen cloth, a quantity of valuable buttons, one piece of cashmere, a number of very valuable books of great variety, a number of vestings, with various other articles of value."[11] A pocketbook that contained a sealed letter and a gold ring was also stolen, and she soon found their stable had been plundered and their saddles, bridles, and a gig and harness taken.

William McLellin, who had lived in Emma's home for three weeks in Kirtland and had been a member of the Quorum of the Twelve until his apostasy in 1836, was the principal culprit. When Emma boldly confronted McLellin and asked him why he did it, "his answer was because he could."[12]

During a subsequent visit to Liberty, Hyrum's wife, Mary Fielding Smith, and her infant son, Joseph F., accompanied Emma and young Joseph, as did Mary's sister, Mercy Thompson, and her baby. Mary had come down with a severe cold soon after the birth of Joseph F. and was unable to nurse him, so her sister was nursing both the infants. According to Mercy, "about the 1st of February, 1839, by the request of her husband, my sister was placed on a bed in a wagon and taken a journey of forty miles, to visit him in the prison. . . . The weather was extremely cold, and we suffered much on the journey."[13]

As the winter temperatures dropped, the Prophet and his companions suffered from the cold. Building a fire was not an option because the jail had no chimney and little ventilation. When Joseph sent word to Emma requesting she send blankets or quilts, she wept because she had none to spare. John Lowe Butler related, "My wife was up there when the word came, and she said that Sister Emma cried and said that they had taken all of her bed clothes, except one quilt and blanket and what could she do? So my wife with some other sisters said, 'Send him them and we will see that you shall have something to cover you and your children.' My wife then went home and got some bed clothes and took them over to her."[14]

Throughout the month of February, many of the Saints were leaving their land and homes in Missouri with hopes of finding refuge elsewhere. Because death and apostasy had taken its toll on the leadership of the Church, Brigham Young, now president of the Quorum of the Twelve, and Heber C. Kimball, oversaw the exodus.

Although Emma had previously said she would not leave Missouri while Joseph remained, Samuel Hadley, the sheriff of Liberty, convinced her to leave: "All the authorities are waiting for is for you to get out of the state . . . [and] the prisoners will be let out."[15] Apparently those in charge knew that when released, Joseph would go immediately to Emma and therefore leave Missouri as well. Consequently on February 7, 1839, she and the children once again left home in the dead of winter. The wagon in which Emma loaded her few possessions was borrowed and shared with the Jonathan Holmes family. Joseph's horses, Charlie and Jim, were hitched to it, and Stephen Markham was their driver.

The night before leaving, she received a welcome visitor with a priceless package. Ann Scott brought to her two cotton sacks filled with the Prophet's papers, including his translation of the Bible. Thinking the mob might hesitate to interfere with a woman, the documents had been entrusted to Miss Scott by the Prophet's secretary and scribe, James Mulholland. So, with her husband's papers sewn into her skirt, Emma helped her children climb aboard the borrowed wagon and find a reasonably comfortable spot in which to make the journey of eight or nine days.

In a letter written to Joseph later in March, Emma shared her feelings regarding her swift departure from Far West: "No one but God knows the reflections of my mind and the feelings of my heart when I left our house and home, and almost all of everything that we possessed excepting our little children, and took my journey out of the State of Missouri, leaving [you] shut up in that lonesome prison. But the reflection is more than human nature ought to bear, and if God does not record our sufferings and avenge our wrongs on them that are guilty, I shall be sadly mistaken."[16]

Their nights along the route were mostly spent sleeping on the ground or in the wagon with very little bedding to keep them warm. One afternoon they were met by a pack of barking dogs when they stopped at a farmhouse along the road. Coming to the door of the house, the farmer assured them the dogs were friendly and when asked if he had room for them to stay the night, the good man said, "Certainly," and invited them into his small but cozy log home. Joseph III recalled: "Mother and we children went in, leaving someone . . . to care for the team. . . . The farmer was a sturdy man and gave us a hearty welcome. The weather was cold, but there was a great fire in one end of the living room and we were soon very comfortable. We had supper and beds were made, some on the bedstead and some on the floor. . . . We slept cozily in the warmth of that big fire."[17]

By the time the small company arrived at the western shore of the Mississippi, the weather had taken a turn for the worse, and the river was frozen but not firm. Deciding to distribute the weight of the team and wagon, Brother Markam hitched Charlie to the wagon tongue and drove the horse on the ice to the opposite riverbank. Emma crossed the frozen river on foot "with her infant son Alexander and his two-year-old brother Frederick in her arms, with six-year-old Joseph and seven-year-old Julia clinging to her dress in terror."[18] As any mother might, she must have wondered how much more she and her children could bear.

Of One Heart: Emma on the Ice

⁓ Chapter Twenty ⁓

As THE THOUSANDS OF REFUGEES crossed the Mississippi River, they were offered shelter, food, and kindness by the citizens of Quincy, Illinois. Emma found sanctuary for the children and herself about three miles from Quincy in the home of Judge John and Sarah Cleveland. In her letter of March 1839, she offers a glimpse into her thoughts, her feelings, and the anxieties she experienced while Joseph sat in that lonely, filthy prison:

"Having an opportunity to send by a friend I make an attempt to write, but I shall not attempt to write my feelings altogether for the situation in which you are, the walls, bars and bolts, rolling rivers, running streams, rising hills, sinking valleys and spreading prairies that separate us, and the cruel injustice that first cast you into prison and still holds you there . . . places my feelings far beyond description. Was it not for conscious innocence and the direct interposition of divine mercy, I am very sure I never should have been able to have endured the scenes of suffering that I have passed through . . . but I still live and am yet willing to suffer more if it is the will of kind heaven, that I should for your sake.

"We are all well at present, except Frederick who is quite sick. Little Alexander who is now in my arms is one of the finest little fellows, you ever saw in your life, he is so strong that with the assistance of a chair he will run all round the room. . . . I left your change of clothes with H. C. Kimball when I came away, and he agreed to see that you had clean clothes as often as necessary. . . . The people in this state are very kind indeed. . . . I have many more things I could like to write but have not time and you may be astonished at my bad writing and incoherent manner, but you will pardon all when you reflect how hard it would be for you to write, when your hands were stiffened with hard work, and your heart convulsed with intense anxiety. But I hope there are better days to come to us yet. Give my respect to all in that place that you respect, and am ever yours affectionately!"[1]

Emma soon became comfortable with the Clevelands and took part in the work of the house and the farm. The children likewise settled in and found interesting and fun playmates nearby. Young Joseph was befriended by the Huntington boys, who lived up the hill from the Cleveland farm, and often went to their home to play. Emma approved of her son's new friends until she found out that Allen, who was two or three years older than young Joseph, was allowed to take his father's rifle into the woods to hunt for rabbits. In an attempt to protect her son, she warned Joseph not to play with the boys if they had the rifle with them. When young Joseph returned home quite late the next evening, Emma questioned him: "I . . . had to admit that I had been out with the boys among the hazel brush, hunting for rabbits, and that Allen had carried the rifle. Thereupon, with the aid of a ready hazel switch, she promptly administered punishment."

The next morning Emma caught Joseph before he left the house and warned, "Joseph, I will not say you must not go to Mrs. Huntington's today, but I will say that if you do go I shall punish you when you return. It is a dangerous thing to play with Allen when he carries the rifle, and I am not going to be responsible for any harm that may come. So just remember what I tell you." Again, not heeding his mother's instructions, Joseph ventured to the Huntingtons. When he returned home, Emma was entertaining guests and said nothing to him. Young Joseph went to bed thinking he had avoided punishment. "However, after the guests departed, I discovered my error, for Mother found me and I received the punishment she had promised, applied vigorously enough to make me feel sorry I had undressed as I went to bed!"

The following morning, Emma warned the boy again, saying, "I will not say you shall not go to play with the Huntington boys while their mother allows Allen to take his father's gun with him to play; but if you go, I will punish you; and I shall punish you harder and harder until you stop." The allure of playing with the boys and the gun was more than Joseph could withstand, so once more he set out to hunt with them. "When I returned my mother punished me with such decidedly increased severity that I—well, comment is needless! I did not go again, for I found that my mother was indeed a woman of her word."[2]

Joseph's next letter to Emma was written on March 21. It contained an epistle to the Saints that is now recorded in Doctrine and Covenants 121 through 123. Wanting his wife and his parents to be the first to read the revelations, he sent them to Emma and asked her to write a copy before giving them to the brethren. His letter records his sentiments for her: "I want to be with you very much. . . . I would ask if Judge Cleveland will be kind enough to let you and the children tarry there until I can learn something further concerning my fate. I will reward him well if he will. . . . My dear Emma, I very well know your toils and sympathize with you. If God will spare my life once more to have the privilege of taking care of you, I will ease your care and endeavor to comfort your heart. . . . Yours forever."[3]

In a letter written in April, Joseph again expressed his love: "If you want to know how much I want to see you, examine your feelings, how much you want to see me, and judge for yourself. I would gladly walk from here to you barefoot, and bareheaded, and half naked, to see you and think it great pleasure, and never count it toil."[4]

On April 22, Emma observed a man riding an unfamiliar horse on the road towards the house. He looked worn and tired in his holey boots, torn pants, and blue cloak. Nevertheless, even with his gaunt face unshaven, his coat collar turned up, and his hat brim pulled over his eyes, she recognized her Joseph. Before he could climb from his horse, Emma was halfway to the gate. After nearly six months of imprisonment Joseph was finally home and holding his "affectionate Emma" in his arms.

Sympathetic to the plight of the Prophet and his fellow prisoners, the sheriff of Daviess County had allowed the men to escape while en route from Gallatin to Boone County for another trial. One night after making camp the lawman lifted a jug of whiskey and said, "I shall take a good drink of grog, and go to bed, and you may do as you have a mind to."[5] Three of the other men guarding Joseph likewise drank from the jug and also went to sleep. Accordingly, the one man left to guard the prisoners helped Joseph and his companions saddle two horses and set off down the road. The brethren made their way north and east over less-traveled routes until they reached the Mississippi River and crossed to Quincy. When asked if he would like to see his father's family, Joseph replied that his first stop would be at the Cleveland farm to see Emma and his children. The day following their tender reunion, she and the children accompanied him to Quincy to visit his parents and others of the family who had gathered for the reunion.

Joseph left Emma in Quincy the next day and traveled north along the Mississippi with several others looking for a place sufficient in size for the Saints to settle. Finding the tiny communities of Commerce City and Commerce, Illinois, swampy but suitable, the Prophet purchased for the Church six hundred acres of land on the eastern side of the Mississippi and about twenty thousand acres on the Iowa side. Before returning to Quincy, he also purchased the Hugh White farm, which would become his and Emma's residence. Furthermore, he fulfilled his promise to repay the Clevelands for caring for Emma and the children by holding for them another piece of property across the street from the Hugh White place.

On May 9, 1839, he and Emma thanked Judge and Sarah Cleveland for their kindness and generosity and left for Commerce. They spent the night with Joseph's uncle John Smith at Green Plains, Illinois, and arrived at their new home on the bank of the Mississippi River the next day. The old farmhouse, which they named the Homestead, was a small two-storied, two-room structure on the southern end of a great bend in the river. On the west end of the ground-level room was a fireplace, and the upstairs level was made comfortable for sleeping. Connected to the back of the house by a shed roof was a smaller log home or summer kitchen in which Father and Mother Smith eventually took up residence. Emma had easy access to a good well in the backyard and a freshwater spring was also nearby. Other out-buildings on the grounds included a log smokehouse and stable and "a smaller log building, one room and a cellar beneath."[6]

As the summer drew near, Emma became wholeheartedly engaged in her household responsibilities. She purchased a cow for young Joseph to milk, and she planted the family garden. She later told Joseph III that she discouraged his father from helping her in the garden, saying, "I never wanted him to go into the garden to work, for if he did it would not be fifteen minutes before there would be three or four, or sometimes a half a dozen men round him and they would tramp the ground down faster than he could hoe it up."[7]

Soon thousands of Saints followed the Prophet northward to settle on both sides of the river. Most lived in their wagons or tents while they drained and cleared land, planted crops, and began to build homes and businesses. During this time Joseph named the new city on the eastern side of the Mississippi *Nauvoo,* which in Hebrew meant "beautiful."

While the refugees continued to pour into the area, a deadly disease known to the Saints as the ague hit with a vengeance. The illness, what we now call malaria, was contracted from mosquitoes from the swamp; the common symptoms were fever, headache, chills, sweats, fatigue, nausea, and vomiting. Before long Emma's home became a hospital and she, the chief nurse. When Joseph found the entire Huntington family sick and getting worse, he loaded them into his wagon and took them home to be cared for. Newel and Elizabeth Whitney's family was brought to live in a small cottage in the yard. Elizabeth had just given birth to her ninth child, and the rest of the family was so sick they "were only just barely able to crawl around and wait upon each other."[8]

Once every available bed in Emma's home was filled, she made beds up in the yard as more and more of the sick went to her for care. Her days were spent rushing from one patient to another with water and "'Sappingtons Pills' which were considered a cleansing agency and were followed by 'Dover's Powders' which were taken just before the next chill was due. The patient also had to drink a strong concoction of what was called 'store tea.'"[9] She and Joseph slept outside in a tent so they could nurse their patients throughout the night. On occasion

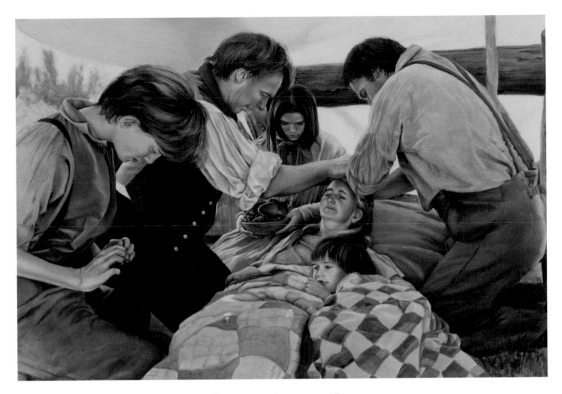

~◦~ Day of God's Power ~◦~

they would saddle their horses and "ride from place to place, visiting the sick, administering to them by laying on of hands and anointing with oil, and relieving their wants."[10]

Young Joseph carried water from the spring in a bucket and then from bed to bed for his mother until he too became ill. Emma lost the Prophet's assistance when he too contracted the disease; however, by then some who were beginning to recover somewhat were able to assist her. While Joseph lay in his sickbed, he worried over his father, who was near death, and contemplated the sad state of the faithful members who were suffering. After several days of lying ill, the Prophet "arose from his bed and commenced to administer to the sick in his own house and door-yard, and . . . commanded them in the name of the Lord Jesus Christ to arise and be made whole" and witnessed that "the sick were healed upon every side of him."[11]

He then walked to the bank of the river where he healed those who lay ill in their tents.

Many of the Saints, including most of the Twelve, were living in Montrose, Iowa, in abandoned military barracks, so in company with Heber C. Kimball, the Prophet crossed the river, entered Brigham Young's home, and healed him. As he went from house to house or tent to tent, those of the Twelve who were healed at his hands followed him as he continued to administer to the sick. Eventually exhausted, the Prophet counseled the Twelve to carry on without him and returned across the Mississippi to his home.

Wilford Woodruff recalled this experience as "the greatest day for the manifestation of the power of God through the gift of healing since the organization of the Church,"[12] and further noted: "There were many sick among the Saints on both sides of the river and Joseph went through the midst of them taking them by the hand and in a loud voice commanding them in the name of Jesus Christ to arise from their beds and be made whole and they leaped from their beds . . . made whole . . . by the power of God."[13]

Emma somehow managed to stay healthy throughout the ordeal and continued to nurse "ten or twelve patients that fall for whom she cared principally by the labor of her own hands."[14] As the sick gradually recovered and left for their own homes, her labors were not lessened because she continued to receive houseguests who were either moving to Nauvoo or traveling to the city to visit the Prophet. So frequent were the visitors that in October the high council published a statement in the *Times and Seasons* that Emma and Joseph's home "be exempt from receiving in future such crowds of visitors as have formerly thronged his house."[15] Although the statement relieved some of the pressure on Emma, her home was once again the headquarters of the Church and the place where Joseph held most of his meetings.

Chapter Twenty-One

As soon as Joseph recovered from malaria, his attention turned to seeking redress for the grievous crimes committed against the Saints and the Church in Missouri. In late October 1839, the Prophet, Sidney Rigdon, Elias Higbee, and Orin Porter Rockwell started for Washington, D.C., to meet with President Martin Van Buren. Joseph's parting with Emma and the children was difficult because little Frederick was ill with a fever and Emma was again experiencing morning sickness from another pregnancy. In a short note written not long after he left Nauvoo, he admonished her to take care of herself and get plenty of rest.

Rest was not on the horizon for Emma, however, because earlier that fall the high council voted to have her expand her hymnbook for a second printing and later approved having ten thousand copies printed when funds became available. Furthermore, soon after Joseph left, young Joseph was hit with another attack of malaria and a severe nosebleed that left the boy weak and very slow to recover.

Before long Emma's home was again overridden with sick guests. Orson Hyde and his wife arrived extremely ill, and the following day the Prophet's scribe, James Mulholland, was brought by his wife to Emma for care. For five weeks Emma nursed the thirty-five-year-old Mulholland, but her efforts were in vain. In a letter to Joseph she informed him of his dear friend's death, saying, "His spirit left its suffering tenement for a better mansion than he had here: he lost his speech the first evening he was here and did not utter a single syllable afterwards, though he retained his mental facilities. His death was sensibly felt by all in this place, and his wife will omit having his funeral, until you return home; his dissolution being so sudden and unexpected."[1]

Meanwhile as the Prophet traveled eastward, he purchased passage with several other travelers on a stagecoach. While the driver was away from the coach at one of their stops, the horses spooked and bolted down a hill. Joseph quieted the frantic passengers and prevented one woman from throwing her infant child from the coach. He then climbed out of the stage window onto the driver's seat and halted the running horses. Everyone on the stage generously congratulated and thanked him for his heroics, but when someone asked his name and he replied he was Joseph Smith the Mormon prophet, he received no more praise or show of thanks.

Once in Washington, the brethren were disappointed with the results of their November 28 meeting with the president of the United States. Said the Prophet of the experience: "I had an interview with Martin Van Buren, the President, who treated me very insolently, and it was with great reluctance he listened to our message, which, when he had heard, he said: 'Gentlemen, your cause is just, but I can do nothing for you;' and 'If I take up for you I shall lose the vote of Missouri.'"[2]

Because Joseph and the brethren preached and proselyted during their return trip, they did not reach Nauvoo until March 4, 1840. He took new clothes to Emma and each of the children, which were received and donned with pleasure. Other than their initial suffering from the fever, she and the children fared relatively well in his absence, though their nutritional mainstay had been vegetables from the garden and "ash cakes," made by adding cornmeal and salt to boiling water and then baked in corn shucks in the ashes of the hearth.

Corn bread seemed to be the family's meager fare throughout that spring and summer. Even so, no one was ever denied a place at Emma's table. "In my early years I used to often eat at the table with Joseph the Prophet," related young Joseph's cousin John Lyman Smith. "At one time I was called to dinner. I being at play in the room with his son Joseph, Jr., he called us to him and we stood one on each side of him. After he had looked over the table he said, 'Lord, we thank thee for this johnny-cake, and ask thee to send us something better. Amen.' The cornbread was cut and I received a piece from his hand.

"Before the bread was all eaten, a man came to the door and asked if the Prophet was at home. Joseph replied he was, whereupon the visitor said, 'I have brought you some flour and a ham.'

"Joseph arose and took the gift and blessed the man in the name of the Lord. Turning to his wife, Emma, he said, 'I knew the Lord would answer my prayer.'"[3]

Children and young adults of the Church seemed to flock to Emma's home, where family prayer, the singing of hymns, and scripture study was held twice a day. Emmeline B. Wells later recalled: "Sister Emma was benevolent and hospitable; she drew around her a large circle of friends, who were like good comrades. She was motherly in her nature to young people, always had a houseful to entertain or be entertained. She was very high-spirited and the brethren and sisters paid her great respect. . . .

"She was a woman of great prominence among the people: large and well proportioned of splendid physique, dark complexion, with piercing eyes that seemingly looked one through; noble in appearance and bearing and certainly favored of the Lord. . . . She was a queen in her home, so to speak, and beloved by the people, who were many of them indebted to her for favors and kindnesses."[4]

Although Emma had a number of individuals who helped in her home and who usually boarded with the family, she was "the first one up in the morning and the last to go to bed at night."[5] The Durfee girls worked for her and lived in the Homestead in 1839. Savilla helped her serve guests and do housework, and Julia was her seamstress. When the sewing was finished, Julia doubled as schoolteacher to Julia and young Joseph.

In the spring of 1840, Joseph built a room on the north end of the house to provide Emma a larger, more efficient kitchen and a good-sized room in which to entertain guests. Joseph III remembered the addition: "It was one-story and but a single room, built of native lumber—oak siding and studding, rived laths, and shaven shingles—but it gave us three rooms, the two in the old part being used for sleeping rooms above and below, and the new one, a rather large room as rooms were counted then, becoming the family living room."[6]

Shortly thereafter, on June 13, 1840, Emma and Joseph were blessed with another son who "brought immense comfort to Emma, and to the whole family. Everyone delighted in watching him grow."[7] The infant was given the name of Don Carlos, for Joseph's faithful younger brother, whom Emma described as "the handsomest man she ever saw," adding, "when in uniform and on horse back . . . he was magnificent."[8]

The joy the new baby brought into their home was overshadowed that fall when Joseph Sr. passed away. Before his death, the revered Patriarch of the Church gathered his family around him and blessed his wife and each of his children. To Joseph he said, "Joseph, my son, you are called to a high and holy calling. You are even called to do the work of the Lord. Hold out faithful and you shall be blest and your children after you. You shall even live to finish your work." Upon hearing these words, Joseph wept and asked, "Oh! my father, shall I?"[9] Indeed, Joseph was comforted by this blessing, and Emma too must have felt more secure after hearing this great promise. She was beginning to be surrounded by security, for Nauvoo was becoming a prosperous and thriving city as more and more Saints gathered from the East and converts began to arrive from Great Britain.

By the end of 1840, an act to incorporate the City of Nauvoo, organize the Nauvoo

Legion, and establish the University of the City of Nauvoo had been signed by Illinois governor Thomas Carlin. The printing press, buried in Missouri to prevent its destruction but recovered before the Saints left the state, was publishing the *Times and Seasons* newspaper. The Homestead was surrounded by more than two hundred and fifty block or framed homes, and more houses were planned or already under construction. Small shops, businesses, mills, and small factories were springing up throughout the city. New fruit and shade saplings and fruit-bearing bushes and vines were being planted and gardens put in on the members' large city lots. Outside Nauvoo, farmers planted grain and potatoes and ran their cattle and sheep on the open land.

In May 1841, Stephen A. Douglas, justice of the supreme court of Illinois and later a candidate for president of the United States, visited Nauvoo. Joseph recorded that Douglas "expressed his satisfaction of what he had seen and heard respecting our people . . . and likewise spoke in high terms of our location and the improvements we had made, and that our enterprise and industry were highly creditable to us, indeed."[10]

The arrival of the many British Saints was due to the faithful and undaunted missionary efforts of the Quorum of the Twelve Apostles. Elders Heber C. Kimball and Orson Hyde had been the first to open the missionary work in England in 1837. Not long after the malaria epidemic and that memorable day of healing in 1839, others of the Twelve left for the British Isles. The fruits of the apostles' labors were plentiful, and converts from England, Wales, Scotland, and Ireland heeded the word of the Lord to gather to Illinois.

The non-Mormon population was also growing in the city, as an ordinance allowed all citizens freedom to practice the religion of their choice. After a short visit to Nauvoo in 1843, Methodist minister Samuel A. Prior addressed a letter to the editor of the *Times and Seasons* newspaper, stating that he felt reluctant to leave the city before thanking the Saints for their kindness: "I had the honor for the first time in my life, to hear the Prophet preach. . . . He commenced preaching not from the Book of Mormon, however, but from the Bible; . . . I listened with surprise . . . he glided along through a very interesting and elaborate discourse . . . and I was compelled to go away with a very different opinion from what I had entertained when I first took my seat to hear him preach. In the evening I was invited to preach, and did so. The congregation was large and respectable—they paid the utmost attention. This surprised me a little, as I did not expect to find any such thing as a religious toleration among them."[11] Indeed, citizens of all faiths in Nauvoo, Emma and Joseph among them, were enjoying a season of peace and plenty.

Chapter Twenty-Two

EMMA'S LIFE WAS FAR FROM QUIET AS Nauvoo continued to grow. Joseph moved his office and therefore the headquarters of the Church into the newly constructed Red Brick Store, but she was still responsible for entertaining and caring for their boarders and many guests.

"Emma was an excellent cook, especially good at cooking meat. . . . [She] served fresh raised biscuits daily to her boarders" and kept a dough start by using "a piece of the raised dough for leven, saving it out as she made up the others to bake and returning it to her crock in the flour box. At night it would be mixed with a fresh supply of materials and in the morning would be ready to bake."[1] She also "understood the hearts of boys and made an excellent concoction called 'sweetened biscuit.' . . . She had also a cookie jar like a small churn which was never empty and the children could go to it whenever they were hungry, day or night. Her cookies were usually a little sweeter and richer than a biscuit but not so rich as regular cookies or doughnuts. Emma's doughnuts were always the twisted kind."[2]

The responsibility of training her five active little ones was a task she took seriously, though she was not one to dote on her children. Joseph III remembered experiencing another bout of the fever and calling for his mother to bring him something. When she did not come immediately, he panicked and got up from his bed. Not strong enough to stand on his own, he became dizzy and let out an anguished cry as he fell to the floor. He recalled: "Mother hurried to me, helped me back into bed, and told me I should not be so foolish, explaining that she had her work to do in addition to waiting on me, and that if she couldn't come at once I should be patient and remember that she would do what she could for me just as soon as she could."[3]

Julia had on several occasions observed her little friend Lucy Rigdon throw temper tantrums if she was not given something she wanted and witnessed the girl's mother rewarding her immediately with that which she demanded. Julia decided to try the same tactic on Emma but obtained entirely different results. One day when she asked her mother for something to eat and Emma told her to wait for a moment, Julia flung herself down and began screaming and pounding her head and heels on the floor. Emma "stepped quickly to her, caught the young miss by the shoulder and straightened her to her feet with the sharp command, 'Stop that! If you want anything, ask for it, but don't try any of that nonsense if you can't have it right away. You just can't come Lucy Rigdon on me!'"[4]

As a curious boy might do, young Joseph went into the yard one cold, blustery day and decided to put his tongue on a frosty axe to see if it would stick. When it did, he picked up the axe and carried it into the house, seeking help from his mother. "A hired man, Ira Willis, had just made a fire in the stove and the water in the teakettle was getting warm so Ira poured it over the tongue and axe and Emma put oil on the swollen tongue and told him to hold some of it in his mouth."[5] She then scolded the boy, telling him she hoped he'd learned a good lesson and that in the future it would be good if he learned his lessons without having to suffer such a painful experience.

In addition to raising her own children, Emma continued to take in other youngsters who needed a warm bed and a hot meal. Lorin Walker and his sisters, Lucy and Catherine, lived in her home for well over two years and were soon considered part of the family. Lucy later recorded that "the Prophet and his wife introduced us as their sons and daughters. Every privilege was accorded us in the home. Every pleasure within reach was ours. He often referred to . . . Lorin as his 'Edwin.' He was indeed his confidential and trusted friend. He was ever by his side . . . and conversed freely on various subjects."[6]

Instances were many of Emma and Joseph taking into their home those less fortunate. Another heartwarming occurrence of love and compassion involved eight African-Americans who had made their way to Nauvoo from Buffalo, New York. Although they were not slaves and therefore free to travel where they pleased, "they were forced to hide from those who might mistake them for runaway slaves. They endured cold and hardship, wearing out shoes and then socks until they walked on bare feet all the way to the City of Joseph." Upon their arrival in the city, Emma welcomed them to stay in her home until each was found a place to live. "But there was one, a girl named Jane, who did not have a place to go, and she wept, not knowing what to do." When Emma and Joseph saw the girl's tears, they made her a place in their home where she lived as a member of the family until she migrated to Utah with the main body of the Saints. Jane said years later that she would still "wake up in the middle of

Time to Laugh

the night, and just think about Brother Joseph and Sister Emma and how good they [were] to me."[7]

Emma always enjoyed joining with family and friends in the many social events in the city. She attended dances, balls, sang in the choirs, quilted, and enjoyed additional recreational activities such as sleigh and horseback riding with the Prophet. In April of 1841, she took part in one of the most celebrated occasions in Nauvoo—the laying of the temple cornerstones.

Joseph had received a revelation in January of 1841, commanding the people to build a temple "for the Most High to dwell therein . . . that he may come to and restore again that which was lost unto you, or which he hath taken away, even the fulness of the priesthood" (D&C 124:27–28). Site preparation for the sacred edifice had begun immediately, and by April 6—precisely eleven years from the time of the organization of the Church on the Whitmer farm in Fayette, New York—the cornerstones were ready to be laid. A grand parade formed in the city, and amidst cannon fire and cheers from onlookers, Joseph and Emma appeared. Emmeline Wells remembered: "Emma Smith was fond of horses and could manage them well in riding or driving. Many can recall seeing her mounted on horseback beside her husband in military parade and a grander couple could nowhere be found. She always dressed becomingly, and a riding costume showed off her shapely figure to the best advantage. She was a woman of commanding presence."[8]

Sister Eunice Billings Snow, who witnessed the Prophet lay the cornerstone of the temple that day, recorded her vivid description of Emma and Joseph on parade: "Some of the most impressive moments of my life were, when I saw the 'Nauvoo Legion' on parade with the Prophet, then Gen. Joseph Smith, with his wife, Emma Hale Smith, on horseback at the head of the troops. It was indeed, an imposing sight, and one that I shall always remember. He so fair, and she so dark, in their beautiful riding-habits. He in full military suit, and she with her habit trimmed with gold buttons, a neat cap on her head, with a black plume in it, while the Prophet wore a red plume in his, and a red sash across his breast, his coat was black, while his white pants had red stripes on the outside seams. He also wore a sword at his side. His favorite riding-horse was named Charlie, a big black steed."[9] Emma's "riding dress was black with a bonnet of a sort of poke style with which she wore a vale which could be pulled back to expose [her] face. Her riding whip had an ivory handle and her side-saddle was also very elegant."[10]

During the April 6 celebration, the Prophet was presented a silk American flag "by the ladies of Nauvoo," which he received and hoisted to cannon fire. Then a hymn was sung from Emma's expanded hymnbook, which she had worked on so determinedly and which had recently come off the press. In the afternoon session, the choir performed a few numbers and the military band played several stirring patriotic songs. Afterward Emma and other sisters served a turkey dinner to the guests in attendance. The Prophet observed, "We never witnessed a more imposing spectacle than was presented on this occasion. . . . Such a multitude of people moving in harmony, in friendship, in dignity. . . . They were a people of intelligence, and virtue and order; in short . . . they were *Saints;* . . . and they were blessed and happy."[11] How Emma must have enjoyed this brief season of peace.

Chapter Twenty-Three

TRAGEDY STRUCK THE SMITH FAMILY not long after the grand celebration in April and left them reeling with grief. Joseph's brother Don Carlos died from pneumonia, and exactly one week later, on August 14, 1841, Emma and Joseph's fourteen-month-old son, also named Don Carlos, died from the swamp fever. In September, Hyrum's seven-year-old son, Hyrum Jr., died of malaria, and in January of 1842, Samuel's wife, Mary, and their infant daughter died. Although the Saints had worked diligently to drain the swamps, the ague continued to plague the people, usually hitting hardest children under ten years of age.

Don Carlos was the fifth child who had been taken in death from Emma and Joseph. She later remarked that it was the most difficult loss she had experienced because she had had him for so long and he had been such a joy to the family.[1] Somehow, though, she had the strength and the ability to mourn his loss while continuing to carry on with the demands of her busy life.

On March 17, 1842, Emma took on an additional role in the Church when under the direction of her prophet-husband, the Nauvoo Female Relief Society was organized. Many of the sisters had previously been meeting together to sew shirts for the men working on the temple and had decided to create a women's society and write up a set of bylaws under which they could operate and serve. Eliza R. Snow was selected to draft the constitution, which would be presented to Joseph for his approval and blessing. After reading the document, the Prophet replied that it was "the best he had ever seen. 'But,' he said, 'this is not what you want. Tell the sisters their offering is accepted of the Lord, and he has something better for them than a written constitution. . . . I will organize the women under the priesthood after the pattern of the priesthood.'"[2]

Twenty sisters, along with John Taylor and Willard Richards, joined the Prophet in that first, historic Relief Society meeting. Joseph suggested the women choose their president and that she should then select her counselors. After the brethren left the room, the women chose Emma to be the president of the organization, and she selected Elizabeth Ann Whitney and Sarah M. Cleveland as her counselors. Her counselors were fitting choices, as both women had provided much relief to Emma and her family when they were in destitute circumstances. Emma chose another of her friends, Eliza R. Snow, to serve as the society's secretary, and Elvira Annie Cowles as the treasurer.

According to Joseph's instruction to the women, Emma's call fulfilled the promise made to her years before in Harmony, Pennsylvania, when the Lord termed her "an elect lady" (D&C 25:3). He further taught that "the elect meant to be elected to a certain work, &c., and . . . the revelation was then fulfilled by Sister Emma's election to the Presidency of the Society, she having previously been ordained to expound the Scriptures."[3] When Elder John Taylor set Emma apart on that historic day, he "blessed her and confirmed upon her all the blessings which had been conferred on her, that she might be a mother in Israel and look to the wants of the needy, and be a pattern of virtue; and possess all the qualifications necessary for her to stand and preside and dignify her office, to teach the females those principles requisite for their future usefulness."[4]

After much discussion and a cordial debate between Emma and Joseph regarding the use of *benevolent* or *relief* in the name of the society, the women agreed to have the society known as the Female Relief Society of Nauvoo and adopted her suggested motto—Charity Never Faileth. Emma said in that first meeting, "We are going to do something extraordinary. . . . We expect extraordinary occasions and pressing calls."[5] During a later gathering of the society, the Prophet counseled the sisters: "As you increase in innocence and virtue, as you increase in goodness, let your hearts expand, let them be enlarged toward others; you must be long-suffering, and bear with the faults and errors of mankind." He concluded his remarks by saying, "I now turn the key in your behalf in the name of the Lord, and this Society shall rejoice, and knowledge and intelligence shall flow down from this time henceforth; this is the beginning of better days to the poor and needy, who shall be made to rejoice and pour forth blessings on your heads."[6] Later the Prophet commented that "the Church was never perfectly organized until the women were thus organized."[7]

Throughout the summer of 1842, Emma and the children joined with audiences of up to eight thousand Saints who gathered to learn from Joseph's Sabbath discourses in a grove of trees on the hillside near the temple site. She and Joseph enjoyed a good deal of time together, whether at home or walking about the city. Although she was expecting another child, she also accompanied him on numerous horseback and carriage rides through the countryside.

Their leisurely walks and rides came to an abrupt halt in early August, however, when Joseph was taken into custody for allegedly "being an accessory before the fact, to an assault with intent to kill" former Missouri governor Lilburn Boggs.[8] In May, Boggs had survived being shot while sitting in his home in Independence and was now—three months later—accusing the Prophet of planning his assassination. Joseph was released the same day when the deputy sheriff admitted the arrest was illegal and returned to seek further direction from Illinois governor Thomas Carlin.

Although Joseph had not been in Missouri since his imprisonment in Liberty Jail, the illegal arrest was taken seriously by him, his associates, and Emma. A month before he was taken into custody, rumors regarding Joseph's being a suspect in the incident had prompted a thousand Relief Society sisters to sign a petition to be presented to Governor Carlin. The document, delivered to him in Quincy by Emma Smith, Eliza R. Snow, and Amanda Smith (whose husband and son had been killed at Haun's Mill), was an effort to convince the governor of the Prophet's integrity and innocence in the Boggs murder attempt and also to persuade Carlin to offer protection to the Saints in Nauvoo that "their families might have the privilege of enjoying their peaceable rights."[9]

Because of the seriousness of the illegal arrest and knowing it would be wise if Joseph was not available if or when the deputy sheriff returned from his visit with Carlin, Joseph crossed the Mississippi River and took up lodging with his uncle John Smith in Zarahemla, Iowa. When the deputy returned two days later and was unable to find the Prophet, he found Emma at the Homestead and attempted to intimidate her with hollow threats. From across the river, Joseph soon sent word for her, Hyrum, and several of the brethren to meet him after dark on an island in the river between Nauvoo and Zarahemla. That night, Emma, now four to five months pregnant, and Hyrum met with the others on the riverbank behind the Red Brick Store and proceeded in a skiff to the island, where they met the Prophet. After some discussion, it was decided it would be best for him to travel up the river and seclude himself at the home of Brother Edward Sayer, who lived on the Nauvoo side of the Mississippi.

Of that island visit Joseph wrote: "How glorious were my feelings when I met that faithful and friendly band . . . on the island . . . between Zarahemla and Nauvoo: with what unspeakable delight, and what transports of joy swelled my bosom, when I took by the hand, on that night, my beloved Emma—she that was my wife, even the wife of my youth, and the choice of my heart. Many were the reverberations of my mind when I contemplated for a moment the many scenes we had been called to pass through, the fatigues and the toils, the sorrows and sufferings, and the joys and consolations, from time to time, which had strewed our paths and crowned our board. Oh what a commingling of thought filled my mind for the moment, again she is here, even in the seventh trouble—undaunted, firm, and unwavering—unchangeable, affectionate Emma!"[10]

Several days later, Emma determined to visit Joseph again. After learning her carriage was being watched by the sheriff in Nauvoo, she walked to a neighbor's home and waited for the driver to pick her up. She then drove about four miles south of Nauvoo, circled the city, and traveled north through the timber where she left the carriage and walked to the Sayer farm. She and Joseph spent the following day "in good spirits and very cheerful" and talked about "various subjects."[11] They read his history and had dinner together before her escorts arrived to take her back to Nauvoo. Because it had rained in the morning and the roads were muddy, the men had come upriver in a skiff to pick her up. Consequently, Emma had to walk quite some distance through the mud before they reached the river's edge and boarded the small boat. The trip home was a harrowing experience due to a strong wind that forced them to take shelter several times near islands in the river before they reached Nauvoo later that evening.

Through her several visits Emma acted as one of Joseph's couriers, delivering correspondence to and from leaders of the Church and of the Nauvoo Legion. One tender letter, however, was addressed specifically to her: "I embrace this opportunity to express to you some of my feelings this morning. First of all, I take the liberty to tender you my sincere thanks for the two interesting and consoling visits that you have made me during my almost exiled situation. Tongue cannot express the gratitude of my heart, for the warm and true-hearted friendship you have manifested in these things towards me."[12]

The Prophet then mentioned to her a suggestion from the brethren that he go north and find temporary safety in Pine Woods, Wisconsin, where lumber had been cut and shipped down the Mississippi for the Nauvoo Temple. He expressed his feeling that going north might be a good thing, but made it very clear that he would leave only if she and the children went with him. As ever, Emma was ready and willing to accompany her husband. She answered his letter with a quick note: "I am ready to go with you if you are obliged to leave; and Hyrum says he will go with me. I shall make the best arrangements I can and be as well prepared as possible. But still I feel good confidence that you can be protected without leaving this country. There are more ways than one to take care of you, and I believe that you can still direct in your business concerns if we are all of us prudent in the matter. If it was pleasant weather I should contrive to see you this evening, but I dare not run too much of a risk. . . . Yours affectionately forever."[13]

After several days of considering Joseph's proposed exile in Wisconsin, Emma tried pleading Joseph's case once again and wrote two letters to Governor Carlin. The first was very respectfully written and detailed the hostile circumstances in which she and her family were forced to live, and she appealed to his sympathies to spare her children further persecution and hardship. The second was also written with respect for Carlin's position as governor but was laced with a bit of insolence relative to his lack of legal knowledge and the courage to protect Joseph and the Saints. Although Carlin "passed high encomiums on Emma . . . and expressed astonishment at the judgment and talent manifest in the manner of her address," he did nothing except suggest Joseph give himself up to the Missourians.[14]

Rumors soon began to spread throughout Nauvoo, "intimating that [Joseph's] retreat had been discovered, and that it was no longer safe for [him] to remain at Brother Sayer's." As soon as Emma heard the rumors, she again visited Joseph, and together they traveled south, where he was welcomed at another home in the northeast part of Nauvoo. Emma visited him there as well. A few days later she sent a note suggesting "she could take care of [him] better at home than elsewhere"[15] and that she expected him home that evening. Taking his wife's good counsel, Joseph waited until nightfall and then left for the Homestead.

Only a few days later another posse of Missourians rudely entered Emma's home while the family was enjoying a quiet dinner. Again their intent was to arrest the Prophet and take him to Missouri. Emma met the men in the front part of the house and kept them in conversation while Joseph went out the back door to Newel and Elizabeth Whitney's, where he stayed until the deputy sheriff had illegally searched the Homestead and left with his men.

The anxiety and fear of this continual harassment, in addition to the stress of her pregnancy, finally wore Emma down until her reserves were depleted and she fell ill with malaria. Her condition worsened until her life was in the balance. Joseph attended to her every need throughout the month of October as her health would be much improved each morning but worsen throughout the day and into the evening. Of the Prophet's constant vigil, Mercy Thompson wrote: "I saw him by the bed-side of Emma, his wife, in sickness, exhibiting all the solicitude and sympathy possible for the tenderest of hearts and the most affectionate of natures to feel."[16]

The Prophet also spent time with their children and kept them busy and out of the house with carriage or horse rides outside the city and to the temple grounds to watch and visit the construction workers. Although Emma's health improved enough to allow her to ride to

Tiny Hands

the temple on a couple of occasions, she continued to have good and bad days throughout the entire fall and into the winter until on December 26, 1842, she felt those familiar pains of labor and delivered a stillborn baby boy. For the second time in just sixteen months she and Joseph mourned the death of a child.

Joseph was compelled to leave the next morning for Springfield, Illinois, where he was acquitted of the charge of participating in the Boggs assassination attempt. He returned as quickly as possible to be with Emma, who was heartbroken and grieving. Having empathy for the depths of her sorrow and in an attempt to console and bring her comfort, he approached William and Anna McIntire with an unusual request.

Anna had given birth to twin girls three months before, so Joseph asked if he could borrow one of the infants during the day to take to Emma to nurse and love. Anna's older daughter, Margarette, recalled, "My mother . . . finally consented for him to take one of them, providing he would bring it home each night. This he did punctually himself, and also came after it each morning. One evening he did not come with it at the usual time, and mother went down to . . . see what was the matter, and there sat the Prophet with the baby wrapped up in a little silk quilt. He was trotting it on his knee, and singing to it to get it quiet before starting out, as it had been fretting. The child soon became quiet when my mother took it, and the Prophet came up home with her."[17] With the passage of time, Emma recovered her physical and emotional health and discontinued keeping little Mary on a daily basis, but she and Joseph often visited the McIntire home "to caress her and play with her." Sadly, when the toddler was two years old, she died, and Emma and Joseph grieved as if they had lost one of their own.

Chapter Twenty-Four

SINCE THE PROPHET'S INCARCERATION IN Liberty Jail, Emma and others witnessed a noticeable change in him. He seemed to have increased in spiritual strength and possessed greater light and intelligence than before his imprisonment. According to Elder B. H. Roberts, Liberty "was more temple than prison, so long as the Prophet was there. It was a place of meditation and prayer."[1] Soon after his release, he entrusted his increased knowledge of eternal doctrines to a few close friends, and within a few short months, he openly began to teach doctrine that even he considered bold.

Elder Parley P. Pratt recalled being personally taught in Philadelphia before the Prophet addressed a congregation of about three thousand people on his way home from Washington, D.C., in 1839: "During these interviews he taught me many great and glorious principles concerning God and the heavenly order of eternity. It was at this time that I received from him the first idea of eternal family organization. . . .

"It was from him that I learned that the wife of my bosom might be secured to me for time and all eternity; and that the refined sympathies and affections which endeared us to each other emanated from the fountain of divine eternal love. It was from him that I learned that we might cultivate these affections, and grow and increase in the same to all eternity; while the result of our endless union would be an offspring as numerous as the stars of heaven, or the sands of the sea shore. . . . It was from him that I learned that the highest dignity of womanhood was, to stand as a queen and priestess to her husband, and to reign for ever and ever as the queen mother of her numerous and still increasing offspring."[2]

Less than a year later, in 1840, at the funeral of Seymour Brunson, the Prophet introduced the doctrine of baptism for the dead and taught the congregation that it was permissible for them to perform this ordinance in behalf of their deceased family members and friends. For Emma, this revealed doctrine was a sweet blessing, and she participated in performing baptisms for her loved ones. She had previously received word that her father had passed away, so in 1841 she was baptized in his behalf. When in 1843 she learned her mother had died, she was baptized for her, for two of her aunts—Eunice Cady and Esther Hale—and her uncle Reuben Hale. That same year, she also acted as proxy in the baptism of her sister Phebe Hale Root, who did not pass away until December of 1856.[3] Obviously, although the doctrine had been set forth, the particulars came "line upon line, precept upon precept" (2 Nephi 28:30), and baptisms that were performed improperly were later redone appropriately.

In March of 1842, the Prophet addressed a group of Saints who had gathered for a child's funeral on the Sabbath day in the grove. In this discourse he revealed another doctrine that perhaps was even more precious and sweet for Emma than that of baptism for the dead. On that occasion the Prophet spoke on the salvation of little children. He prefaced his talk by reading from the book of Revelation and said: "Why it is that infants, innocent children, are taken away from us, especially those that seem to be the most intelligent and interesting. The strongest reasons that present themselves to my mind are these: This world is a very wicked world. . . . In the earlier ages of the world a righteous man, and a man of God and of intelligence, had a better chance to do good . . . than at the present day. . . . The Lord takes many away, even in infancy, that they may escape the envy of man, and the sorrows and evils of this present world; they were too pure, too lovely, to live on earth; therefore, if rightly considered, instead of mourning we have reason to rejoice as they are delivered from evil, and we shall soon have them again."[4]

The remainder of the Prophet's discourse that day was about baptism. After the meeting, he invited all who wished to participate in the ordinance to meet at the river's edge at two o'clock that afternoon. When he left the Homestead and walked down the hill to the river at the appointed time, "the bank of the Mississippi was lined with a multitude of people, and President Joseph Smith went into the river and baptized eighty persons for the remission of their sins."[5] The first to enter the river that day to be baptized by Joseph was Emma's nephew Lorenzo Wasson, after herself the first of her father's family to accept the restored gospel. When the baptisms were concluded, the congregation walked to the grove, where the Prophet confirmed fifty of those he had baptized.

In 1843, Joseph referred to his 1842 discourse about the salvation of little children and explained to the sisters that they would have the opportunity of rearing their lost children. "The Prophet wanted to comfort us, and he told us that we should receive those children in the morning of the resurrection just as we laid them down, in purity and innocence, and we should nourish and care for them as their mothers . . . that the children would grow and develop in the Millennium, and that the mothers would have the pleasure of training and caring for them, which they had been deprived of in this life."[6]

Emma's heart must have thrilled when she heard this revealed doctrine. She now knew it would actually be possible for her to rear her children who had been taken in death. In addition, the time was fast approaching when she could partake of all the ordinances of the temple, including the reception of her endowment and the blessing of entering into the new and everlasting covenant of marriage with her beloved Joseph.

After the completion of the Kirtland Temple in 1835, many of the brethren had received a preparatory endowment, and now in Nauvoo the time had come for a select few to receive their full endowment. On May 4, 1842, the Prophet invited nine of his most trusted confidants—including his brother Hyrum and Brigham Young—to privately meet with him at the Red Brick Store. The day before the meeting, Joseph called for several of the brethren to help him prepare his office located above the store to resemble the interior of the temple as closely as possible. "He told us that the object he had was for us to go to work and fit up that room preparatory to giving endowments to a few Elders. . . . We therefore went to work making the necessary preparations, and everything was arranged representing the interior of a temple as much as the circumstances would permit."[7] The men divided the room with partitions made of canvas, built an altar, and brought in additional furniture. Trees, plants, and shrubbery were carried up the stairs and put in place to represent the various instruction rooms of the temple.

When the Prophet and the nine men gathered, Joseph, with Hyrum's assistance, washed, anointed, and administered the endowment to the eight men. The following day, the ceremony was performed in like manner for the Prophet and his brother. Brigham Young remembered: "When we got our washings and anointings under the hands of the Prophet Joseph at Nauvoo we had only one room to work in with the exception of a little side room or office where we were washed and anointed, and had our garments placed upon us." Receiving the endowment set these brethren apart from the general membership of the Church; however, their meetings were sporadic and infrequent until May 28, 1843, when Emma was invited to meet with them. Though she had yet to receive the endowment, she and Joseph became the first husband and wife to be sealed for time and all eternity in the dispensation of the fulness of times.

Four months later, on September 28, 1843, Emma became the first woman of this dispensation to receive the endowment and then participated in the administration of the initiatory ordinances in late 1843 and early 1844. She either presided over or personally administered washings and anointings to a number of sisters, including her mother-in-law, Lucy Mack Smith; Hyrum's wife, Mary Fielding Smith; Vilate Kimball; and Bathsheba W. Smith.

Chapter Twenty-Five

 URING THE PROPHET'S LIFETIME thirty-six men and twenty-nine women received their temple endowment, and many were also sealed in what the Saints called "prayer meetings." Though Emma was a ready participant in receiving these temple blessings, she balked decisively at another teaching Joseph introduced—the principle of plural marriage. When she was first made aware of the principle is unknown; however, Joseph learned it through revelation as early as 1831 in Ohio, while he was working on the revision of the Old Testament.

By the summer of 1841, Joseph was discussing plural marriage extensively with the Quorum of the Twelve and had actually married a plural wife (Louisa Beaman) in a private ceremony in April of that year. Emma vacillated between acceptance and rejection of the principle. Elder Orson Pratt related that she "at times fought against him with all her heart; and then again she would break down in her feelings, and humble herself before God and call upon His holy name, and would then lead forth ladies and place their hands in the hands of Joseph, and they were married to him according to the law of God."[1]

Bathsheba W. Smith remembered at the time she received her washings and anointings that Emma counseled the sisters present: "Your husbands are going to take more wives, and unless you consent to it, you must put your foot down and keep it there." Bathsheba further related that "much more was said in regard to plural marriage at that time by Sister Emma Smith, who seemed opposed to the principle."[2]

In May of 1843, Emma gave approval for the Prophet to take Eliza and Emily Partridge as his wives but afterward seems to have treated them unkindly and with suspicion. "She often made things very unpleasant," wrote Emily years later. "I know it was hard for [her], and any women to enter plural marriage . . . , and I do not know as anybody would have done any better than Emma did under the circumstances."[3]

Emma's wrestle with the principle heightened over the next three months, and by mid-July Joseph was worried and anxious. He spent several days with her and the children riding in their carriage about the city and the countryside and then on the following day took counsel with Hyrum about her struggle. During their meeting, the Prophet dictated the "Revelation on the Eternity of the Marriage Covenant, including the Plurality of Wives," and his clerk, William Clayton, recorded it.[4] Among the many great and important principles contained in this revelation was the most important reason for Joseph and a select few of the brethren to take plural wives—because the Lord commanded it! In addition the Lord spoke directly to Emma and explained that the commandment was given "to prove you all" and admonished her to "receive all those that have been given unto my servant Joseph, . . . who are virtuous and pure before me" (D&C 132:51–52).

Because he had enjoyed a close relationship with his sister-in-law for many years, Hyrum felt he could help Emma with her struggle if Joseph would allow him to take the revelation and show it to her. Joseph reluctantly agreed but smiled and said to his brother before he left, "You do not know Emma as well as I do." Nonetheless, the confident Hyrum headed to the Homestead with the revelation in hand, only to return shortly to tell Joseph "he had never received a more severe talking to in his life." Joseph responded, "I told you you did not know Emma as well as I did."[5] On the following day, Joseph recorded, "I was in conversation with Emma most of the day"; although the Prophet gives no further details, we may assume plural marriage was the primary topic of their discussion.[6]

Conversely, about a month later, it appears that Hyrum had much better success discussing the practice with Emma. She and Joseph had been talking quietly in their room late one night when Joseph came out and asked one of the hired girls, Maria Jane Woodward, to bring Hyrum to the house. When he arrived, Jane heard him say as he entered the room, "Well Sister Emma, what is the matter?" Though the nineteen-year-old girl heard no more of the conversation that night, Emma must have thought she had. Jane later related that the following day Emma sat her down on one of the beds she was making and said, "It was you that Joseph came to when he sent for Hyrum last night was it?" When the girl answered in the affirmative, Emma went on: "The principle of plural marriage is right, but I am like other women, I am naturally jealous hearted and can talk back to Joseph as long as any wife can talk back to her husband, but what I want to say to you is this. You heard me finding fault with the principle. I want to say that that principle is right, it is from our Father in Heaven. . . . What I said I have got [to] repent of. The principle is right but I am jealous hearted. Now never tell anybody that you heard me find fault with Joseph of that principle. The principle is right and if I or you or anyone else finds fault with that principle we have got to humble ourselves and repent of it."[7]

Persistent gossip circulated throughout Nauvoo, and third- and fourthhand accounts of unsubstantiated rumors were recorded in members' journals regarding Emma's difficulty with the principle. The most popular story that filtered through the community was that she lashed out in anger toward Eliza R. Snow, one of Joseph's plural wives. Eliza was a faithful journal keeper, but such an incident never appears in her writings. A sister who did record a brief account of the alleged incident admitted that she had heard the story from a friend and finished her account by adding, "This I give as rumor only."[8] Over the years this report was embellished by so many that it escalated into a folktale in which Emma angrily pulled Eliza's hair or hit her with a broomstick and either pushed or pulled her down a flight of stairs, causing her to lose the unborn child she was carrying.[9] Sadly, without proper documentation, this story, as well as several others, was perpetuated by word of mouth until 1886, when it was published by an anti-Mormon author whose only source was "they say."

Emma was not alone in her struggle with plural marriage. Brigham Young spoke of his internal struggle with the practice: "I was not desirous of shrinking from any duty, nor of failing in the least to do as I was commanded, but it was the first time in my life that I had desired the grave, and I could hardly get over it for a long time. And when I saw a funeral, I felt to envy the corpse its situation, and to regret that I was not in the coffin."[10]

Though the practice of plural marriage caused no small stir among the Saints, only a few of the brethren were commanded to take more than one wife, and the women married as plural wives kept their marriages secret. Eliza Partridge recalled: "A woman living in polygamy dare not let it be known, and nothing but a firm desire to keep the commandments of the Lord could have induced a girl to marry that way. I thought my trials were very severe in this line, and I am often led to wonder how it was that a person of my temperament could get along with it and not rebel. But I know it was the Lord who kept me from opposing his plans, although in my heart I felt like I could not submit to them. But I did, and I am thankful to my Heavenly Father for the care he had over me in those troublous times."[11]

Although additional rumors spread that Emma and Joseph's marriage was strained on account of the practice, Joseph III later gave an account of his parents' close and enduring relationship up to the time of the Prophet's death. "It has been charged by certain ones advocating plural marriage that she was a thorn in his side, opposing his policies, and leading him an ill life. This is absolutely not true. I was old enough at the time to know what was going on around me, and was closely associated with both my parents. The sleeping room I shared with my brothers was never more than a door away from where Father and Mother slept. Because of the great love and concern Mother had for her children she never wanted us far from her, in order that she might be on hand to take care of us herself in case of necessity. So, I am sure that if there ever were angry words between my parents I should have known it, and I can truthfully state that nothing of the kind ever occurred."[12]

Chapter Twenty-Six

CERTAINLY THE PRACTICE OF PLURAL MARRIAGE and the gossip related to it complicated Emma's life but did not bring it to a standstill. She continued on with dignity and grace, supporting her husband in his personal life and in his public life as the Prophet and president of the Church. On January 18, 1843, while living in the Homestead, Emma and Joseph hosted a dinner party, which seventy-four visitors attended. Because the dining area in their home was small, the guests ate in four shifts and were served by the Prophet and Emma. Joseph tenderly observed that it had been sixteen years "this day since I was married to Emma Hale."[1]

In early May she and Joseph boarded the *Maid of Iowa* steamer and, with about one hundred friends and acquaintances, spent an enjoyable time traveling upriver as far as Fort Madison, Iowa. Joseph vividly described the excursion: "We had an excellent address from our esteemed friend, Parley P. Pratt. The band performed its part well. Much good humor and hilarity prevailed. The captain and officers on board did all they could to make us comfortable, and we had a very agreeable and pleasant trip."[2]

Soon afterward a more extensive family excursion was planned, and on June 13, 1843, Emma and Joseph left Nauvoo with their children to visit her sister Elizabeth Wasson, who lived about two hundred miles north of Nauvoo in Dixon, Illinois. Unfortunately, this journey was not nearly as enjoyable as their day trip up the river. Just five days after their departure, Hyrum Smith sent Stephen Markham and William Clayton to Dixon to warn the Prophet that another writ had been issued and the Missourians were again after him. Though the brethren arrived in time to alert the Prophet, he chose to stay with Emma and the children rather than escape.

Disguised and "represent[ing] themselves as Mormon elders who wanted to see the prophet," the Missouri sheriff, Joseph Reynolds, and the constable of Carthage, Illinois,

Harmon Wilson, obtained information along the route to lead them straight to the Wasson residence. Joseph was outside when the men arrived and recorded: "I was in the yard going to the barn when Wilson stepped to the end of the house and saw me. He accosted me in a very uncouth, ungentlemanly manner, when Reynolds stepped up to me, collared me, then both of them presented cocked pistols to my breast, without showing any writ or serving any process. Reynolds cried out, ' . . . if you stir I'll shoot.' . . . I enquired, 'What is the meaning of all this? . . . I am not afraid of your shooting; I am not afraid to die.' I then bared my breast and told them to shoot away. 'I have endured so much oppression, I am weary of life; and kill me, if you please. I am a strong man, however, and with my own natural weapons could soon level both of you; but if you have any legal process to serve, I am at all times subject to law, and shall not offer resistance.' Reynolds replied, 'G—d—you, if you say another word I will shoot you. . . .' I answered, 'Shoot away; I am not afraid of your pistols.'"[3]

All the while Emma stood in horror, watching as Joseph was hustled into a wagon while taking repeated jabs to his ribs with the law officers' pistols. When he asked for permission to get some clothes and say good-bye to his family, they ignored him and prepared to drive away. Stephen Markham, who initially tried to help the Prophet but was instructed by Joseph to not obstruct the officers, ran to the front of the wagon and grabbed the horse's bits and held them just long enough for Emma to give Joseph his coat and hat before the wagon rumbled away.

While Joseph was being held prisoner and "shamefully abused,"[4] she and the children were driven home to Nauvoo in their carriage by Lorenzo Wasson, her nephew, and Lorin Walker, who with his two sisters lived with Emma and Joseph. During their four-day return trip, Emma had no way of knowing Joseph's whereabouts or whether he was dead or alive. Young Joseph remembered well the journey back to Nauvoo because on the second day of travel after stopping for lunch and to feed the horses, two of his fingers were accidentally smashed in the carriage door. "The wounds bled freely and Mother bound them up with some cloths from her bag, and we traveled on. My fingers became very painful, and after a while we stopped at a farmhouse. Mother unwrapped them, soaking the temporary dressing off with warm water and rewrapped them with fresh cloths. Taking from her trunk a little bottle of whiskey and wormwood, she turned the tips of my fingers upward, and poured the liquid upon them, into the dressings—at which for the first time in my life I promptly fainted! It seemed as if she had poured the strong medicine directly upon my heart, so sharply it stung and so quick was its circulatory effect. When I returned to consciousness I was lying on a lounge against the wall and Mother was bathing my face most solicitously. I soon recovered and we proceeded on our journey, reaching home in good time and without further mishap."[5]

When Emma and the children reached Nauvoo, she soon learned that Joseph—though still under arrest—had been aided by a posse of the brethren sent out from the city and was not far behind her. On the morning of June 30, in company with a brass band and many anxious Saints, she rode out to meet her husband and welcome him home. She wept as she and Joseph embraced and then celebrated with him and the others present as the brass band began to play a favorite melody. Joseph, who had been riding in a carriage, then mounted his favorite horse, Charlie, and with "Emma riding by [his] side," returned to Nauvoo.[6]

They entered the city to an enthusiastic greeting by members who lined the streets to convey their love and respect. When they reached the Homestead, Joseph's mother, Lucy, was at the door to greet her son, and his children enthusiastically ran from the house and clung to him. That afternoon Emma served dinner to Joseph and more than fifty friends and family members. Because he was still under the guard of the sheriff and constable who had so rudely arrested him at the Wasson home in Dixon, Emma invited the lawmen to dinner and seated them at the head of the table, where they were served and treated with every kindness. Afterward, Joseph spent the rest of that day and the next in court. Once the evidence was examined and witnesses testified, the case against the Prophet was again dropped, and he was released to return home. The disastrous family excursion was finally over.

Chapter Twenty-Seven

JOSEPH ALWAYS TRIED TO PROVIDE for his family in the little private time he had. In Nauvoo he owned and operated the Red Brick Store, and he also farmed a small piece of ground outside the city. Emma had taken care of most of the family's domestic affairs and accommodated the needs of their many visitors. Joseph III remembered "scarcely a Sunday in ordinary weather that the house and yard were not crowded—the yard with teams and the house with callers. This made a great deal of bustle and confusion, and also a heavy burden of added toil for Mother and unnecessary expense for Father."[1]

In an attempt to lessen the confusion and provide a home with more living space and better accommodations for guests, the Mansion House was built for Joseph and Emma across the street and northeast of the Homestead. In August 1843 they moved into the two-storied, six-room home; however, before long it too was overridden with folks wanting to see and talk with the Prophet. As a result, Joseph added a number of additional sleeping rooms on the east side of the building and on September 15, 1843, put up a sign at the front of the Mansion House which read in part:

Nauvoo Mansion.

In consequence of my house being constantly crowded with strangers and other persons waiting to see me . . . I found myself unable to support so much company free of charge. . . . My house has been a home and resting-place for thousands, and my family many times obliged to do without food, after having fed all they had to visitors. . . . I have been reduced to the necessity of opening 'The Mansion' as a hotel. I have provided the best table accommodations in the city; and the Mansion . . . renders travelers more comfortable than any other place on the Upper Mississippi.[2]

Soon after the public announcement, W. W. Phelps was invited to the Mansion to enjoy an intimate dinner with the Prophet and Emma. Joseph recorded: "I took dinner in the north room, and was remarking to Brother Phelps what a kind, provident wife I had,—that when I wanted a little bread and milk, she would load the table with so many good things, it would destroy my appetite. At this moment Emma came in, while Phelps, in continuation of the conversation said, 'You must do as Bonaparte did—have a little table, just large enough for the victuals you want yourself.' Mrs. Smith replied, 'Mr. Smith is a bigger man than Bonaparte: he can never eat without his friends.' I remarked, 'That is the wisest thing I ever heard you say.'"[3]

The first large gathering Emma hosted in her new home was an open house in which over one hundred people enjoyed dinner. Later that evening and after a full day of festivities, the company had the benefit of participating in the wedding of a young couple and then a select few witnessed the Prophet solemnize their marriage.

While Joseph recorded numerous occasions where "prayer meeting" was held in the Mansion, Emma had the task of preparing the ordinance room for the sacred meetings. She also accepted the responsibility for washing and ironing the temple clothing, which was hung to dry outdoors "between sheets" to prevent it from being exposed to the public eye.[4]

At about one o'clock in the morning on Christmas Day of 1843, Emma and Joseph were awakened to the caroling of a group of Saints outside the Mansion House. Having had little rest, they hosted a dinner that afternoon with about fifty couples in attendance and celebrated the birth of the Savior with music and dancing throughout the evening. Observing the new year of 1844 was no less festive and began at midnight when "about fifty musicians and singers sang" under Emma and Joseph's bedroom window.[5] New Year's Day culminated with their hosting another large dinner followed by music and dancing.

Music and singing were part of the family's routine. William Holmes Walker, who was sent to Nauvoo to conduct some business with the Prophet, stayed at the Mansion House. He said, "I arrived at his house . . . , just as his family was singing, before the accustomed evening prayer. His wife Emma was leading the singing. I thought I had never heard such sweet heavenly music before. I was equally interested in the prayer offered by the Prophet."[6]

To be sure, Emma had an influential presence in her home, and amid the celebrations and parties she also dealt with the more mundane activities that come with raising children and the hard work involved in running a business. Managing a hotel required additional furniture, rugs, curtains, linens, food, and other supplies, which necessitated her occasionally making a trip down the Mississippi to St. Louis.

Fiddle Dance

During Emma's absence on one such journey, Joseph's good friend and bodyguard, Orin Porter Rockwell, sought the Prophet's help with a business enterprise. Rockwell was building a bar and barbershop across the street, and because the construction was going more slowly than he had anticipated, he asked if he could temporarily open his tavern in the Mansion House. Joseph, ever ready to give assistance, approved of the venture, and Rockwell soon opened up for business in Emma's parlor. Joseph III remembered "a bar, with counter, shelves, bottles, glasses, and other paraphernalia customary for a fully-equipped tavern bar, and Porter Rockwell in charge as tender."[7]

When Emma returned home not many days later, she saw the bar but said nothing for a few hours. When she met young Joseph in the hallway, she asked him to go tell his father she wished to speak with him. With his son on his heels, Joseph soon went to see Emma. Joseph III recalled his mother asking, "Joseph, what is the meaning of that bar in this house?"

Her husband assured her it was only a short-term arrangement until Rockwell could finish his building. Joseph III recalled: "There was no excitement or anger in Mother's voice, nor in what she said as she replied, but there was a distinctness and earnestness I have never forgotten, and which had its effect upon Father as well. 'How does it look,' she asked, 'for the spiritual head of a religious body to be keeping a hotel in which is a room fitted out as a liquor-selling establishment?'"

When the Prophet once again attempted to justify the bar, Joseph III remembered his mother quietly said, "'Well, Joseph, the furniture and other goods I have purchased for the house will come, and you can have some other person look after things here. As for me, I will take my children and go across to the old house [the Homestead] and stay there, for I will not have them raised up under such conditions as this arrangement imposes upon us, nor have them mingle with the kind of men who frequent such a place. You are at liberty to make your choice; either that bar goes out of the house, or we will!'

"It did not take Father long to make the choice, for he replied immediately, 'Very well, Emma; I will have it removed at once'—and he did."[8]

Chapter Twenty-Eight

ALTHOUGH 1844 OPENED WITH SINGING and a splendid celebration, Emma must have been aware of the escalating turmoil surrounding Joseph's life. She may have been aware of the sense of urgency with which he was acting to instruct the brethren and to lay the foundation for the future of the kingdom of God on the earth. He began to place more and more responsibility on the Twelve, often choosing to spend evenings with Emma and the children rather than attend endowment sessions presided over by Brigham Young at the Homestead or in the Red Brick Store.

A series of events caused serious conflict to develop, which inevitably led to increased persecution of the Prophet and Hyrum, who by the end of 1843 was Assistant President and Patriarch of the Church and vice mayor of Nauvoo.

Because 1844 was an election year, Joseph contacted each of the more viable candidates running for president of the United States. He requested that they state their views on several political issues but particularly on the Mormon issue in Illinois and Missouri. When none of the candidates' views were satisfactory, Joseph, supported by the First Presidency and the Quorum of the Twelve, announced his intention to run for president. Before long an effective campaign was organized, and the Prophet's views on various key political issues were nationally publicized. His candidacy increased in popularity until he had gathered a good deal of support throughout the country and posed a real threat to the other candidates.

This development, of course, irritated not only those with national political ambition but also civic leaders throughout the state of Illinois and particularly in Hancock County, where Nauvoo was located. The large number of Mormons in the county enabled the Saints to wield substantial political control locally, which incited the non-Mormon population in Warsaw and in Carthage, the county seat.

Undoubtedly Emma supported Joseph in his political ambitions; nonetheless, she showed her true feelings about politics when she fed a number of politicians at the Mansion House. Because she had not been informed that they were to visit, she hastily prepared puffed pastries that were deep fried, hollow in the middle, and served with sugar and cream. When one of the gentlemen told her the pastries were delicious and asked her what she called them, "she smiled and answered soberly that they were called 'candidates.'"[1]

The Prophet might have endured all the political pressure and persecution if leaders of the Church had not begun to apostatize. In late December 1843, Joseph said to members of the Nauvoo police: "My life is more in danger from some little dough-head of a fool in this city than from all my numerous and inveterate enemies abroad. I am exposed to far greater danger from traitors among ourselves than from enemies without. . . . We have a Judas in our midst."[2]

Arguably the most dangerous among the apostates was John C. Bennett, who had come to Nauvoo in 1840 and was soon a prominent force among the people. Within a year he helped draw up and establish the Nauvoo Charter, became the first elected mayor of the city, and was sustained for a brief period as an Assistant President of the Church. Interestingly, Emma did not like the man and never trusted him. When Bennett first arrived in Nauvoo, he lived for a time at the Homestead, but no matter how much Joseph esteemed him, Bennett's manner and habits annoyed and agitated her. On one occasion when she was very ill and Bennett, who professed to have great medical knowledge, prescribed a medication for her, she refused to take it. But the incident that really annoyed her was his insistence on pulling one of young Joseph's teeth before it was sufficiently loose. The tooth finally came out; nevertheless, Joseph III bled so profusely that Emma had to apply a poultice of saltpeter and leather shavings to stop the bleeding.

Trouble began to brew between Bennett and the Prophet when Hyrum heard a rumor that Bennett had run out on his wife and child in Ohio. When he checked further, he found the story was indeed true, even though Bennett had told Joseph he had never been married. Additionally, the Prophet had not instructed Bennett to marry plural wives, but wanting to satisfy his own unbridled lust Bennett duped several women into engaging in what he termed "spiritual wifery," which was no less than adultery.

When his many immoral activities were eventually brought to light and proven true, Bennett was excommunicated and became revengeful. He engineered a scheme to assassinate Joseph and take over leadership of the Church by organizing a mock battle for the Nauvoo Legion. One division was to come against the other and engage in feigned combat; in the scuffle, the Prophet would be killed. Joseph sensed the danger and refused to position himself where Bennett had proposed.

Bennett quickly left Nauvoo and before long began to stir up anti-Mormon feelings throughout the entire state of Illinois. He had been the force behind Joseph's being accused of attempting to assassinate former Missouri governor Boggs in 1842, which had led to the Prophet's living in exile and his arrest while visiting Emma's sister in Dixon. Other key players in the mounting persecution were the Prophet's former second counselor in the First Presidency, William Law, and his brother Wilson, who had been a major general in the Nauvoo Legion. Together with other prominent apostates, they declared Joseph a fallen prophet and formed their own church with William Law as their president.

The apostates purchased a printing press and published in June 1844 the first and only issue of the *Nauvoo Expositor,* a newspaper in which they accused the Prophet—among other things—of teaching false doctrine, committing adultery, and using his influence among the Saints to gain political power. When the paper was released, the city council met to determine the course they should take to combat the libelous publication. After long consideration and examination of legal codes and opinions, the council and Joseph, as mayor of Nauvoo, ordered the city marshal to destroy the press and any remaining papers.

When the publishers learned what the marshal had done, they brought legal action in Carthage. But their appeal was denied, and it was determined that the city council and mayor had acted within their legal authority. Soon riot actions and vigilante behavior began to materialize, and Joseph and Hyrum were forced to leave their families and cross the river. Late in the evening of June 22, Joseph bade a sorrowful farewell to his four children and Emma, who was now about four months pregnant and in delicate health. With tears streaming down his face, the Prophet left the Mansion House with Hyrum. Before boarding the skiff at the river's edge, he "told Stephen Markham that if I and Hyrum were ever taken again we should be massacred, or I was not a prophet of God. I want Hyrum to live to avenge my blood, but he is determined not to leave me."[3] Porter Rockwell rowed the leaky boat that carried the Prophet, his brother, and Willard Richards to the Iowa side of the Mississippi. A plan had been devised before they left that Emma and the children and Hyrum's family would soon follow and together they would "go away to the West."[4]

The next morning Wandle Mace and his brother Hyrum were "walking together up the street towards Joseph's house, talking over the events of the last few days. Two men came up to us in a great hurry from an opposite direction; they were very much excited over the present situation, and thought it was absolutely necessary that Joseph should return. We took an opposite view of the case and did not want him to return into the very jaws of death.

"But they argued, 'If Joseph don't come back the Governor will put the city under martial law, and then nothing can be brought into the city, neither can anything be taken out, and then what will all our property be worth.' They further said, 'the Governor is our friend, and he will protect Joseph from harass if he would come back.'

"I returned answer with considerable warmth. . . . These men, Reynolds Cahoon and Hiram Kimball, then left us, and walked towards Joseph's house, when they reached it, and before entering, they leaned on the fence and talked together for some time. They then went into the house, we . . . both felt the impression that they were going to persuade Sister Emma . . . to write to him and prevail on him to return. This feeling came upon us so forcibly we were uneasy as to the result. Afterwards, from [Orin Porter] Rockwell who was with Joseph . . . I learned our impressions were correct."[5]

Emma was convinced by the men to write to Joseph, because she soon called for Porter Rockwell and sent him with Cahoon, Kimball, and her nephew Lorenzo across the river with a letter. What the note actually said is not known; however, when the messengers reached the Iowa side of the Mississippi, they gave the letter to Joseph and also told him and Hyrum the negative talk of a few in Nauvoo who thought them cowards for leaving the city. The Prophet replied, "If my life is of no value to my friends it is of none to myself." He counseled with Hyrum, who said, "Let us go back and give ourselves up, and see the thing out." The Prophet responded, "If you go back I will go with you, but we shall be butchered."[6]

Emma later revealed to an acquaintance the anxiety she felt when Joseph returned home to the Mansion House well after dark. She said, "When he came back I felt the worst I ever did in my life, and from that time I looked for him to be killed."[7] Before leaving the next morning for Carthage, he turned to her and asked, "Emma, can you train my sons to walk in their father's footsteps?" to which she answered, "Oh, Brother Joseph, you are coming back!" Joseph asked the same question twice again, and "Emma gave the same answer each time."[8]

Emma watched on the morning of June 24, 1844, as Joseph left for Carthage with his brother Hyrum, John Taylor, Willard Richards, and fifteen members of the Nauvoo city council. When the company was within four miles of the county seat, they were met by a group of about sixty Illinois militiamen, and the Prophet was asked to return with them to Nauvoo to collect from the Nauvoo Legion the weapons which had been lent them by the state.

Joseph's complying with this request afforded Emma another opportunity to see him, and this time, before she said good-bye, she asked that he give her a blessing. Joseph was unable to do so, but he later sent word to Emma "that he had not time to write as he would like, but I could write out the best blessing I could think of and he would sign the same on his return."[9] Emma sat and penned the desires of her heart:

"First of all that I would crave as the richest of heaven's blessings would be wisdom from my Heavenly Father bestowed daily, so that whatever I might do or say, I could not look back at the close of the day with regret, nor neglect the performance of any act that would bring a blessing. I desire the Spirit of God to know and understand myself, that I desire a fruitful, active mind, that I may be able to comprehend the designs of God, when revealed through his servants without doubting. I desire a spirit of discernment, which is one of the promised blessings of the Holy Ghost.

"I particularly desire wisdom to bring up all the children that are, or may be committed to my charge, in such a manner that they will be useful ornaments in the Kingdom of God, and in a coming day arise up and call me blessed.

"I desire prudence that I may not through ambition abuse my body and cause it to become prematurely old and care-worn, but that I may wear a cheerful countenance, live to perform all the work that I covenanted to perform in the spirit-world and be a blessing to all who may in any wise need aught at my hands.

"I desire with all my heart to honor and respect my husband as my head, ever to live in his confidence and by acting in unison with him retain the place which God has given me by his side, and I ask my Heavenly Father that through humility, I may be enabled to overcome that curse which was pronounced on the daughters of Eve. I desire to see that I may rejoice with them in the blessings which God has in store for all who are willing to be obedient to his requirements. Finally, I desire that whatever may be my lot through life I may be enabled to acknowledge the hand of God in all things."[10]

Sadly, Joseph never enjoyed the opportunity of reading the blessing Emma wrote or to know in this way of his beloved wife's most intimate and private desires.

Chapter Twenty-Nine

ᏞEAVING EMMA AND NAUVOO FOR THE last time, the Prophet soberly said to the company with which he rode: "I am going like a lamb to the slaughter, but I am calm as a summer's morning. I have a conscience void of offense toward God and toward all men. If they take my life I shall die an innocent man, and my blood shall cry from the ground for vengeance, and it shall be said of me 'He was murdered in cold blood!'"[1]

The city of Carthage was in an unruly state when Joseph and his company arrived at the Hamilton Hotel about midnight. The following day, he and Hyrum voluntarily surrendered to the constable and were arrested and eventually charged with treason, a capital offense, and that evening taken to jail. They were permitted to have a number of their friends stay with them at the jail, where they were held in an upstairs room for most of the next two days.

On the morning of June 27, 1844, Joseph wrote Emma about the court's proceedings and in a postscript said, "I am very much resigned to my lot, knowing I am justified, and have done the best that could be done. Give my love to the children and all my friends . . . and as for treason, I know that I have not committed any . . . so you need not have any fears that anything can happen to us on that account. May God bless you all. Amen."[2]

By midafternoon all of the prisoners' associates but John Taylor and Willard Richards had left the jail. As the four men endured the sweltering heat of the day, Elder Taylor related: "We all of us felt unusually dull and languid, with a remarkable depression of spirits. In consonance with those feelings, I sang a song . . . entitled, 'A Poor Wayfaring Man of Grief.' . . . After a lapse of some time, Brother Hyrum requested me again to sing that song. I replied, 'Brother Hyrum, I do not feel like singing;' when he remarked, 'Oh, never mind; commence singing, and you will get the spirit of it.' At his request I did so. Soon afterwards I was sitting at one of the front windows of the jail, when I saw a number of men, with painted faces, coming around the corner of the jail, and aiming towards the stairs. The other

Going as a Lamb

brethren had seen the same, for, as I went to the door, I found Brother Hyrum Smith and Dr. Richards already leaning against it. . . . While in this position, the mob, who had come upstairs and tried to open the door, probably thought it was locked and fired a ball through the keyhole. At this Dr. Richards and Brother Hyrum leaped back from the door, with their faces towards it. Almost instantly another ball passed through the panel of the door, and struck Brother Hyrum on the left side of the nose, entering his face and head. At the same instant, another ball from outside entered his back, passing through his body. . . . Immediately, when the ball struck him, he fell flat on his back, crying as he fell, 'I am a dead man!' . . .

"I shall never forget the deep feeling of sympathy and regard manifested in the countenance of Brother Joseph as he drew nigh to Hyrum, and, leaning over him, exclaimed, 'Oh! my poor, dear brother Hyrum!' He, however, instantly arose, and with a firm, quick step, and a determined expression of countenance, approached the door, and pulling the six-shooter left by Brother Wheelock from his pocket, opened the door slightly, and snapped the pistol six successive times. Only three of the barrels, however, were discharged. . . . The firing of Brother Joseph made our assailants pause for a moment. Very soon after, however, they pushed the door some distance open, and protruded and discharged their guns into the room, when I parried them off with my stick, giving another direction to the balls.

"It certainly was a terrible scene. Streams of fire as thick as my arm passed by me as these men fired. . . . While I was engaged in parrying the guns, Brother Joseph said, 'That's right, Brother Taylor, parry them off as well as you can.' These were the last words I ever heard him speak on earth. . . .

"After parrying the guns for some time, which now protruded farther and farther into the room, . . . it occurred to me that we might have some friends outside, and that there might be some chance of escape in that direction. . . . I made a spring for the window . . . and was on the point of leaping out [when] I was struck by a ball from the door about midway of my thigh. . . . I think some prominent nerve must have been severed or injured, for as soon as the ball struck me, I fell like a bird when shot, . . . and lost entirely and instantaneously all power of action or locomotion. I fell upon the window sill, and cried out, 'I am shot!' Not possessing any power to move, I felt myself falling outside of the window, but immediately I fell inside, from some, at that time, unknown cause. When I struck the floor, my animation seemed restored. . . . As soon as I felt the power of motion I crawled under the bed. . . . While on my way and under the bed, I was wounded in three other places; one ball entered a little below the left knee . . . another entered the forepart of my left arm, a little above the wrist.

. . . Another struck me on the fleshy part of my left hip and tore away the flesh as large as my hand, dashing the mangled fragments of flesh and blood against the wall. . . .

"It would seem that immediately after my attempt to leap out of the window, Joseph also did the same thing. . . . A cessation of firing followed, the mob rushed downstairs, and Dr. Richards went to the window. Immediately afterward I saw the doctor going towards the jail door, . . . and I said to him, 'Stop, Doctor, and take me along.' He proceeded to the door and opened it, and then returned and dragged me along to a small cell prepared for criminals.

"Brother Richards was very much troubled, and exclaimed, 'Oh! Brother Taylor, is it possible that they have killed both Brother Hyrum and Joseph? It cannot surely be, and yet I saw them shoot them;' and elevating his hands two or three times, he exclaimed, 'Oh Lord, my God, spare Thy servants!' He then said, 'Brother Taylor, this is a terrible event;' and he dragged me farther into the cell . . . and, taking an old filthy mattress, he covered me with it, and said, 'That may hide you, and you may yet live to tell the tale, but I expect they will kill me in a few moments!' . . .

"Soon afterwards Dr. Richards came to me, informed me that the mob had precipitately fled, and at the same time confirmed the worst fears that Joseph was assuredly dead. . . . The poignancy of my grief, I presume, however, was somewhat allayed by the extreme suffering that I endured from my wounds. Soon afterwards I was taken to the head of the stairs and laid there, where I had a full view of our beloved and now murdered brother, Hyrum. . . .

"Brother Richards was busy during this time attending to the coroner's inquest, and to the removal of the bodies, and making arrangements for their removal from Carthage to Nauvoo. When he had a little leisure, he again came to me, and . . . I was removed to Hamilton's tavern. . . . It was with difficulty that sufficient persons could be found to carry me to the tavern, for immediately after the murder a great fear fell upon all the people, and men, women, and children fled with great precipitation."[3]

Evidence later revealed that Elder Taylor lived only because his watch in his breast pocket stopped a fatal ball from hitting him in the chest and was the force which caused him to fall back into the room when he attempted to jump from the window. Elder Richards was miraculously untouched except for a ball that grazed his ear.

Unconfirmed news of the murders reached Nauvoo quickly. Frantic to know the welfare of his brothers, Samuel rode swiftly to Carthage and arrived that evening to find Joseph's body lying in the yard and Hyrum's in the jail. He and Elder Willard Richards moved the corpses and the wounded Elder Taylor to the Hamilton House. The next morning the bodies of Joseph and Hyrum were placed in separate wagons, covered with buffalo robes and green branches to protect them from the hot sun, and driven to Nauvoo by Samuel Smith, Willard Richards, and Artois Hamilton.

Emma's nephew Lorenzo was the first to reach the Mansion House that morning to inform her that Joseph had indeed been murdered. Stunned, she told the dreadful news to her children and her mother-in-law and then sat in a chair, weeping uncontrollably with her hands covering her face. When a minister from another church in the city tried consoling her, she sobbed, "Why, O God, am I thus afflicted? Why am I a widow and my children widows? Thou knowest I have always trusted in the law."

As the minister tried to comfort her grief by suggesting "that this affliction would be to her a crown of life," Emma replied without hesitation, "My husband was my crown; for him and my children I have suffered the loss of all things; and why, O God, am I thus deserted, and my bosom torn with this ten-fold anguish?"

"One wild scream of childish despair" was heard in another room as the children lamented the loss of their father. Frederick and Alexander were lying on the floor, and Julia and young Joseph were "kneeling over them." In shock and with dry eyes, "her anguish seem[ing] too deep for tears," Mother Smith paced the floor in another room and asked "with a gaze of wild despair . . . why they had shot her dear children."

The wagons bearing the bodies of the dead Prophet and Patriarch reached Nauvoo about three o'clock that afternoon. Weeping mourners thronged the streets of the city, and as the wagons passed by the grieving Saints, "the groans and sobs and shrieks grew deeper and louder, till the sound resembled the roar of a mighty tempest, or the slow, deep, roar of the distant tornado."[4] The bodies were carried inside the Mansion House and placed in the dining room, where they were washed and prepared for burial. "Cotton soaked in camphor was put in each wound, and the bodies laid out with fine plain drawers and shirt, white neckerchiefs, white cotton stockings and white shrouds."[5]

Emma, with the help of two attendants, was the first of the family to enter the room to view the bodies. As she walked towards Hyrum's body, she "swooned and fell to the floor. Her friends raised her up and gave her water, but she fainted again, and was carried out insensible." She endeavored six times to enter the room, but on each attempt fainted until she was eventually taken to Hyrum's body, where she gained her strength and whispered, "Now I can see him; I am strong now." Without assistance she then made her way to her husband's body and "kneeling down, clasped him around his face, and sank upon his body. Suddenly her grief found vent; and sighs and groans and words and lamentations filled the room. 'Joseph, Joseph,' she said, 'are you dead? Have the assassins shot you?'"[6]

The children gathered around their mother as grief enveloped everyone in the room. Joseph III remembered his mother "in grief-stricken accents" saying, "Oh, Joseph, Joseph! My husband, my husband! Have they taken you from me at last!"[7] When Mother Smith entered the room she first hesitated and then walked to her sons and resting a hand on each cried out, "My God, my God, why hast thou forsaken this family!"[8]

At eight o'clock the following morning, nearly ten thousand people began to file through the dining room of the Mansion House to pay their final respects to their Prophet and his brother. The bodies lay in their "coffins which were covered with black velvet fastened with brass nails. Over the face of each corpse a lid was hung with brass hinges, under which was a square of glass to protect the face, and the coffin was lined with white cambric."[9] Early that evening the doors were closed, and because a reward had been posted for the Prophet's head, the brothers' coffins were removed from the outer pine caskets and taken to a back room. Quickly a few of the brethren placed sandbags in the empty pine boxes, loaded them into waiting wagons and proceeded to the public funeral. Later that night Joseph's and Hyrum's bodies were taken across the street to the unfinished Nauvoo House, where they were buried in the basement without further ceremony.

Chapter Thirty

$\mathcal{E}$MMA MOURNED HER HUSBAND'S DEATH as would any woman whose husband had been murdered, though within a week worried creditors began to contact her about Joseph's business affairs. Because he was trustee-in-trust of the Church, most of his and Emma's personal holdings were indistinguishable from those of the Church, and it was impossible for her to know what she owned and what she did not.

Anxious to have her financial affairs in order, Emma understandably but perhaps inappropriately pressed ahead of the Twelve and within two weeks attempted to convince Church leaders who were in the city to appoint William Marks, Nauvoo's stake president, as trustee-in-trust of the Church. Because most members of the Quorum of the Twelve had been serving missions in the East at the time of the Martyrdom and were then en route to Nauvoo, Parley P. Pratt spoke for the Quorum and adamantly objected to Emma's proposal, saying that a decision of that magnitude was for the Twelve to make. This did not set well with her. In consequence she rode to Carthage and at the courthouse filed the necessary papers designating her as the legal administrator of Joseph's estate.

Amid all her financial and legal concerns, another tragedy struck Emma's household and the Smith family the day after her return from the county seat. Joseph's brother Samuel had been experiencing severe pains in his side since the murder of his brothers, and the ache and an ensuing fever grew worse until he died on July 30, 1844. He left behind his wife, Levira, and their two children, his three older children from his previous marriage, and his poor mother, Lucy, who within four years had lost her husband and four of her sons.

Brigham Young, the senior apostle, arrived in Nauvoo the first of August and moved quickly to establish proper order and leadership of the Church. Emma and her attempt to move forward was a minute problem for him compared to Sidney Rigdon's claim to have had a vision in which he was appointed guardian of the Church. Rigdon had been living with his family in Pittsburgh, Pennsylvania, at the time of the Martyrdom but was now in the city campaigning among the Saints.

Because of his prolonged absence, Rigdon was unaware of Joseph's concerted efforts to instruct the brethren and confer the keys of the kingdom upon them before his death. Elder Parley Pratt recorded a glimpse into this time of intense tutoring: "This great and good man [Joseph Smith] was led, before his death, to call the Twelve together, from time to time, and to instruct them in all things pertaining to the kingdom, ordinances, and government of God. He often observed that he was laying the foundation, but it would remain for the Twelve to complete the building. Said he, 'I know not why; but for some reason I am constrained to hasten my preparations, and to confer upon the Twelve all the ordinances, keys, covenants, endowments, and sealing ordinances of the priesthood, and so set before them a pattern in all things pertaining to the sanctuary and the endowment therein.'

"Having done this, he rejoiced exceedingly; for, said he, 'the Lord is about to lay the burden on your shoulders and let me rest awhile; and if they kill me,' continued he, 'the kingdom of God will roll on, as I have now finished the work which was laid upon me, by committing to you all things for the building up of the kingdom according to the heavenly vision, and the pattern shown me from heaven.' With many conversations like this, he comforted the minds of the Twelve, and prepared them for what was soon to follow.

"He proceeded to confer on Elder Young, the President of the Twelve, the keys of the sealing power, as conferred in the last days by the spirit and power of Elijah, in order to seal the hearts of the fathers to the children, and the hearts of the children to the fathers, lest the whole earth should be smitten with a curse."[1]

Elder Wilford Woodruff wrote: "Joseph Smith was what he professed to be, a prophet of God, a seer and revelator. He laid the foundation of this Church and kingdom, and lived long enough to deliver the keys of the kingdom to the Elders of Israel, unto the Twelve Apostles. He spent the last winter of his life, some three or four months, with the Quorum of the Twelve, teaching them. It was not merely a few hours ministering to them the ordinances of the Gospel; but he spent day after day, week after week and month after month, teaching them and a few others the things of the kingdom of God."[2]

After several days of controversy among some of the members, a special meeting was held in the grove on August 8. Rigdon spoke for an hour and a half about his vision and claim to guardianship of the Church. Following his address, Brigham Young rose, and as he began to speak he was transfigured to look and sound like the Prophet Joseph Smith. Many in the audience recorded the miraculous experience, including fifteen-year-old George Q. Cannon:

"It was the voice of Joseph himself; and not only was it the voice of Joseph which was heard; but it seemed in the eyes of the people as though it was the very person of Joseph which stood before them. . . . They both saw and heard with their natural eyes and ears, and then the words which were uttered came, accompanied by the convincing power of God, to their hearts, and they were filled with the Spirit and with great joy."[3]

It is not known whether Emma attended the meeting and witnessed what others saw and heard. She did, however, confide in James Monroe, the children's young schoolteacher living in the Mansion House, that "Mr. Rigdon is not the proper successor of President Smith, . . . but Elder Marks should be the individual."[4] Probably not coincidentally, Marks shared Emma's views of plural marriage and toward the end of 1843 was adamantly pushing for the abandonment of the principle.

Nevertheless, in October and well after Church leadership was in the hands of the Twelve, Heber C. Kimball noted in his journal that the brethren "met in council at Sister Emma Smith's . . . and expressed our feelings to her and [what] our intentions were. She seemed to be pleased with our course. It seemed like old times."[5] Over the next fifteen months, however, events occurred that resulted in hard feelings and a loss of respect between Emma and Brigham. Though most of the ensuing offenses can be attributed to misunderstandings and misinterpretations caused by others, Emma tended to shift responsibility for all the hurtful happenings directly to President Young.

The transition was challenging to Emma in several ways. For example, Joseph had often counseled with her regarding Church business and on more than one occasion had invited her to sit in counsel with the Brethren. Emma had also assisted her husband in reconciling the finances of the Church. She therefore mistakenly felt she should continue to have some say in the decisions being made about the affairs of the kingdom and was confused, hurt, and even angry when the Twelve failed to consult her at all. In fact, because Brigham Young was inundated with Church problems and business upon his return to Nauvoo, it was five weeks before he met with Emma to discuss her estate.

Emma was particularly chagrined when the Twelve made decisions without conferring with her about her finances because she knew that such decisions would have a lasting effect on her and her children. Although the Brethren eventually agreed that she could keep several properties—including the Mansion House, the Nauvoo Mansion, the Red Brick Store, the farm outside the city, and the Cleveland farm that was three or four miles from Quincy, Illinois, and gave her a cash allowance they felt was adequate for her support—she still felt slighted and worried it would not be enough.

Another incident that raised Emma's ire happened when she went to retrieve some papers and books she had left in Joseph's desk before it was taken to Brigham Young's home. Because President Young was not at home when Emma arrived, she was denied possession of her husband's property and was sent away empty-handed. Though President Young later did return to her most of the books and papers left in the desk, Emma offered her own offense and angered the Brethren by refusing to relinquish Joseph's translation of the Bible when Willard Richards asked for it in August 1844.

Joseph III told of an occurrence that certainly caused sore feelings between him and Brigham Young and may have added to Emma's mistrust. President Young sent a note to Emma one morning asking to borrow Joe Duncan, a favorite horse of the family, to ride on parade. When she received the note, she immediately told young Joseph to prepare the horse for riding. The boy hesitated to obey because Joe Duncan had been ridden hard just two days before, but she "sharply directed me to do as I was bidden, saying that . . . the horse would be carefully used and would only be needed during the parade."[6]

Around four o'clock that afternoon the horse was seen being ridden hard on the city streets by President Young's clerk, so Emma sent a message to Brigham asking that Joe Duncan be taken home immediately. The note surprised him because he thought the horse had been returned hours earlier. About an hour later Joe Duncan was returned but in pitiful condition. His entire body was lathered with sweat and foam, and it was obvious he had not been watered nor fed. Joseph III recorded: "To say I was disturbed is to put the matter mildly. I was thoroughly indignant, furiously angry, and utterly heart-broken! All the while I was caring for him and trying to comfort him, I was crying bitterly. . . . I sponged his coat with warm water . . . gave him food and drink and sympathy. I made a vow then and there, while washing that horse and giving him proper nourishment, that never again would I put saddle or bridle upon him for Elder Young. Going to the house I told Mother so, adding that if ever in the future she wished to loan one of our horses to that man she would have to get someone else to saddle it, for I would not do it." Though Brigham Young later sent a note of apology, the deed had been done, and the offense inflicted.[7]

Offense was again taken when in January 1845, the state legislature repealed the Nauvoo Charter and ordered the Nauvoo Legion to disband, leaving Nauvoo and the Saints virtually unprotected. Armed guards were stationed outside the city and at the homes of the Twelve. Because Emma and her family were also a likely target for violence, a sentinel was sent to safeguard her door as well. When Emma realized her house was being guarded, she mistakenly concluded that Brigham Young had placed her under house arrest. Joseph III related how Brigham's guard was interpreted by Emma and the unfortunate suspicions that followed: "This unpleasant state of affairs was caused, apparently, by Mother's having become obnoxious to some of the leading men of the church, including Brigham Young. . . . This . . . did not suit my mother; and besides, she could not fellowship some other things that were occurring. She spoke openly against them, with the result that a certain degree of hostility grew up against her."[8]

Other rumors that have been perpetuated through the years about Emma's relationship with the Church, the Brethren, and particularly Brigham Young stemmed from several articles printed in various newspapers throughout the country. Some declared Emma's faith was wavering; others asserted that she was soon to be excommunicated. One false editorial in which Emma's signature was forged stated she had written and planned to publish an exposé that would discredit Mormonism and the current leadership of the Church. In an attempt to refute the false accounts, the Brethren wrote and published a rebuttal in the *Times and Seasons,* which confirmed that Church leaders still had respectful feelings toward her:

"Suppose we say a word concerning the 'prophet's wife,' Mrs. Emma Smith; she honored her husband while living, and she will never knowingly dishonor his good name while his martyred blood mingles with mother earth! Mrs. Smith is an honorable woman and if we are not deceived, is as far from the corrupt insinuations in this ninety-ninth exposé of Mormonism, as a fixed star is from a gambler's lamp at midnight. The very idea that so valuable and beloved a lady, could be coaxed into a fame of *disgrace* . . . is as cruel and bloody as the assassination of her husband at Carthage. . . . The fact is, the story must have been put in circulation to injure the Latter-day Saints; and as Mrs. Smith was one of them, to destroy, or murder her reputation, and create division in the church."[9]

In October of 1845, Emma wrote to Joseph Heywood about his renting the Red Brick Store from her: "My family are all in good health at present, and the brethren are generally well with the exception of Amasa Lyman who has been very sick but is better now."[10] Even after all that had transpired since the Martyrdom between her and the leaders of the Church, Emma still felt tender concern for the welfare of the leading brethren.

Chapter Thirty-One

Because the Mansion House provided little privacy and took much of Emma's time and attention away from her children, she leased the hotel to William Marks for one year and two hundred dollars and moved back into the Homestead. One of Samuel's older daughters, Mary Bailey Smith (named for her mother), had gone to live with Emma soon after her father's death. Mary was a godsend. She helped with the children and housework and provided loving care for her grandmother Lucy, who had lived with Emma for well over a year.

Three months after the move, on November 17, 1844, Emma gave birth to another son, whom she named David Hyrum. Although the baby was born healthy, he soon developed behavior that would drive Emma to her wits' end. He was quiet and content during the day, but when night fell, he cried incessantly and deprived the household, especially Emma, from getting any rest. When the infant's nighttime screaming intensified, she was finally compelled to counsel with the family doctor, John Bernhisel, from whom she received medication that quieted the infant and thus enabled Emma to sleep.

Soon after David's birth, Emily Partridge visited the Homestead and said Emma "was very gracious, for there was no Joseph to be jealous of then."[1] Eliza R. Snow also went to visit and see the baby. She later composed a poem for David, which was printed in the *Times and Seasons*:

Sinless as celestial spirits—
Lovely as a morning flow'r,
Comes the smiling infant stranger
In an evil-omen'd hour.

In an hour of lamentation—
In a time—a season when

Zion's noblest sons are fallen,
By the hands of wicked men.

In an hour when peace and safety
Have the civil banner fled—
In a day when legal justice
Covers its dishonor'd head.

In an age when saints must suffer
Without mercy or redress:
Comes to meet a generation
That has made it fatherless.

Not to share a father's fondness—
Not to know its father's worth—
By the arm of persecution
'Tis an orphan at its birth!

Smile, sweet babe! thou art unconscious
Of thy great, untimely loss!
The broad stroke of thy bereavement,
Zion's pathway seem'd to cross!

Till in childhood thou had'st known him,
Had the age, thy father spar'd;
The endearment of remembrance,
Through thy life time thou had'st shar'd.

Thou may'st draw from love and kindness
All a mother can bestow;
But alas! on earth, a father
Thou art destin'd not to know![2]

After David Hyrum's birth, Emma seemed to grow more suspicious of the Brethren and others who had close association with them. Her mistrust, particularly of those who were practicing plural marriage, caused her to think and do things that brought suspicion upon her. When she and Hyrum's wife, Mary Fielding, began to worry that their husbands' bodies might be discovered in the basement of the Nauvoo House, the women set a date and time in the night to move them to the backyard of the Homestead. For some reason, however, Emma contacted Mary to postpone their meeting and then secretly had the bodies moved at the predetermined time.

Because Mary was having trouble sleeping that night, she decided to go for a walk down by the river. As she passed the Homestead, she saw Emma with some men behind the house. When Mary walked over and discovered what Emma was doing, she was hurt and felt betrayed. Even so, she stayed and watched until the bodies were buried, but Emma's deception put a strain on their relationship from that time forward.

Joseph III remembered being with his mother that night. "I saw the features of my father as they were exposed, and a lock of hair was cut from his head."[3] Emma kept the hair and, according to her son, put it in a brooch that she often wore throughout the rest of her life.

Emma's problems were compounded in early May when Joseph's younger brother William arrived with his family from the East. Emma graciously received them into her home, and while William met with the Brethren regarding his role in the Church, Emma cared for his wife, Caroline, who had been extremely ill for several years. Sadly, Emma was able to do little more than comfort Caroline, and within three weeks of their arrival she passed away.

Though William was at first in agreement with the Twelve and was ordained Patriarch of the Church on the day of his wife's funeral, his thirst for additional authority intensified. Finally, by October of 1845, William was at such odds with Brigham Young and others that he "declared the authority of the Twelve to be null and void."[4] He even claimed that before his death Joseph had ordained him to be guardian of the Church. Emma was cautiously supportive of William's claim for a short time, but she distanced herself from him when she learned that it was possible he too was practicing plural marriage. Unfortunately, though, William's discontent with the Twelve and their decisions fueled Emma's negative feelings toward the leadership of the Church.

Meanwhile anti-Mormon sentiment and oppression towards the Saints heightened in and around Nauvoo until the Quorum of the Twelve was forced to promise antagonists in the neighboring counties that the Saints would leave the state the next spring. With that announcement, work on the temple hastened, and as soon as rooms were finished, they were dedicated and used for the bestowal of ordinances. Brigham Young described the sense of urgency the Saints were feeling in January of 1846 about receiving their temple ordinances: "I have given myself up entirely to the work of the Lord in the Temple night and day, not taking more than four hours sleep, upon an average, per day, and going home but once a week."[5]

According to Bathsheba Smith, by this time Emma was so far "out of harmony with the twelve and with the church"[6] that she did not administer the initiatory ordinances or assist with endowment sessions in the Nauvoo Temple. Furthermore, when Heber C. Kimball and others visited her home on various occasions and attempted to persuade her to go west with the main body of the Church, she firmly declined their invitations.

Because of increased persecution and threats by state officials to destroy the Saints before they could begin their trek west, Emma watched the first of many wagons and teams depart the city earlier than planned on February 4, 1846. Before their departure, many Church members rode to Carthage and legally deeded their city lots to her.

Joseph III remembered several of the Brethren presenting him with gifts. Brigham Young called him to his home, where he gave him a dueling pistol; however, when Emma discovered the gun had a treacherous hair trigger—as dueling pistols commonly did—she persuaded him to get rid of it. George A. Smith gave Joseph III a weapon commonly called a bowie knife or "Arkansas toothpick." It was "sharp as a razor [and] accompanied by a scabbard," but when he returned home and showed it to his mother, she looked at the gift with disgust and said, "Pshaw! Why couldn't he have given you something useful?"[7] Later, when the boy traded the knife to a friend for a large cherry wood rolling pin, he remembered his mother saying, "Now, *that* is something useful. Why could not Elder Young and Cousin George have given you something like that instead of things with which you might injure yourself or your companions?"[8]

Before Newel K. Whitney and his family left the city, he also gave young Joseph a present. Joseph III recalled: "He had me come to his home on Parley Street . . . There he presented me with his writing-desk, a very convenient and attractive piece of furniture for those times. He said he preferred to give it to me rather than to sell it for what little it might bring or to have the risk and bother of taking it with him on the journey. I accepted the gift gratefully, and the desk was removed to my room where I used it for many years. . . . I remember when Bishop Whitney gave me the desk he remarked that Elder Young and Cousin George A. had given me weapons of war, but he wished to impress upon me the sentiment that 'the pen is mightier than the sword.' I seemed to feel at the time that his intention was to foster within me a spirit of peace rather than one of conflict."[9]

As hundreds of Saints and their loaded wagons lined Parley Street, waiting for their turn to leave their beautiful city of Nauvoo and cross the Mississippi River, we can only imagine

Forgive Me, Joseph

what Emma's thoughts and feelings were. William Marks's lease had expired, so she and the children were once again living in the Mansion House, where she welcomed friends and family members who called on her before they departed the city. She had a very cordial visit with Wilford and Phoebe Woodruff and gave Phoebe a handkerchief and Wilford a pair of white cotton gloves and a cane that she had had fashioned from the rough oak box that carried Joseph's body from Carthage to Nauvoo. Brigham Young and his wife Mary Ann also paid her one last visit, and Mary Ann gave Emma some dishes and other household items she could not carry with her.

Precisely why Emma refused to travel to the Rocky Mountains with the Saints is unknown. She later expressed at least one reason why she refused to leave Nauvoo when she said, "You may think I was not a very good Saint not to go West, but I had a home here and did not go because I did not know what I should have there."[10] Certainly the unfortunate interactions with members of the Twelve and others also played a role in her staying behind, but the continued practice of plural marriage was likely a greater deterrent. She was unquestionably aware of the revelation regarding plural marriage and that the Prophet Joseph practiced the principle, but she later taught her children that Brigham Young was the founder of the practice and that their father had no plural wives.

Chapter Thirty-Two

𝒩OT LONG AFTER THE SAINTS' EXODUS, antagonistic neighbors, land speculators, and other unseemly characters began coming to Nauvoo, which caused "considerable confusion and excitement."[1] This turmoil in the city gave Emma good reason to worry for the safety and welfare of her children, so in late August she determined to lease the Mansion House to Dr. Abram Van Tuyl and relocate until order was restored. Days later she and the children boarded the *Uncle Tobey* steamship and traveled upriver about one hundred and forty miles to Fulton, Illinois.

She left for Van Tuyl most of her furniture, bedding, dishes, cooking utensils, and all else he would need to run a hotel. Her horses, wagon, carriage, and a few household items were taken overland as a favor by Lorin Walker and Wesley Knight. In Fulton she was met by William Marks, who had moved his family into the area, and before long Emma was settled in a small cottage near the edge of town and the children were enrolled in the local school. In early February of 1847, however, she received word from her friend Dr. Bernhisel that Van Tuyl was building a houseboat and outfitting it with her furniture and goods from the hotel. Without hesitation, Emma packed up the children and their few possessions, hitched the horse to the wagon, and started for Nauvoo.

Though the roads were thawing and muddy, she and her family reached the city on February 19 and "pulled up in front of the . . . Mansion, much to the astonishment and discomfiture of the dishonest landlord!" Emma recovered most of her belongings, but she never received the money Van Tuyl owed her for the lease.[2] She immediately went to work managing the hotel, but the patrons she fed and housed were "men of all classes," and most of the people then living in Nauvoo were of a different social class than the Saints had been. "Saloons were many and ran wide open, proprietors and patrons alike being shiftless, thieving, drinking, boisterous, and thoroughly unprofitable citizens."[3]

Fortunately, however, because the Saints had left Nauvoo earlier than originally planned, Brigham Young left behind several men, including John Bernhisel and Almon W. Babbitt, to tie up the financial affairs of the Church. In consequence of their assignment, Emma had extensive dealings with both men and particularly enjoyed having Dr. Bernhisel live at the hotel until he departed for the Salt Lake Valley in October of 1847.

Bernhisel treated Emma with respect and appreciation and by early 1845 had become her trusted confidant. In fact, her trust in him was so complete that in May of 1845, after denying the Brethren access to Joseph's translation of the Bible, she invited him to examine the Prophet's revision. Dr. Bernhisel later wrote: "I had great desire, to see the New Translation, but did not like to ask for it; but one evening, being at Bro. Joseph's house about a year after his death, Sister Emma to my surprise asked me if I would not like to see it. I answered, 'Yes.' She handed it to me the next day and I kept it in my custody about three months. She told me it was not prepared for the press, as Joseph had designed to go through it again. I did not copy all that was translated leaving some few additions and changes that were made in some of the books. But so far as I did copy, I did so as correctly as I could."[4]

Dr. Bernhisel expressed his admiration for and gratitude to "Dear Sister Emma" in a letter penned before he left for Utah: "I cannot take my departure from this place, without acknowledging the debt of gratitude that I am under to you. And in making this acknowledgment, I especially desire to be understood that I am observing no mere form or idle custom, nor empty ceremony. During the three years that I was a member of your family, I found every necessary provided for my comfort, with much order and neatness, and from yourself and family, I experienced not only kindness and respect, but such affectionate regard, tenderness and delicacy as to make me feel more than your grateful friend. I may never be permitted to pay you all; but the bond of obligation shall ever remain binding on my heart and life. And I beg you to accept my profound and grateful acknowledgments for your uniform kindness and attention to me, and for your trouble of me during so long a period; and I fervently pray that God may reward you in this world a thousand fold, and in the world to come with life everlasting."[5]

Regrettably, Emma's relationship with Almon Babbitt was quite the opposite. His abrupt and insensitive manner irritated her, and because the man represented the Church, she credited Babbitt's every offense to Brigham Young. Joseph III recalled an argument between his mother and the boorish man that offers insight into just how far Emma's regard for President Young had deteriorated. On one visit to the Mansion House, Babbitt attempted to persuade Emma to go with him to Utah. She declined his invitation, stating she could never move west and support the Brethren in their practice of plural marriage. Babbitt responded that "it had been determined to make her so poor that she would be willing and glad to come out for protection" and added "that he had been appointed to accomplish that purpose and he proposed to do it." To this bold and tactless statement Emma replied: "Almon Babbitt, it may be possible for you to make me poor, but you could never make me poor enough to induce me to follow Brigham Young!"[6]

It was not long before word spread that the woman running the Mansion House was the widow of Joseph Smith, the Mormon prophet, nor did it take many months for suitors to come calling. Emma was an attractive woman of forty-three, and though she may have been cash poor, she was the principal landowner in the city. Two gentlemen paid particular attention to her during the summer of 1847, but she seemed from the first more attracted to Major Lewis Crum Bidamon, a widower from Canton, Ohio.

Joseph III recalled a story related to the Major's courting that caused him and his mother "considerable amusement." One evening when Bidamon entered the yard dressed in a broadcloth suit and high-crowned hat to pay a visit, he noticed Emma sewing in an upstairs window. Wanting to make an impression, he removed his hat and "made her a very polite and widely-sweeping bow. Regaining his erect posture after this elaborate ceremony, he replaced his hat upon his head and stepped forward briskly, when suddenly a clothesline he had failed to observe caught him right across the forehead, just under the brim of his hat! Off flew the hat, but alas, along with it flew a very fine toupee with which he had been concealing the bald spot on his head!"[7] Both Emma and young Joseph witnessed the awkward episode, and when the boy went laughing uncontrollably from the stable to offer assistance, he heard the Major say as he picked up the toupee and put it back onto his head, "Damn that wig!"[8]

The embarrassing event did not deter the Major, for on December 23, 1847, Emma and Lewis C. Bidamon were married by a Methodist minister in Nauvoo. Bidamon was a good-looking, well-dressed man who was very opinionated, passionate about his likes and dislikes, and easy to anger. He stood about six feet tall. Joseph III remembered that "he made friends easily, but, unfortunately for him, lost them quite as easily. His love for intoxicating liquors and his lack of religious convictions were the two most serious drawbacks to the happiness of our home. . . . While his moral character might not be considered to be of the highest quality he did possess a certain pride of manhood, a deeply-rooted dislike of being in debt or under obligation to anyone, and, so far as the ordinary transactions of life are concerned, a desire to deal honorably with his fellow men."[9]

Word of Emma's marriage soon made its way west to the Salt Lake Valley, and members asked the question that lingers in the minds of many in the Church today: Why would Emma, who had been married to a prophet of God and a man of Joseph's distinction, stoop to marry a man so lacking in character? When a visitor to Nauvoo interviewed Emma in 1869 and asked her that very question, Emma candidly said, "I had my own reasons for so doing to protect my children,"[10] adding that she had become aware of a plot to kidnap young Joseph.

Smith family researcher Buddy Youngreen offered another plausible explanation for her marriage to Bidamon. "Here, at last, was the relaxation she had longed for. Life with Joseph had been so intense, so driving, so momentous. Now, with Lewis Bidamon, little mattered but the day-by-day necessities. Life was so simple. Bidamon was not ambitious. He was not trying to establish a kingdom. He was not difficult to please—and he loved her in his way, not with the intensity, the fierceness of Joseph's love, but with a matter-of-factness which was never threatening, at least at first, to her need to belong and to possess."[11]

Though the Major certainly had his faults, together they lived comfortably from their genius and hard labor. Emma ran the hotel while he and the boys worked the farm outside the city and fed and cared for the livestock. He also raised three fields of grapes from which he made wine that he stored in the basement of the Mansion House until the market price was right.

Every spring they planted a large garden in the yard, and every fall they preserved fruits and vegetables and stored potatoes, onions, turnips, squashes, and cabbages. "They did their own butchering of pigs and cured hams and bacon but bought their beef. Emma did much of the milking, especially in later years when they had only one cow."[12]

Each morning and evening after milking, she would lug the full bucket down the steep stairs to the cellar of the Mansion House where the milk would be cool. This was no easy task and was particularly tricky when several of the boards in the stairwell became danger-ously loose. After asking the Major several times to fix the boards, she finally "delivered an ultimatum that she would not again carry milk down the stairs until they were fixed." That evening after she finished her milking, the boards in the stairwell were still loose, so Emma—ever a woman of her word—tossed the bucket of milk down the stairs "and quietly proceeded with her kitchen duties."[13] The stairs were fixed before she finished milking the next morning.

Emma welcomed many visitors to the Mansion House. Some came on business, and oth-ers came for no other reason than to see Nauvoo, the "City of Joseph." One such visitor,

Henry Lewis, sailed up the Mississippi in July of 1848 to paint a mural of the city. John Frances McDermott, a friend of the artist who accompanied Lewis on his journey, recounted: "At sunset on the twenty-ninth of July the sketching party stopped at the 'celebrated city' of Nauvoo. Lewis immediately 'hurried to take a look at the temple and see it by sun set.' He was much impressed: 'Taking into consideration the circumstances under which it was built, it is a wonderful building and considering too that it is of no particular style it does not in the least offend the eye by it uniqueness.' . . . The following day, [the artist] explored the interior of the Temple" and then paid an inquisitive visit to the Mansion to see Emma, "who, though married to 'a man by the name of Bideman . . . is always call'd the widow Smith.' Lewis describe[d] [Emma] as 'a remarkably fine looking woman I should judge of some 35 or 40 years of age with a strongly mark'd tho' kind and intelligent face on whose surface are the marks of much care and suffering.' . . . She 'supports herself and family by keeping one of the largest and best hotels in the place and seems to be doing a thriving business.'"[14]

Unfortunately, Henry Lewis and his party were among the last visitors to Nauvoo to see the temple in its beauty and splendor. On the night of October 8, 1848, young Joseph had just retired to bed when he was awakened by someone on the street shouting "Fire!" As he hurried down the stairs, he met a man who told him the temple was burning. Joseph joined Emma and his brothers and sister at an upstairs window in the Mansion House, and together they watched the sacred edifice go up in flames. The light of day revealed that the entire interior of the temple was burned and great damage done to the walls both inside and out. Not long after the fire, a great storm blew much of the south wall to the ground, and in time the remaining walls fell. Joseph III remembered the temple site "became a veritable quarry and provided the materials with which many homes, wine cellars, and saloons in the town were built."[15]

Chapter Thirty-Three

IF EMMA'S MARRIAGE TO LEWIS BIDAMON was one of convenience or simply for protection, a letter she wrote to him while he was working in the gold fields of California in 1849 and 1850 indicates she had grown to love the man and was concerned for his well-being. In the correspondence Emma confessed she had "scarcely enjoyed any good thing since [he] left home" and went on to write, "some may think that I might be content, but I am not, neither can I be until you are within my grasp, then, and not till then shall I be free from fears for your safety, and anxieties for your welfare."[1] Her sons also became quite attached to their stepfather, and in several of the many letters they wrote to their mother in later years, they sent their love to "Pa Bidamon."

The Major likewise esteemed Emma and did not seem to mind the portrait of the Prophet Joseph that she left hanging in the Mansion House nor the case containing Joseph's "razor, strop, combs, brushes, jars for salves, and a pair of 'pulls' for boots"[2] that remained on a dresser in their bedroom. Also to his credit, he would not allow anyone to speak ill of the Prophet in his presence.

Although Emma avoided any in-depth discussion with her children about the Church and its doctrines, David Hyrum later indicated that a religious environment continued to pervade their home:

> *Remember how she taught us five*
> *In faithfulness to pray*
> *That God would guard us through the night*
> *And watch us through the day.*[3]

Sometime in 1851, Mother Smith returned to live with Emma and her family. Lucy had expressed a desire to go west at the time of the exodus, but her health was declining and her husband and four sons were buried in Nauvoo. She continued to live with Emma and her children until Emma moved to Fulton, Illinois. Lucy lived in several homes in Nauvoo and then with her daughter Lucy Milliken in Fountain Green, Illinois. Once Emma returned to live in Nauvoo, so did Mother Smith.

Even though Lucy's body was crippled with arthritis, her mind was sharp and her memory outstanding. Eventually her arthritis worsened until she was confined to a wheelchair, which was made for her by the Major, and ultimately she was unable even to feed herself. Emma lovingly cared for her mother-in-law until her death in 1856 at the age of eighty-one.

Joseph III recorded a vivid description of Mother Smith's passing: "Grandma died the morning of the 14th of May last easily and with her senses to the last moment and we trust she has no wish to return from the 'bourne.' She appeared somewhat fearful of death a little while before he came yet appeared resigned afterwards. I sat by her and held her hand in mine till death relieved her—the first death scene I ever witnessed—Long may I be spared the death scene of my mother."[4]

Several months after Lucy passed away, two guests arrived at the Mansion House, and though their visit certainly affected Emma's future, it dramatically changed young Joseph's life forever. The men were Edmund C. Briggs and Samuel Gurley from Wisconsin, missionaries of the Reorganized Church of Jesus Christ of Latter Day Saints. When the Major greeted the men at the hotel on that cold December morning, he initially assumed they were missionaries from Utah, because it was customary for Mormon elders to stop at the Mansion House either going to or coming from the East. In fact, just several days before Briggs and Gurley's visit, George A. Smith and Erastus Snow from Utah had stopped by the hotel.

Once the Major realized who the men were and that they had come to speak to Joseph III, "he spoke very highly of young Joseph" and boldly said "that his wife, Emma, was the best woman that ever lived, and that she believed her former husband was a prophet of God." He added, "And I believe she is honest in her convictions. She tells so many things that took place in connection with the writing of the Book of Mormon, that I can't help but believe there is something in it. . . . I believe Joseph Smith was an honest man . . . [and that] my wife wrote a part of the Book of Mormon as Smith translated it from the plates he had found."[5]

Bidamon took the men into the dining room to meet Emma, where they introduced themselves as missionaries of the Reorganized Church who had come to Nauvoo to preach the gospel. Briggs related, "She appeared quite reserved; seemed inclined to talk very little with us, and we avoided telling our special object of visiting Nauvoo at this time."[6]

Emma's reticent behavior may have been caused by an inkling she had that their "special object" in coming to Nauvoo was to persuade her son to join with them and become president of their church. Before this visit she and Joseph III had been made aware of their organization through numerous letters and pamphlets, and neither of them wanted anything to do with their church.

The following afternoon the men journeyed to see Joseph III at his farm, where he lived with his new bride, Emmeline Griswold. Joseph greeted the missionaries with reservation, and when he realized the purpose for their visit, he emphatically declared, "Gentlemen, I will talk with you on politics or any other subject, but on religion I will not allow one word spoken in my house."

Mr. Briggs replied, "Mr. Smith, while we respect your feelings as a man, and do not wish to injure your feelings, yet we will not allow you to hinder us in doing our duty, as we have been sent . . . to tell you what we know and most surely believe in relation to your calling as the successor of your father."

At this Joseph III stood and sharply replied, "When men come to my house and tell me what I must do, I tell them there is the door and they can go out."[7]

Eventually, however, tempers were calmed, and Briggs and Gurley convinced Joseph III to meet with them the next day at the Mansion House. The meeting was held and Joseph softened somewhat, but he still refused their offer to lead the Reorganized Church. That evening the missionaries had a cordial visit with Emma and explained precisely the purpose for their coming to Nauvoo. "She made several inquiries about our meetings and the interests of the Church, . . . and we informed her of the evidence we had received of her son taking the leadership of the Church, as it was his right by lineage. She seemed to wish to avoid any reference about her children having anything to do with the Church [and] spoke of her former husband with tears in her eyes."[8]

Before the men left the hotel the following morning, they again spoke to Emma, who said candidly, "I have always avoided talking to my children about having anything to do in the Church, for I have suffered so much, I have dreaded to have them take any part in it. But I have always believed if God wanted them to do anything in the Church, the same One who called their father would make it known to them, and it was not necessary for me to talk to them about it." Briggs and Gurley then recorded that Emma once again openly conversed with them about her beloved Joseph and when she spoke "the tears flowed from her large, bright eyes like rain."[9]

Elder Gurley was extremely homesick and returned to Wisconsin after their visit, but Briggs stayed on in Nauvoo for nearly a year and developed a cordial friendship with Joseph

III. As the next few years passed and correspondence continued between Joseph III and the RLDS leaders—particularly William Marks—both he and Emma began to lean toward the Reorganized Church and away from the Church in Utah. It was certainly not coincidental that the RLDS leaders abhorred the practice of plural marriage and supported both Emma and Joseph III in their false assertion about the introduction and practice of the principle.

In the spring of 1860, Emma and her son crossed the Mississippi River and took a train from Montrose, Iowa, to Amboy, Illinois, where on April 6 Joseph III was ordained and sustained as prophet, seer, revelator, and president of the Reorganized Church of Jesus Christ of Latter Day Saints. Emma was enthusiastically welcomed as a member that day, and in response to a request by church leaders worked through the remainder of that year and into the next compiling a hymnbook for them. When the book was published in 1861, it contained 249 hymns and was entitled *The Latter Day Saint's Selection of Hymns.*

Within a short time the Olive Branch of the RLDS church was established in Nauvoo and meeting in the Red Brick Store. Emma was esteemed as one of the small fledgling congregation's leading members, and in the ensuing years became the most renowned and revered member of the Reorganized Church. In later years, when she was asked if she "had trained Joseph with any idea that he was to be head of the Church . . . [she] emphatically said, 'No!'" Emma "taught [him] to be religious . . . and she had no idea that Joseph would head the church until . . . the Re's began to [contact] him."[10]

Although in 1895 Joseph III moved with his family to Plano, Illinois, where he became editor of the *Saints' Herald* newspaper, Emma maintained possession of the Prophet Joseph's "New Translation of the Bible" until April 1866, when she turned it over to the Reorganized Church and authorized its publication. Prior to that time she had been very reluctant to give up the precious papers, feeling that having the manuscript in her home was a protection for her and the children. She wrote just before the book went on sale: "I have often thought the reason why our house did not burn down when it has been so often on fire was because of them and I still feel there is a sacredness attached to them."[11]

A few months after Emma officially joined with the Reorganized Church, Hyrum's son Joseph F. Smith and his cousin Samuel stopped by the Mansion House en route from Utah to the eastern seaboard, where they were to sail to England for missionary service. They were presented to Emma by "her son Frederick G., who said: 'Mother, do you know these young men?' She looked up and said: 'Why, as I live, it is Joseph. Why, Joseph, I would have known you [anywhere], you look so much like your father.'"[12] Joseph F. remembered that Emma was very kind to them throughout their visit.

Chapter Thirty-Four

EMMA CONTINUED INTO OLD AGE WITH grace and dignity. She was dearly loved by all with whom she had association and was "very democratic and would gather Church people into her home for prayer meetings and socials without distinction whatever being made." She kept a melodeon in her home and although she did not play, David did, and he would accompany her and their many visitors as they sat "about the dying embers of the fireplace and [sang] hymns hour after hour."[1]

She loved taking walks out to the flatlands, where she picked herbs to use for medicinal purposes, and she grew saffron, peppermint, sage, hoarhound, and other herbs in her garden. From the catnip she grew she made a tea that she fed "to her horde of cats to keep them in good health to catch the mice and rats."[2] She became quite famous in the area for one of her homemade salves that was used to heal cuts, bruises, rheumatism, and other aches and pains. Folks traveled for miles to procure the concoction that she made from sweet elder bark, jimsonweed, beeswax, mutton tallow, and camphor gum.[3] She also developed a reputation for being the best midwife in Nauvoo.

Working in her beautiful flowers brought Emma great joy, and "the walks at the Mansion House were bordered by pansies and violets."[4] She "loved lilacs and called them 'laylocks'"[5] and enjoyed sweet alyssum and roses.

Emma was neat and comely in her appearance and "not so deeply wrinkled as most women." When working around the house she wore "plain dresses that she made herself, [with] a plain waist and full gathered skirt." For special occasions she wore "dresses made of calico with sprigged patterns." She "always wore a white collar or fine white neckerchief with her dresses which were usually cut rather low in the neck" and "the collar was fastened with a brooch." Emma "loved shades of lavender and purple and particularly in her later years wore much of this color." She "often wore shawls, a plain wool one for chilly days at home and a handsome one for going out made of silk and with long knotted fringe."[6]

The only jewelry Emma wore was the brooch containing a lock of Joseph's hair and a string of pea-sized gold beads, which she wore "until there were holes in some of them, and they were flattened and bent."[7] She eventually gave the well-worn necklace to her grand-daughter Emma as a wedding gift in 1876.

Even in old age, she rose from bed at four in the summer and well before daybreak in the winter. Once her morning work was completed, she "would recomb and redress" her iron gray hair, which was "parted in the middle with rills above the ears."[8]

On most days Emma's life was simple and yet busy. Usually after her noon meal, she would nap in her chair for half an hour or so and then, though her eyes were growing dim and she needed the aid of spectacles, she would read from the *Chicago Tribune* and the *Saints' Herald.* In an 1866 letter to Joseph III she wrote: "I must now tell you about myself. . . . I never lived a winter with so little hard work to do . . . and I am blessed with a good appetite and eat more and sleep more than I ever did before. One trouble I have, that is I often go to bed without being either tired or sleepy and find it hard to rest when I am not weary and sleep without being sleepy."[9]

Having family and friends visit was a joy in her life, but she was not a gossip. She once wrote, "You say news to me. Why, I have none. I do not believe I have any of any kind, not even lies. I believe the tattlers have all got tired of telling me any thing. I cannot tell why, unless it is because they have to tell somebody else their tales before they can get them into circulation."[10]

Although she lived in relative comfort and security in her later years, Emma's life continued to be laced with tragedy and heartache. Before returning to Nauvoo after the April 1860 conference of the RLDS church, she and Joseph III visited her younger sister, Tyral Morse, who lived outside Amboy, Illinois. Sadly, though, in June Emma received word that Tyral and her twenty-nine-year-old daughter, Emma, were killed when a tornado whipped through their small farm. Tyral's body was found nearly one hundred feet from the house, and her daughter suffered two broken legs and other injuries that shortly took her life.

The following year Frederick became extremely ill, and on Christmas Day of 1861 Emma had him moved from his home into the Mansion House so she could better care for him. Frederick was always a gentleman and "was very affectionate to his mother, and often saluted her with a loving kiss and good morning or good-by."[11] When he died of pneumonia on April 13, 1862, she was filled with grief. He left behind his wife, Annie Maria, and their baby daughter, Alice Fredricka.

Emma received further heart-wrenching news in 1864 when she learned that Lewis had had an affair and his mistress, Nancy Abercrombie, had given birth to a son she named Charles Edwin. Bidamon apparently kept in contact with his son and the child's mother, because four years later, when Abercrombie was struggling to make ends meet, Emma invited Charles into her home and raised him as her own.

Many years later, when Charles was in his seventy-sixth year, he wrote the following tribute to Emma: "I was taken into the home of Emma Smith Bidamon in 1868, at the age of [four] years, and was considered as one of the family up to and including the year of her death in 1879.

"As to my recollection of her, she was a person of very even temper. I never heard her say an unkind word, or raise her voice in anger or contention. She was loved and respected by the entire community, (all who knew her). And at her funeral, which the whole countryside attended, many tears flowed, showing grief at her passing. She had a queenly bearing without the arrogance of a queen. A noble woman, showing and living charity for all. Loving and beloved. . . .

"I am the only living person, who had the opportunity of knowing her in every day life, which was that of a very lovely person. Her children, and grandchildren, visited her ofttimes and loved and esteemed her highly, but I was there [for] a period of [eleven] years. I should know her disposition and character thoroughly. Her ideals were high, and her disposition kindly."[12]

Sometime later, Emma asked Nancy Abercrombie to move into her home so she could be near her young son and foster a meaningful relationship with him. Moreover, she exacted a promise from Lewis and Nancy that they would marry after her death.

It seems strange that Emma would acquiesce to such an arrangement when years before she had such a difficult time reconciling herself to the God-given doctrine of plural marriage. After all, was not the relationship between Bidamon and Abercrombie a de facto form of the very principle she had grown to abhor? As strange as it may seem, could the arrangement have been an attempt by Emma to atone for her rejection of the Lord's will? Then again, quite possibly her actions represented pure charity—a quality given to her by her Heavenly Father.

Chapter Thirty-Five

After nearly thirty years of living in the Mansion House, Emma turned it over to Alexander and David in 1871 and moved across the street, near the bank of the Mississippi, into the Riverside Mansion, where she continued to rent rooms and feed boarders. Formerly known as the Nauvoo House, the building had initially been designed to have only a single story; however, Lewis Bidamon removed part of the original structure and salvaged the bricks to add a second level.

Emma's new residence provided her a better view of the beautiful Mississippi and allowed the neighborhood boys easier access to her kitchen. One day when a few of the boys were playing near the river's edge, one fell in. His friends pulled him out of the ice-cold water and took him to Emma's kitchen, where she gave him dry clothing and fed the boys from her cookie jar. "From that time on, falling in the river became a frequent occurrence."[1]

One of the neighborhood boys, Joseph S. Jemison, lived just up the street from Emma and wrote years later: "I saw Mrs. Smith Bidamon at least once a day most of the time. The young people of the community were in the habit of gathering of evenings at the Bidamon home. . . . I can still taste Mrs. Smith Bidamon's cookies after all these years. Everyone in town liked them."[2]

Though she was comfortable in the Riverside Mansion and had all the amenities and comforts of the time, reminiscing about the past and sharing her testimony of the restoration of the gospel seemed for her almost therapeutic. Julius Chambers, a noted journalist for the *Brooklyn Eagle,* happened on Nauvoo and recorded a delightful and vivid description of Emma and his visit to the town:

"In the summer of 1872 I was paddling down the Mississippi in a canoe. . . . At the nightfall of a July evening, after a long day's work, I saw on the Illinois shore, upon a fine bluff, a red brick building that indicated a town of more than village size. Making a landing,

I climbed to the top of the plateau and learned that the building that had attracted my attention was the only hotel in the place. What was much more important, I was told that the town was Nauvoo, for six years (1840 to 1846) the seat of Mormonism.

"When I applied at the office for supper I was received by an elderly woman. My eye-memory of the face and the figure of the distinguished old lady is quite distinct. She was tall, for her sex; her hair was gray, not white, and was combed straight over her temples. Her face was thin; her nose lean, aquiline, and pointed. Her mouth was small; her chin was badly shaped and protruded; her eyes were very noticeable, although their color can not be recalled. . . . I also remember her hands, which were small and had well-cared-for nails. . . .

"This lady was the widow of Joseph Smith. . . . Mrs. Smith was a sincere believer in her husband's faith, but she took the earliest occasion to say that she did not believe in polygamy. She denounced the practice as 'vile and infamous.' She said it had 'blighted and dishonored a beautiful doctrine that came direct from an angel of God, inscribed upon plates of gold.'

"The dear old woman put me to shame with her dignified forbearance when I asked if she ever had seen those plates, or the miraculous pair of spectacles, known in Mormon history as 'Urim and Thummim.' She had not; but they veritably existed. Had I seen the 'Tables of Stone' that Moses received? Did I doubt the miracles of the Savior? Faith was comprised in the acceptance of things not seen, she said to me.

"We talked long into the evening, for this aged woman appeared glad to see even a boy from the great east. . . . She asked me a thousand questions, many of which I could not answer; . . . her waking hours were largely passed seated in a tall-backed rocking-chair, near the edge of the bluff, with her eyes fixed upon the majestic Mississippi before her. . . .

"She was a picture of a fine woman, stranded on the ice-shore of age, amid surroundings with which she was entirely out of sympathy and among people who did not appreciate her intellect or her innate refinement. I believe she had a husband about the place, . . . but the pride of living she felt was not as his spouse. What earthly honor and renown she claimed was solely as 'the widow of Joseph Smith, a sincere believer, a devout man, and a loving husband.' Thus did she speak of the dead Prophet to me.

"My last sight of this venerable woman occurred next forenoon, as she stood upon the bluff in front of the red hotel and waved her hand when I headed for the center of the broad stream to get into deep water on the [Mississippi]."[3]

Emma's great-great-granddaughter Gracia N. Jones offers another dramatic account that depicts Emma's yearning for past relationships and seemingly reveals that her decision not to join with the Saints in Utah was still an emotional one. "A woman who served as a maid in

Emma's home . . . related the fact that each evening after the chores were done, Emma would climb the stairs to her room, sit in her low rocker, and gaze out the window at the western sunset over the Mississippi River. No one dared approach to offer comfort, because they did not know how to touch the depth of sorrow evidenced by the tears that coursed down her cheeks."[4]

The decision Emma made soon after the Martyrdom and that haunted her until her death was her denial both to her children and to the public that the Prophet Joseph had practiced plural marriage. As evidenced in letters and in other communication, Emma suffered great anxiety regarding this deception, particularly when her sons served missions for the RLDS church in Utah, Idaho, and Nevada. Although some of her worry was certainly for their safety and welfare, much of her angst was from fear they would learn the truth about their father and his plural wives.

All three of her sons heard numerous stories and saw affidavits on their western missions that contradicted Emma's statements regarding the principle of plural marriage. Although Joseph III and Alexander held fast to their mother's word, David did not. When he returned from Utah in 1872, it was reported that he held back from Emma's welcoming embrace and asked, "Mother, why have you deceived us?"[5]

Still, Emma continued to deny publicly that her prophet-husband had practiced plural marriage. She made several statements to that effect in an interview with Joseph III and Alexander in February of 1879. The dialogue between mother and sons was published after her death in an October 1879 edition of the *Saints' Herald* as an article entitled "Last Testimony of Sister Emma."

Nevertheless, soon after the interview but before its publication, Emma was visited by a son of Thomas B. Marsh, who frankly asked her if the Prophet had had plural wives. The younger Marsh later related that she "broke down and wept, and excused herself from answering directly, assigning as a reason . . . that her son Joseph was the leader of the Re-organized Church."[6] Although many have attempted to offer explanations of Emma's dishonesty regarding the practice—the first and foremost being to protect her children and to keep the Prophet Joseph's name unsullied—no one but Emma will ever know her precise motives for her deception.

Chapter Thirty-Six

WITH THE EXCEPTION OF A BROKEN LEFT ARM in 1872, Emma remained generally vital and strong until the spring of 1879 when her health began to decline rapidly. In mid-April, Alexander stopped by the Riverside Mansion for a visit and was stunned at her failing condition. He and his wife, Lizzie, had moved from Nauvoo to Andover, Missouri, about a year before, so he had not seen his mother since he and Joseph III had interviewed her in February.

Of that heart-wrenching visit Alexander remembered, "I went in at the front door, and through the hall, and into the kitchen, where I knew my mother was usually to be found. My mother was not there. Another woman was there. I said to her, where is mother? Don't you know that your mother is sick? She is in the other room, . . . and as I opened the door and went into the room I saw my mother on the bed, and I had the testimony from God that [she] was dying." Immediately, Alexander sent a telegram to Joseph III in Plano, Illinois, saying, "Joseph if you expect to see mother alive, come quick."[1]

Joseph arrived at the Riverside Mansion the following day and together with Alexander, Julia, and Lewis kept a constant vigil at her bedside for the next ten days. In a letter dated April 27, 1879, Alexander wrote to his wife, "Mother is still alive, but oh, how she suffers. . . . [She] needs someone constantly by her, she must be lifted up about every fifteen or twenty minutes. . . . Mr. Bidamon is very kind and gentle to her, but is nearly worn out. . . . [She] is gradually failing, she can not recognize anyone now. Her mind wanders constantly. . . . [We] do all we can for her and she still suffers fearfully."[2]

So it was a blessing when, at a little after four o'clock in the morning of April 30, 1879, Emma died. Alexander remembered, "Just before she passed away she called, 'Joseph, Joseph.' I thought she meant my brother. He was in the room, and I spoke to him, and said, Joseph, mother wants you. I was at the head of the bed. My mother raised right up, lifted her left hand as high as she could raise it, and called, Joseph. I put my left arm under her shoulders, took her hand in mine, saying, Mother, what is it, laid her hand on her bosom, and she was dead; she had passed away."[3]

Emma's nurse, Elizabeth Revel, later asked Alexander if he understood the significance of his mother's calling out for Joseph. When he replied that he didn't, she offered this comforting explanation: "Well, a short time before she died she had a vision which she related to me. She said that your father came to her and said to her, 'Emma, come with me, it is time for you to come with me.' And as she related it she said, 'I put on my bonnet and my shawl and went with him; I did not think that it was anything unusual. I went with him into a mansion, a beautiful mansion, and he showed me through the different apartments of that beautiful mansion. And one room was the nursery. In that nursery was a babe in the cradle.' She said, 'I knew my babe, my Don Carlos that was taken away from me.' She sprang forward, caught the child up in her arms, and wept with joy over the child. When she recovered herself sufficient, she turned to Joseph and said, 'Joseph, where are the rest of my children?' He said to her, 'Emma, be patient, and you shall have all of your children.' Then she saw standing by his side a personage of light, even the Lord Jesus Christ."[4]

Emma was dressed for burial in a plum colored dress that was "brocaded with flowers and leaves in a raised design"[5] and laid in the parlor of the Riverside Mansion in preparation for the viewing and funeral. From twelve noon until two P.M. on May 2, 1879, friends and relatives filed past her casket until "the rooms were filled, and a large number in attendance who could not find entrance . . . stood gathered near the open doors to listen."[6] Among the many mourners present were the Prophet Joseph's younger sisters, Katharine Smith Salisbury and Lucy Smith Milliken. Both were accompanied by immediate family members and several of their sons served as pallbearers.

After the services and before Emma was laid to rest beside her beloved Joseph behind the old Homestead, numerous mourners passed through the parlor. "There was often noted the silent gaze of sorrow, the gently-falling tears, or the touch of living hands upon those folded in death, all mute testimonies of the love and appreciation which had been cherished for her in the hearts of her friends and neighbors."[7] Suppressed emotion surfaced when one grieving friend extended her hand as she passed by the casket and "laid it tenderly upon [Emma's] cheek, and bending down, kissed her on the forehead, whispering with falling tears as she moved on, 'She was the very best friend I ever had.' Tears had already been flowing freely, but this simple tribute of genuine grief, added a new impulse to the weeping, as others freshly realized their own loss and loving ministry of the departed Saint."[8]

Epilogue

ONE QUESTION IN THE HEARTS of some members of The Church of Jesus Christ of Latter-day Saints is whether the Prophet Joseph will have Emma as his eternal companion in the celestial kingdom of our Heavenly Father. Often they refer to a statement by Brigham Young regarding her eternal welfare: "Joseph used to say that he would have her hereafter, if he had to go to hell for her, and he will have to go to hell for her as sure as he ever gets her."[1] Though President Young certainly made that statement, it was after Emma had publicly denied that the Prophet Joseph practiced plural marriage, and he was further angered when her sons served missions in Utah for the Reorganized Church and perpetuated their mother's deception regarding the principle.

Conversely, it should be noted that Brigham Young is also quoted as saying, "I have prayed from the beginning for sister Emma and for the whole family. There is not a man in this Church that has entertained better feelings toward them."[2] At the 1892 jubilee celebration of the Nauvoo Relief Society in Salt Lake City a sister made "a motion to hang a life-size portrait of Emma" in the Tabernacle to commemorate the role she played in those initial formative years of the organization. When several sisters in attendance raised objection to the action, Zina D. H. Young, then president of the Relief Society, talked over the matter with President Wilford Woodruff, who responded that "anyone who opposed it . . . must be very narrow minded indeed."[3]

When I am asked questions about Emma's exaltation by members of the Church with whom I visit, my usual response is something like this: I have no more information than anyone else regarding Emma's eternal future. What I do know is that if ever I am blessed with the opportunity to meet Emma, I hope and pray that as we embrace, rather than my having to whisper in her ear, "I'm sorry," she will whisper in mine, "Thank you."

Publisher's Note

THE CHURCH OF JESUS CHRIST OF LATTER-DAY SAINTS abandoned the practice of polygamy (or plural marriage) at the end of the nineteenth century. An official statement by the Church on polygamy can be found on the Church's website, lds.org, which states:

"In obedience to direction from God, Latter-day Saints followed this practice for about 50 years during the 1800s but officially ceased the practice of such marriages after the Manifesto was issued by President Woodruff in 1890. Since that time, plural marriage has not been approved by The Church of Jesus Christ of Latter-day Saints and any member adopting this practice is subject to losing his or her membership in the Church."

Occasionally questions still arise as various news media report on activities and individuals within polygamous sects. These reports can be confusing, particularly when the term "Mormon" is misleadingly applied to polygamist groups and individuals.

In an October 1998 general conference address, President Gordon B. Hinckley declared: "I wish to state categorically that this Church has nothing whatever to do with those practicing polygamy. They are not members of this Church. Most of them have never been members. . . .

"If any of our members are found to be practicing plural marriage, they are excommunicated, the most serious penalty the Church can impose. Not only are those so involved in direct violation of the civil law, they are in violation of the law of this Church. . . .

"There is no such thing as a 'Mormon Fundamentalist.' It is a contradiction to use the two words together. More than a century ago God clearly revealed unto His prophet Wilford Woodruff that the practice of plural marriage should be discontinued, which means that is now against the law of God. Even in countries where civil or religious law allows polygamy, the Church teaches that marriage must be monogamous and does not accept into its membership those practicing plural marriage" (*Ensign,* November 1998, 71).

Information regarding the Church's stand on polygamy can be found at newsroom.lds.org.

~Notes~

CHAPTER ONE

1. Von Wymetal, *Joseph Smith,* 75.
2. Jones, *Emma's Glory and Sacrifice,* 5.
3. Vesta Crawford, Notes, MS 125, box 2, folder 11, Marriott Library, University of Utah, Salt Lake City, Utah. Vesta Crawford received her bachelor of arts degree from Brigham Young University, studied at Stanford University, and received her master's degree in 1928 from the University of Wyoming. In 1945, she was appointed editorial secretary of the *Relief Society Magazine* and in 1947 was named associate editor. In her notes are interviews with Emma's granddaughters Mary Audentia Smith Anderson, Emma McCallum, and Vida Smith Yates. See website of University of Utah Marriott Library Special Collections for more information.
4. Blackman, *Susquehanna County,* 103.
5. Kennedy, *Recollections,* 96.
6. George Peck Account, 1843, "Mormonism and the Mormons," *Methodist Quarterly Review,* Jan. 1843, 112.
7. G. Peck Account, 1874, 67–68, in Vogel, *Early Mormon Documents,* 4:281.
8. George Peck Account, 1843, "Mormonism and the Mormons," *Methodist Quarterly Review,* Jan. 1843, 112.
9. Blackman, *Susquehanna County,* 104; William Thompson, *Montrose (PA) Susquehanna Register* 9 (May 1, 1834); spelling standardized.
10. Blackman, *Susquehanna County,* 207.
11. Clarke, Centennial Celebration program, March 1912.
12. Anderson, *Ancestry and Posterity,* 301–2.
13. Mark H. Forscutt, "Commemorative Discourse, on the Death of Mrs. Emma Bidamon," *Plano (IL) Saints' Herald* 26, no. 14 (July 15, 1879): 209.
14. Ibid.
15. Crawford, Notes, MS 125, box 2, folder 11, University of Utah.
16. Kennedy, *Recollections,* 96.
17. Mehetable Doolittle Reminiscence, 1877, in Vogel, *Early Mormon Documents,* 4:338.
18. "The Early Mormons: Joe Smith Operates at Susquehanna," *Binghamton (NY) Republican,* Mar. 29, 1877.
19. Crawford, Notes, MS 125, box 2, folder 11, University of Utah.

CHAPTER TWO

1. "School Reports, 1813–1867," Broome County Courthouse, Binghamton, N.Y., as cited in Porter, *Origins,* 73.
2. Smith, *History of Joseph Smith by His Mother,* ed. Nibley, 92.
3. Porter, Backman, and Black, *New York,* 98.
4. Smith, *History of the Church,* 1:17.
5. Blackman, *Susquehanna County,* 578.
6. Marvin S. Hill, "Joseph Smith and the 1826 Trial: New Evidence and New Difficulties," *BYU Studies* 12 (Winter 1972): 223.

7. Smith, *History of the Church,* 1:17.

8. Hill, *Joseph Smith,* 68.

9. "Newell Knight's Journal," in *Classic Experiences,* 48.

10. Roberts, *Comprehensive History,* 1:85.

11. Josiah Stowell Jr. to John S. Fullmer, Feb. 17, 1843, MS 2823, LDS Church Archives, Salt Lake City, 2.

12. Smith, *History of Joseph Smith by His Mother,* ed. Nibley, 93.

CHAPTER THREE

1. Smith, *History of Joseph Smith by His Mother,* ed. Nibley, 89, 87.

2. Joseph Knight Sr. (1772–1847), "Reminiscences," n.d., MS 3470, LDS Church Archives, Salt Lake City; spelling and punctuation standardized.

3. Smith, *History of Joseph Smith by His Mother,* ed. Nibley, 93.

4. Jones, *Emma's Glory and Sacrifice,* 4.

5. Bradford, *Of Plymouth Plantation.*

6. "Last Testimony of Sister Emma," *Saints' Herald* 26, no. 10 (Oct. 1, 1879): 289–90.

7. Nan Hill, "Joe Smith Lived and Married Here," *Afton (NY) Enterprise,* July 20, 1939, U. Grant Baker Collection, Papers 1930–1950, MS 2851, LDS Church Archives, Salt Lake City.

8. Blackman, *Susquehanna County,* 578.

CHAPTER FOUR

1. Smith, *History of Joseph Smith by His Mother,* ed. Nibley, 94.

2. Smith, *History of Joseph Smith by His Mother,* ed. Nibley, 65.

3. Blackman, *Susquehanna County,* 578.

4. Porter, Backman, and Black, *New York,* 102.

5. Smith, *History of Joseph Smith by His Mother,* ed. Nibley, 100.

6. Smith, *History of Joseph Smith by His Mother,* ed. Nibley, 101.

7. Smith, *History of Joseph Smith by His Mother,* ed. Nibley, 102.

8. Smith, *History of the Church,* 1:18.

9. Smith, *History of Joseph Smith by His Mother,* ed. Nibley, 107–8.

10. Smith, *History of Joseph Smith by His Mother,* ed. Nibley, 103–4.

11. Smith, *History of Joseph Smith by His Mother,* comp. Ingleton, 163–64. The title page of this version describes it as "an up-to-date reprint of the original 1853 edition in its entirety, with additional information from the rough-draft manuscript and corrections resulting from subsequent research."

12. Smith, *History of the Church,* 1:18–19.

13. Smith, *History of Joseph Smith by His Mother,* ed. Nibley, 106.

14. Smith, *History of Joseph Smith by His Mother,* ed. Nibley, 110.

15. Smith, *History of Joseph Smith by His Mother,* ed. Nibley, 109.

16. Smith, *History of Joseph Smith by His Mother,* ed. Nibley, 112.

17. Mary Salisbury Hancock, "Three Sisters of the Prophet Joseph Smith," *Saints' Herald* (Jan. 11, 1954): 36.

18. Bean, *History of Palmyra,* 46.

CHAPTER FIVE

1. "Martin Harris's Testimony," Martin Harris to Edward Stevenson, *Millennial Star* 55, no. 49 (Dec. 4, 1893): 794.

2. Smith, *History of Joseph Smith by His Mother,* ed. Nibley, 118.

3. Bean, *History of Palmyra,* 35.

4. Smith, *History of the Church,* 1:19.

5. Porter, *Origins,* 83. See also Smith, *History of Joseph Smith by His Mother,* ed. Proctor and Proctor, 159, n. 5.

6. Bean, *History of Palmyra,* 48.

7. Bean, *History of Palmyra,* 46.

8. Smith, *History of the Church,* 1:19.

9. Porter, *Origins,* as cited in Smith, *History of Joseph Smith by His Mother,* ed. Proctor and Proctor, 195, n. 2.

10. *Montrose (PA) Susquehanna Register,* May 1, 1834, as cited in Porter, *Origins,* 51.

11. Rex B. Hawes, Oakland, Susquehanna County, Pennsylvania, to Elder and Sister Abner H. Baird, Oct. 7, 1957, as cited in Porter, *Origins,* 51.

12. Smith, *History of the Church,* 1:20.

13. Smith, *History of Joseph Smith by His Mother,* ed. Nibley, 121.

14. Smith, *History of Joseph Smith by His Mother,* ed. Nibley, 122.

15. Smith, *History of the Church,* 4:537.

16. Smith, *History of the Church,* 4:537.

17. Smith, *History of Joseph Smith by His Mother,* ed. Nibley, 111.

18. "Last Testimony of Sister Emma," *Saints' Herald* 26, no. 10 (Oct. 1, 1879): 290.

19. Stocker, *Centennial History of Susquehanna County,* 554.

CHAPTER SIX

1. Smith, *History of the Church,* 1:21.

2. Smith, *History of the Prophet Joseph,* ed. Smith and Smith, 118.

3. Smith, *History of Joseph Smith by His Mother,* ed. Nibley, 128–29.

4. Smith, *History of Joseph Smith by His Mother,* ed. Proctor and Proctor, 160–67.

5. Smith, *History of Joseph Smith by His Mother,* ed. Nibley, 133.

6. Edmund C. Briggs, "A Visit to Nauvoo in 1856," *Journal of History* 9 (Oct. 1916): 454. The name *Sariah* was written *Sarah.*

7. "Last Testimony of Sister Emma," *Saints' Herald* 26, no. 10 (Oct. 1, 1879): 290.

8. Smith, *History of Joseph Smith by His Mother,* ed. Nibley, 133, 137.

9. Joseph Smith III to Mrs. E. Horton, Mar. 7, 1900, as cited in Vogel, *Early Mormon Documents,* 1:546–47. See also "Last Testimony of Sister Emma," *Saints' Herald* 26, no. 10 (Oct. 1, 1879): 290.

10. Dean C. Jessee, "Joseph Knight's Recollection of Early Mormon History," *BYU Studies* 17, no. 1 (1976): 36.

CHAPTER SEVEN

1. Jenson, *Biographical Encyclopedia,* 1:264.

2. Jenson, *Biographical Encyclopedia,* 1:267.

3. Smith, *History of Joseph Smith by His Mother,* ed. Nibley, 148.

4. Smith, *History of Joseph Smith by His Mother,* ed. Nibley, 148–49.

5. Jenson, *Biographical Encyclopedia,* 1:267; see also Roberts, *Comprehensive History,* 1:126–27.

6. Roberts, *Comprehensive History,* 1:131.

7. Roberts, *Comprehensive History,* 1:131.

8. Smith, *History of the Church,* 1:59.

9. Smith, *History of Joseph Smith by His Mother,* ed. Nibley, 151.

10. Smith, *History of Joseph Smith by His Mother,* ed. Nibley, 152.

11. Roberts, *Comprehensive History,* 1:127.

12. Young, *Journal of Discourses,* 19:38.

13. Smith, *History of Joseph Smith by His Mother,* ed. Nibley, 156.

14. Smith, *History of the Church,* 1:75, 64.

15. Gordon B. Hinckley, "150-Year Drama: A Personal View of Our History," *Ensign,* Apr. 1980, 11.

16. Smith, *History of Joseph Smith by His Mother,* ed. Nibley, 168.

17. Hinckley, "150-Year Drama: A Personal View of Our History," *Ensign,* Apr. 1980, 11.

CHAPTER EIGHT

1. Smith, *History of the Church,* 1:86.

2. Joseph Knight Jr. Autobiography, 1862, MS F 564, no. 24, LDS Church Archives, Salt Lake City.

3. Smith, *History of the Church,* 1:88.

4. Smith, *History of the Church,* 1:91.

5. Smith, *History of the Church,* 6:395.

6. Smith, *History of the Church,* 1:96.

7. Smith, *History of the Church,* 1:97.

8. Smith, *History of the Church,* 1:106.

9. Smith, *History of the Church,* 1:108.

10. Smith, *History of the Church,* 1:108.

11. Isaac Hale, Affidavit to Peter Ingersoll, 1833, as cited in Jones, *Emma's Glory and Sacrifice,* 29.

CHAPTER NINE

1. Pratt, *Autobiography,* ed. Proctor and Proctor, 32.
2. Pratt, *Autobiography,* ed. Proctor and Proctor, 32.
3. Smith, *History of the Church,* 1:115.
4. Smith, *History of Joseph Smith by His Mother,* ed. Nibley, 190.
5. Smith, *History of Joseph Smith by His Mother,* ed. Nibley, 192.
6. "History of Joseph Smith," *Times and Seasons* 4, no. 18 (Aug. 1, 1843): 290.
7. A.W. Cowles, *Moore's Rural New Yorker* (Jan. 23, 1843): 61, as cited in Anderson, *Joseph Smith's Kirtland,* 4.
8. Orson F. Whitney, Conference Report, Apr. 1912, 50.
9. Orson F. Whitney, Conference Report, Apr. 1912, 50.
10. Smith, *History of the Church,* 1:146.

CHAPTER TEN

1. Smith, *History of the Church,* 1:146.
2. Diary of Levi W. Hancock, 1960, L. Tom Perry Special Collections, Brigham Young University, Provo, Utah, 42.
3. Kent P. Jackson, "Joseph Smith's Cooperstown Bible: The Historical Context of the Bible Used in the Joseph Smith Translation," *BYU Studies* 40, no. 1 (2001): 58.
4. Kent P. Jackson, "Joseph Smith's Cooperstown Bible: The Historical Context of the Bible Used in the Joseph Smith Translation," *BYU Studies* 40, no. 1 (2001): 60.
5. Smith, *History of Joseph Smith by His Mother,* ed. Nibley, 199.
6. Smith, *History of Joseph Smith by His Mother,* ed. Nibley, 199.
7. Smith, *History of Joseph Smith by His Mother,* ed. Nibley, 204–5.
8. Smith, *History of Joseph Smith by His Mother,* ed. Nibley, 207.
9. Young, *Journal of Discourses,* 11:295.
10. Smith, *History of the Church,* 1:175–77.
11. Smith, *History of the Church,* 1:188.
12. *Messenger and Advocate,* Sept. 1835, 179.
13. Smith, *History of the Church,* 1:197.
14. "Newel Knight's Journal," in *Classic Experiences,* 70.

CHAPTER ELEVEN

1. Smith, *History of Joseph Smith by His Mother,* ed. Nibley, 190–91.
2. Smith, *History of the Church,* 1:207.
3. Smith, *History of the Church,* 1:215.
4. Smith, *History of the Church,* 1:216.
5. Sue Foster, "They Kept Home Fires Burning," *Western Reserve,* Nov.-Dec. 1976, 46. See also Newell and Avery, *Mormon Enigma,* 41.
6. Smith, *History of the Church,* 1:245.
7. Philo Dibble, "Recollections of the Prophet Joseph Smith," *Juvenile Instructor* 27, no. 10 (Mar. 15, 1892): 303–4.
8. Smith, *History of the Church,* 1:252.
9. Young, *Journal of Discourses,* 6:281.
10. Smith, *History of the Church,* 1:261–62.
11. Smith, *History of the Church,* 1:263.
12. Smith, *History of the Church,* 1:263.
13. Smith, *History of the Church,* 1:263.
14. Smith, *History of the Church,* 1:264.

CHAPTER TWELVE

1. Elizabeth Ann Whitney, "A Leaf from an Autobiography," *Woman's Exponent* 7, no. 7 (Sept. 1, 1878): 51.
2. Smith, *History of the Church,* 1:271.
3. Joseph Smith to Emma Smith, June 6, 1832, Greenville, Indiana; spelling and punctuation standardized. Original in Chicago History Museum, Mormon Collection, folder 1 of 6, 1832–1844.
4. Smith, *History of Joseph Smith by His Mother,* ed. Ingleton, 327.
5. *History of Geauga and Lake Counties, Ohio,* 248.
6. Joseph Smith to Emma Smith, Oct. 13, 1832, Pearl Street House, New York, Community of Christ Archives, Independence, Missouri; spelling and punctuation standardized.

CHAPTER THIRTEEN

1. Cook, *David Whitmer,* 204.
2. Young, *Journal of Discourses,* 12:158.
3. Smith, *History of Joseph Smith by His Mother,* ed. Nibley, 230.
4. Smith, *History of the Church,* 5:423.
5. Tullidge, *Women of Mormondom,* 76.
6. George A. Smith, "Memoirs of George A. Smith," 10, typescript, Harold B. Lee Library, Brigham Young University, Provo, Utah, cited in Anderson, *Joseph Smith's Kirtland,* 24.
7. Pratt, *Autobiography,* ed. Proctor and Proctor, 112.
8. Roberts, *Missouri Persecutions,* 73–74. See also Roberts, *Comprehensive History,* 1:323.
9. Smith, *History of the Church,* 1:391.
10. Pratt, *Autobiography,* ed. Proctor and Proctor, 121.
11. Smith, *History of the Church,* 3:438–39.
12. Smith, *Personal Writings,* 306.
13. Cowley, *Wilford Woodruff,* 39.
14. *Church History in the Fulness of Times,* 143.
15. Porter and Black, *Prophet Joseph,* 203.

CHAPTER FOURTEEN

1. Smith, as cited by Wilford Woodruff, Conference Report, Apr. 1898, 57.
2. Anderson, *Joseph Smith's Kirtland,* 41.
3. Smith, *History of the Church,* 2:281, 286.
4. Caroline Barnes Crosby (1807–1884), as cited in Godfrey, Godfrey, and Derr, *Women's Voices,* 55–56.
5. Anderson, *Memoirs,* 12.
6. Caroline Barnes Crosby (1807–1884), as cited in Godfrey, Godfrey, and Derr, *Women's Voices,* 49.
7. Smith, *History of the Church,* 2:362.
8. Emma Hale Smith, patriarchal blessing by Joseph Smith Sr., Dec. 9, 1834, Emma Smith Papers, P4, f22, Community of Christ Archives, Independence, Missouri.
9. William R. Hine, affidavit, ca. Mar. 1885, *Oakland (CA) Naked Truths about Mormonism* 1, no. 1 (Jan. 1888): 2.
10. Pratt, *Journal of Discourses,* 20:65.
11. Smith, *History of the Church,* 2:235.
12. Smith, *History of the Church,* 2:348.

13. Smith, *History of the Church,* 2:273.
14. Smith, *History of the Church,* 2:304.
15. Smith, *History of the Church,* 2:334–35.
16. Smith, *History of Joseph Smith by His Mother,* ed. Proctor and Proctor, 324.
17. Smith, *History of the Church,* 2:345.

CHAPTER FIFTEEN

1. Larson, *Erastus Snow,* 466.
2. Heber C. Kimball, *Times and Seasons* 6, no. 13 (July 15, 1845): 972.
3. Anderson, *Joseph Smith's Kirtland,* 181.
4. Smith, *History of the Church,* 2:428.
5. Smith, *History of the Church,* 2:428.
6. Bruce R. McConkie, "The Keys of the Kingdom," *Ensign,* May 1983, 22.
7. Smith, *Doctrines of Salvation,* 3:129.
8. Anderson, *Joseph Smith's Kirtland,* 173.
9. Smith, *History of the Church,* 6:184.
10. Smith, *Doctrines of Salvation,* 2:52.

CHAPTER SIXTEEN

1. Smith, *History of Joseph Smith by His Mother,* ed. Nibley, 239–40.
2. Snow, *Biography and Family Record,* 20.
3. "History of Brigham Young," *Deseret News,* Feb. 10, 1858, 386.
4. Caroline Barnes Crosby (1807–1884), as cited in Godfrey, Godfrey, and Derr, *Women's Voices,* 56; spelling standardized.
5. Emma Smith to Joseph Smith, May 3, 1837, Joseph Smith letterbooks, 35, McKay Library, Brigham Young University–Idaho, Rexburg, Idaho.
6. Emma Smith to Joseph Smith, April 25, 1837, Joseph Smith letterbooks, 35, McKay Library, Brigham Young University–Idaho,
7. Emma Smith to Joseph Smith, May 3, 1837, Joseph Smith letterbooks, 36, McKay Library, Brigham Young University–Idaho; grammar standardized.
8. Emma Smith to Joseph Smith, May 3, 1837, Joseph Smith letterbooks, 36, McKay Library,

Brigham Young University–Idaho; some grammar standardized.

9. Mary Fielding to Mercy Thompson, July 8, 1837, MS 2779, LDS Church Archives, Salt Lake City.

10. Smith, *History of the Church*, 2:492–93.

11. Anderson, *Joseph Smith's Kirtland*, 60.

12. Mary Fielding Smith (1801–1852), as cited in Godfrey, Godfrey, and Derr, *Women's Voices*, 63.

13. Smith, *History of the Church*, 2:323.

14. Smith, *History of the Church*, 2:529.

15. Whitney, *Life of Heber C. Kimball*, 101.

CHAPTER SEVENTEEN

1. Smith, *History of the Church*, 2:429.

2. Smith, *History of the Church*, 2:294.

3. Anderson, *Memoirs*, 2.

4. Jones and DeMille, *History of Fredonia*, 49.

5. Young, *Manuscript History of Brigham Young*, 25–26.

6. Young, *Manuscript History of Brigham Young*, 26–27.

7. Young, *Manuscript History of Brigham Young*, 27.

8. Smith, *History of the Church*, 3:8.

9. Allen and Leonard, *Story of the Latter-day Saints*, 107.

10. Smith, *History of the Church*, 3:9.

11. Joseph Smith to the Church Presidency in Kirtland, Ohio, Mar. 29, 1838, in Joseph Smith, "Scriptory Book," 23–26, MS 8955, LDS Church Archives, Salt Lake City, as cited in Smith, *Personal Writings*, 396.

12. Smith, *History of the Church*, 3:25.

13. Crawford, Notes, MS 125, box 2, folder 3, University of Utah.

CHAPTER EIGHTEEN

1. Smith, *History of the Church*, 3:335.

2. Smith, *History of the Church*, 3:35, 39.

3. Smith, *History of the Church*, 3:41.

4. Pratt, *Autobiography*, ed. Proctor and Proctor, 218.

5. Smith, *History of Joseph Smith by His Mother*, ed. Nibley, 254–55.

6. Smith, *History of Joseph Smith by His Mother*, ed. Nibley, 255–56.

7. Smith, *History of the Church*, 3:175.

8. Crawford, Notes, MS 125, box 1, folder 13, University of Utah.

9. Smith, *History of Joseph Smith by His Mother*, ed. Nibley, 257.

10. Crawford, Notes, MS 125, box 1, folder 13, University of Utah.

11. Smith, *History of the Church*, 3:189.

12. Pratt, *Autobiography*, ed. Proctor and Proctor, 235.

13. Smith, *History of the Church*, 3:189.

14. Pratt, *Autobiography*, ed. Proctor and Proctor, 235.

15. Smith, *History of the Church*, 3:190–91.

16. Smith, *History of the Church*, 3:193.

17. Anderson, *Memoirs*, 2.

18. Mark H. Forscutt, "Commemorative Discourse, on the Death of Mrs. Emma Bidamon," *Saints' Herald* 26, no. 14 (July 15, 1879): 213.

19. Smith, *History of Joseph Smith by His Mother*, ed. Nibley, 291.

CHAPTER NINETEEN

1. Anderson, *Memoirs*, 3.

2. Smith, *History of the Church*, 3:203.

3. Joseph Smith to Emma Smith, Nov. 4, 1838, Community of Christ Archives, Independence, Missouri; spelling and some punctuation standardized.

4. Smith, *History of Joseph Smith by His Mother*, ed. Nibley, 291.

5. Pratt, *Autobiography*, ed. Proctor and Proctor, 262.

6. Pratt, *Autobiography*, ed. Proctor and Proctor, 262–63.

7. Joseph Smith to Emma Smith, Nov. 12, 1838, Richmond, Missouri, in Smith, *Personal Writings*, 405–6; spelling and punctuation standardized.

8. John Rigdon, *Friendship (NY) Sesquicentennial Times*, as cited in Jones, *Emma's Glory and Sacrifice*, 89.

9. John Rigdon, *Friendship (NY) Sesquicentennial Times*, as cited in Jones, *Emma's Glory and Sacrifice*, 90.

10. Anderson, *Memoirs*, 2.

11. Smith, *History of the Church,* 3:287.

12. John Lowe Butler, Autobiography, MSS 390, Special Collections, Brigham Young University, Provo, Utah, 16.

13. Mercy Fielding Thompson, as cited in Tullidge, *Women of Mormondom,* 254.

14. John Lowe Butler, Autobiography, MSS 390, Special Collections, Brigham Young University, Provo, Utah, 16.

15. Joseph Smith III, notes of an interview with Emma Smith Bidamon, Feb. 1879, Community of Christ Archives, Independence, Missouri, as cited in Newell and Avery, *Mormon Enigma,* 78.

16. Emma Smith to Joseph Smith, Mar. 9, 1839, Joseph Smith letterbooks, 37, McKay Library, Brigham Young University–Idaho; punctuation and grammar standardized.

17. Anderson, *Memoirs,* 4.

18. Anderson, *Ancestry and Posterity,* 76.

CHAPTER TWENTY

1. Emma Smith to Joseph Smith, Mar. 9, 1839, Joseph Smith letterbooks, 37, McKay Library, Brigham Young University–Idaho.

2. Anderson, *Memoirs,* 5.

3. Joseph Smith to Emma Smith, Mar. 21, 1839, Liberty Jail, Missouri, in Smith, *Personal Writings,* 448–49; spelling and punctuation standardized.

4. Joseph Smith to Emma Smith, Apr. 4, 1839, Emma Smith Collection, Community of Christ Archives, Independence, Missouri; spelling, punctuation, and grammar standardized.

5. Smith, *History of the Church,* 3:321.

6. Crawford, Notes, MS 125, box 1, folder 13, University of Utah.

7. Emma Smith Bidamon to Joseph Smith III, 1 Aug. [no year], P4, F17, Community of Christ Archives, Independence, Missouri,

8. Elizabeth Ann Whitney, "A Leaf from an Autobiography," *Woman's Exponent* 7, no. 12 (Nov. 15, 1878): 91.

9. Crawford, Notes, MS 125, box 1, folder 13, University of Utah, 14.

10. Wandle Mace (1809–1890) Autobiography (ca. 1890), MS 1924, LDS Church Archives, Salt Lake City, 41.

11. Smith, *History of the Church,* 4:3.

12. Woodruff, *Leaves from My Journal,* 115.

13. Woodruff, *Journal,* entry of July 22, 1839, 1:347–48; grammar standardized.

14. Anderson, *Memoirs,* 7.

15. Smith, *History of the Church,* 4:16.

CHAPTER TWENTY-ONE

1. Emma Smith to Joseph Smith, Dec. 6, 1839, Joseph Smith letterbooks, 110, McKay Library, Brigham Young University–Idaho.

2. Smith, *History of the Church,* 4:80.

3. Parry, *Stories about Joseph Smith the Prophet,* 34–35. See also Andrus and Andrus, *They Knew the Prophet,* 146.

4. Emmeline B. Wells, "L.D.S. Women of the Past: Personal Impressions," *Woman's Exponent* 36, no. 7 (Feb. 1908): 49.

5. Crawford, Notes, MS 125, box 1, folder 13, University of Utah.

6. Anderson, *Memoirs,* 19.

7. Jones, *Emma's Glory and Sacrifice,* 109.

8. Mary Bailey Smith Norman to Ina Coolbrith, n.d. [ca. Mar. 1908], P13, f2290, Community of Christ Archives, Independence, Missouri.

9. Smith, *History of Joseph Smith by His Mother,* ed. Nibley, 309.

10. Smith, *History of the Church,* 4:357.

11. Samuel A. Prior, "A Visit to Nauvoo," *Times and Seasons* 4, no. 13 (May 15, 1843): 198; spelling standardized.

CHAPTER TWENTY-TWO

1. Crawford, Notes, MS 125, box 1, folder 13, and box 1, no folder number, University of Utah.

2. Crawford, Notes, MS 125, box 1, folder 13, University of Utah; punctuation standardized.

3. Anderson, *Memoirs,* 17.

4. Anderson, *Memoirs,* 4.

5. Crawford, Notes, MS 125, box 1, folder 13, University of Utah.

6. Lucy Walker Kimball, Autobiographical sketch, MS 4942, LDS Church Archives, Salt Lake City, 4.

7. Joseph B. Wirthlin, "The Abundant Life," *Ensign*, May 2006, 101.

8. Emmeline B. Wells, "L.D.S. Women of the Past: Personal Impressions," *Woman's Exponent* 36, no. 7 (Feb. 1908): 49,

9. "A Sketch of the Life of Eunice Billings Snow," *Woman's Exponent* 39, no. 3 (Sept. 1910): 22.

10. Crawford, Notes, box 1, folder 13, University of Utah, 19.

11. Smith, *History of the Church,* 4:331.

CHAPTER TWENTY-THREE

1. Jones, *Emma's Glory and Sacrifice,* 112.

2. Sarah M. Kimball, "Auto-biography," *Woman's Exponent* 12 (Sept. 1, 1883): 51.

3. Smith, *History of the Church,* 4:552–53.

4. Susa Young Gates, "A Record of the Organization and Proceedings of the Female Relief Society of Nauvoo, Illinois," Mar. 17, 1842, LDS Church Archives, Salt Lake City.

5. Susa Young Gates, "A Record of the Organization and Proceedings of the Female Relief Society of Nauvoo, Illinois," Mar. 17, 1842, LDS Church Archives, Salt Lake City.

6. Smith, *History of the Church,* 4:606–7.

7. Sarah M. Kimball, "Auto-biography," *Woman's Exponent* 12 (Sept. 1, 1883): 51.

8. Smith, *History of the Church,* 5:86.

9. Smith, *History of the Church,* 5:71.

10. Smith, *History of the Church,* 5:107.

11. Smith, *History of the Church,* 5:92.

12. Smith, *History of the Church,* 5:103.

13. Smith, *History of the Church,* 5:110.

14. Smith, *History of the Church,* 5:118.

15. Smith, *History of the Church,* 5:117, 129.

16. Mercy R. Thompson, "Recollections of the Prophet Joseph Smith," *Juvenile Instructor* 27, no. 13 (July 1892): 399.

17. Margarette McIntire Burgess, "Recollections of the Prophet Joseph Smith," *Juvenile Instructor* 27, no. 2 (Jan. 1892): 67.

CHAPTER TWENTY-FOUR

1. Roberts, *Comprehensive History,* 1:526.

2. Pratt, *Autobiography,* ed. Proctor and Proctor, 361; paragraphing altered.

3. Black and Black, *Annotated Record of Baptisms for the Dead, 1840–1845, Nauvoo, Hancock County, Illinois,* 6:3354–56.

4. Smith, *History of the Church,* 4:553.

5. Smith, *History of the Church,* 4:557.

6. Smith, *History of the Church,* 4:556.

7. Dimick B. Huntington, Statement, Dec. 12, 1878, Zina Y. Card Papers, Archives and Manuscripts, Brigham Young University, as cited in Ehat, "Joseph Smith's Introduction of Temple Ordinances," 26.

CHAPTER TWENTY-FIVE

1. Pratt, *Journal of Discourses,* 13:194.

2. Smith and Evans, *Blood Atonement,* 105.

3. Emily Dow Partridge Smith Young, "A Testimony That Cannot Be Refuted," *Woman's Exponent* 12, no. 21 (Apr. 1, 1884): 165.

4. Smith, *History of the Church,* 5:501.

5. William Clayton statement, in Smith, *History of the Church,* 2:106.

6. Smith, *History of the Church,* 5:509.

7. Maria Jane Woodward statement, attached to letter from George H. Brimhall to Joseph F. Smith, Apr. 21, 1902, Incoming Correspondence, Joseph F. Smith Papers, LDS Church Archives, Salt Lake City.

8. Journal of Mary A. Boice, in John Boice Blessing Book, 1884–1885, MS 8129, LDS Church Archives, Salt Lake City, 40.

9. James B. Allen, "The Historians Corner," *BYU Studies* 22, no. 1 (Winter 1982): 91.

10. Young, *Journal of Discourses,* 3:266.

11. Eliza Partridge Lyman (1820–1886), Journal, Feb. 1846–Dec. 1885, MS 1527, LDS Church Archives, Salt Lake City, 6.

12. Anderson, *Memoirs,* 12.

CHAPTER TWENTY-SIX

1. Smith, *History of the Church,* 5:253. Emma and Joseph were married January 18, 1827.
2. Smith, *History of the Church,* 5:385.
3. Smith, *History of the Church,* 5:440.
4. Smith, *History of Joseph Smith by His Mother,* ed. Nibley, 318.
5. Anderson, *Memoirs,* 142–43.
6. Smith, *History of the Church,* 5:459.

CHAPTER TWENTY-SEVEN

1. Anderson, *Memoirs,* 34.
2. Smith, *History of the Church,* 6:33.
3. Smith, *History of the Church,* 6:165–66.
4. Maria Jane Woodward statement, attached to letter from George H. Brimhall to Joseph F. Smith, Apr. 21, 1902, Incoming Correspondence, Joseph F. Smith Papers, LDS Church Archives, Salt Lake City.
5. Smith, *History of the Church,* 6:153.
6. Diary of William Holmes Walker, BX 8670.1. W158d, L. Tom Perry Special Collections, Harold B. Lee Library, Brigham Young University, Provo, Utah, 7.
7. Anderson, *Memoirs,* 34.
8. Anderson, *Memoirs,* 34.

CHAPTER TWENTY-EIGHT

1. Crawford, Notes, MS 125, box 1, folder 13, University of Utah, 13.
2. Smith, *History of the Church,* 6:152.
3. Smith, *History of the Church,* 6:546.
4. Smith, *History of the Church,* 6:546.
5. Wandle Mace Autobiography (1809–1890), MS 1924, LDS Church Archives, Salt Lake City; punctuation standardized.
6. Smith, *History of the Church,* 6:549–50.
7. Edmund C. Briggs, "A Visit to Nauvoo in 1856," *Journal of History* 9 (Oct. 1916): 454.
8. "Edwin Rushton, Bridge Builder and Faithful Pioneer," Pioneer Journals, BX 8670.P659, L. Tom Perry Special Collections, Harold B. Lee Library, Brigham Young University, 3.
9. Emma Hale Smith (1804–1879), Blessing [1844], MS 5135, LDS Church Archives, Salt Lake City.
10. Emma Hale Smith (1804–1879), Blessing [1844], MS 5135, LDS Church Archives, Salt Lake City.

CHAPTER TWENTY-NINE

1. Smith, *History of the Church,* 6:555.
2. Smith, *History of the Church,* 6:605.
3. Taylor, *Gospel Kingdom,* 359–64; paragraphing altered.
4. McGavin, *Nauvoo, the Beautiful,* 144–45. See also statement of B. W. Richmond in "The Prophet's Death!" *Salt Lake City (UT) Deseret Evening News* 24, no. 45 (Dec. 8, 1875): 715.
5. Smith, *History of the Church,* 6:627.
6. McGavin, *Nauvoo, the Beautiful,* 145–46. See also statement of B. W. Richmond in "The Prophet's Death!" *Salt Lake City (UT) Deseret Evening News* 24, no. 45 (Dec. 8, 1875): 715.
7. Anderson, *Memoirs,* 37.
8. Smith, *History of Joseph Smith by His Mother,* ed. Nibley, 324.
9. Smith, *History of the Church,* 6:627.

CHAPTER THIRTY

1. Parley P. Pratt, "Proclamation," *Millennial Star* 5 (Mar. 1845): 151.
2. Woodruff, *Journal of Discourses,* 13:164.
3. "Joseph Smith, the Prophet," *Juvenile Instructor* 5, no. 22 (Oct. 29, 1870): 175.
4. James Monroe Diary, Apr. 24, 1845, Beinecke Rare Book and Manuscript Library, New Haven, Connecticut, as cited in Newell and Avery, *Mormon Enigma,* 207.
5. Journal of Heber C. Kimball, Oct. 4, 1844, LDS Church Archives, Salt Lake City.
6. Anderson, *Memoirs,* 27.
7. Anderson, *Memoirs,* 27; paragraphing altered.
8. Anderson, *Memoirs,* 38.
9. "Another Mormon Expose," *Times and Seasons* 6 (Jan. 15, 1845): 776–77; paragraphing altered.

10. Emma Smith to Joseph L. Heywood, Oct. 18, 1845, P4, f27, Emma Smith Papers, Community of Christ Archives, Independence, Missouri.

CHAPTER THIRTY-ONE

1. Emily Partridge Dow Young (1824–1899), Diary and Reminiscences, Feb. 1874–Nov. 1899, MS 2845, LDS Church Archives, Salt Lake City, 3.
2. Eliza R. Snow, "Lines, Written on the Birth of the Infant Son of Mrs. Emma, Widow of the Late General Joseph Smith," *Times and Seasons* 5 (Dec. 1, 1844): 735.
3. Anderson, *Memoirs,* 37.
4. Walker, *United by Faith,* 279.
5. Smith, *History of the Church,* 7:567.
6. McGavin, *Nauvoo Temple,* 53.
7. Anderson, *Memoirs,* 28.
8. Anderson, *Memoirs,* 28.
9. Anderson, *Memoirs,* 28.
10. Nels Madsen, "Visit to Mrs. Emma Smith Bidamon," Nov. 27, 1931, MS 852, LDS Church Archives, Salt Lake City.

CHAPTER THIRTY-TWO

1. Anderson, *Memoirs,* 39.
2. Anderson, *Memoirs,* 39.
3. Anderson, *Memoirs,* 39.
4. John Bernhisel statement, preserved in extracts from the Diary of L. John Nuttall, Sept. 10, 1879, BX 8670.1.N963t, L. Tom Perry Special Collections, Brigham Young University, Provo, Utah, 335–36; some punctuation standardized.
5. Dr. John Bernhisel to Emma Smith, Nauvoo, Illinois, Oct. 9, 1847, P4, f29, Emma Smith Papers, Community of Christ Archives, Independence, Missouri.
6. Anderson, *Memoirs,* 38.
7. Anderson, *Memoirs,* 42.
8. Anderson, *Memoirs,* 42.
9. Anderson, *Memoirs,* 42.
10. Nancy J. Tharpe, "Reminiscence of Sister N. J. Tharpe, *Journal of History* 11 (Jan. 1918): 120.

11. Youngreen, *Reflections of Emma,* 40.
12. Crawford, Notes, MS 125, box 1, folder 13, University of Utah, 19.
13. Crawford, Notes, MS 125, box 1, folder 13, University of Utah, 19.
14. "Nauvoo Observed by William Mulder," *BYU Studies* 32, nos. 1 and 2 (Winter-Spring 1992): 95.
15. Anderson, *Memoirs,* 44.

CHAPTER THIRTY-THREE

1. Emma Smith Bidamon to Lewis C. Bidamon, Jan. 7, 1850, Emma Smith Papers, P4, f30, Community of Christ Archives, Independence, Missouri.
2. Crawford, Notes, MS 125, box 1, folder 13, University of Utah, 20.
3. Youngreen, *Reflections of Emma,* 83.
4. Joseph Smith III to John M. Bernhisel, Jan. 24, May 7, and Aug. 6, 1856, MS 370 fd 4, microfilm of holograph, LDS Church Archives, Salt Lake City; paragraphing altered.
5. Briggs, *Early History,* 446.
6. Briggs, *Early History,* 448.
7. Briggs, *Early History,* 449–50.
8. Briggs, *Early History,* 452–53.
9. Briggs, *Early History,* 453–54.
10. Crawford, Notes, MS 125, box 1, University of Utah; spelling standardized.
11. Emma Smith to Joseph Smith III, Nauvoo, Illinois, Dec. 2, 1867, Emma Smith Papers, P4, f16, Community of Christ Archives, Independence, Missouri.
12. Smith, *Life of Joseph F. Smith,* 198.

CHAPTER THIRTY-FOUR

1. Crawford, Notes, MS 125, box 1, folder 13, University of Utah.
2. Crawford, Notes, MS 125, box 1, folder 13, University of Utah, 20.
3. Emma Smith to Joseph Smith III, Nauvoo, Illinois, Jan. 20, 1867, Emma Smith Papers, P4, f13, Community of Christ Archives, Independence, Missouri.

4. Crawford, Notes, MS 125, box 1, folder 13, University of Utah.

5. Crawford, Notes, MS 125, box 1, folder 13, University of Utah, 12.

6. Crawford, Notes, MS 125, box 1, folder 13, University of Utah.

7. Crawford, Notes, MS 125, box 1, folder 13, University of Utah.

8. Crawford, Notes, MS 125, box 1, folder 13, University of Utah.

9. Emma Smith to Joseph Smith III, Nauvoo, Illinois, Feb. 2, 1866, Emma Smith Papers, P4, f14, Community of Christ Archives, Independence, Missouri.

10. Emma Smith to Joseph Smith III, Emma Smith Papers, P4, f13, Community of Christ Archives, Independence, Missouri.

11. Edmund C. Briggs, "A Visit to Nauvoo in 1856," *Journal of History* 9 (Oct. 1916): 458.

12. Charles E. Bidamon to Warren L. Van Dine, Sept. 9, 1940, P13, f1741, Community of Christ Archives, Independence, Missouri; paragraphing altered.

CHAPTER THIRTY-FIVE

1. Newell and Avery, *Mormon Enigma,* 299.

2. Joseph S. Jemison, statement, Aug. 29, 1940, Biographical Folder Collection, P21, f73, Community of Christ Archives, Independence, Missouri; some paragraphs combined.

3. "Recollections of Nauvoo," *Des Moines (IA) Register and Leader,* June 13, 1907, reprinted in *Saints' Herald* 54 (June 19, 1907): 541–42.

4. Gracia N. Jones, "My Great-Great-Grandmother, Emma Hale Smith," *Ensign,* Aug. 1992, 37.

5. Crawford, Notes, MS 125, box 1, University of Utah.

6. Lorenzo Snow to Francis M. Lyman, Aug. 10, 1901, First Presidency letterpress copybooks, Jan. 1901–May 1902, vol. 36, LDS Church Archives, Salt Lake City.

CHAPTER THIRTY-SIX

1. Alexander H. Smith, "Second Coming of Christ, the Home of the Redeemed," *Zion's Ensign* (Dec. 31, 1903): 4, 6–7.

2. Alexander Smith to Lizzie Smith, Apr. 27, 1879, in Crawford, Notes, box 1, folder 1, University of Utah, 34.

3. Alexander H. Smith, "Second Coming of Christ, the Home of the Redeemed," *Zion's Ensign* (Dec. 31, 1903): 7.

4. Alexander H. Smith, "Second Coming of Christ, the Home of the Redeemed," *Zion's Ensign* (Dec. 31, 1903): 7.

5. Crawford, Notes, MS 125, box 1, folder 13, University of Utah, 19.

6. Obituary of Emma Smith Bidamon, *Saints' Herald* 11 (June 1, 1879).

7. Anderson, *Memoirs,* 186.

8. Anderson, *Memoirs,* 186.

EPILOGUE

1. Young, *Journal of Discourses,* 17:159.

2. Young, *Journal of Discourses,* 8:69.

3. Ludlow, et al., *Encyclopedia of Mormonism,* 4:1326.

Books Cited

Allen, James B., and Glen M. Leonard. *The Story of the Latter-day Saints.* 2d ed. Salt Lake City: Deseret Book, 1992.

Anderson, Karl Ricks. *Joseph Smith's Kirtland: Eyewitness Accounts.* Salt Lake City: Deseret Book, 1989.

Anderson, Mary Audentia Smith. *Ancestry and Posterity of Joseph Smith and Emma Hale.* Independence, Mo.: Herald Publishing House, 1929.

———. *The Memoirs of President Joseph Smith III, 1832–1914.* Independence, Mo.: Price Publishing, 2001.

Andrus, Hyrum L., and Helen M. Andrus, comps. *They Knew the Prophet.* Salt Lake City: Bookcraft, 1974.

Bean, Willard. *A.B.C. History of Palmyra and the Beginning of "Mormonism."* Palmyra, N.Y.: Palmyra Courier Co., 1938.

Black, Susan Easton, and Harvey Bischoff Black. *Annotated Record of Baptisms for the Dead, 1840–1845, Nauvoo, Hancock County, Illinois.* 6 vols. Provo, Utah: Brigham Young University Press, 2002.

Blackman, Emily C. *History of Susquehanna County, Pennsylvania.* Philadelphia, Pa.: Claxton, Remsen, & Haffelfinger, 1873.

Bradford, William. *Of Plymouth Plantation, 1620–1647.* Edited by Samuel Eliot Morison. New York: Random House, 1952.

Briggs, Edmund C. *Early History of the Reorganization.* Independence, Mo.: Price Publishing, 1998.

Church History in the Fulness of Times. Institute manual prepared by the Church Educational System. Rev. ed. Salt Lake City: The Church of Jesus Christ of Latter-day Saints, 1992.

Clarke, Albert. Program of the Centennial Celebration of the Methodist Episcopal Church, Lanesboro, Pennsylvania, 3–5 Mar. 1912.

Classic Experiences and Adventures. Salt Lake City: Bookcraft, 1969.

Cook, Lyndon W., ed. *David Whitmer Interviews: A Restoration Witness.* Orem, Utah: Grandin Book, 1991.

Cowley, Matthias F. *Wilford Woodruff: History of His Life and Labors As Recorded in His Daily Journals.* Salt Lake City: Deseret News, 1909.

Ehat, Andrew F. "Joseph Smith's Introduction of Temple Ordinances and the 1844 Succession Question." Master's thesis, Brigham Young University, Provo, Utah, 1982.

Godfrey, Kenneth W., Audrey M. Godfrey, and Jill Mulvay Derr. *Women's Voices: An Untold History of the Latter-day Saints, 1830–1900.* Salt Lake City: Deseret Book, 1982.

Hill, Donna. *Joseph Smith, the First Mormon.* Midvale, Utah: Signature Books, 1977.

History of Geauga and Lake Counties, Ohio. Philadelphia: J. B. Lippincott and Co., 1878.

Jenson, Andrew. *Latter-day Saint Biographical Encyclopedia.* 4 vols. 1901. Reprint, Salt Lake City: Western Epics, 1971.

Jones, Gracia N. *Emma's Glory and Sacrifice: A Testimony.* Hurricane, Utah: Homestead, 1987.

Jones, Gracia N., and Janice F. DeMille. *History of Fredonia, Arizona, 1885–1985.* Hurricane, Utah: Homestead, 1986.

Journal of Discourses. 26 vols. London: Latter-day Saints' Book Depot, 1854–86.

Kennedy, Inez. *Recollections of the Pioneers of Lee County.* Dixon, Ill.: Inez A. Kennedy, 1893.

Larson, Andrew Karl. *Erastus Snow: The Life of a Missionary and Pioneer for the Early Mormon Church.* Salt Lake City: University of Utah Press, 1971.

Ludlow, Daniel H., ed. *Encyclopedia of Mormonism.* 4 vols. New York: Macmillan, 1992.

McGavin, E. Cecil. *Nauvoo, the Beautiful.* Salt Lake City: Bookcraft, 1972.

———. *The Nauvoo Temple.* Salt Lake City: Deseret Book, 1962.

Newell, Linda King, and Valeen Tippetts Avery. *Mormon Enigma: Emma Hale Smith.* New York: Doubleday, 1994.

Parry, Edwin F., comp. *Stories about Joseph Smith the Prophet.* Salt Lake City: Deseret News Press, 1951.

Porter, Larry C. *A Study of the Origins of The Church of Jesus Christ of Latter-day Saints in the States of New York and Pennsylvania, 1816–1831.* Dissertations in Latter-day Saint History Series. Provo, Utah: Brigham Young University, 2000.

Porter, Larry C., and Susan Easton Black, eds. *The Prophet Joseph: Essays on the Life and Mission of Joseph Smith.* Salt Lake City: Deseret Book, 1988.

Porter, Larry C., Milton V. Backman Jr., and Susan Easton Black, eds. *New York.* Regional Studies in Latter-day Saint History Series. Provo, Utah: Brigham Young University Department of Church History and Doctrine, 1992.

Pratt, Parley P. *Autobiography of Parley P. Pratt.* Edited by Scot Facer Proctor and Maureen Jensen Proctor. Revised and enhanced edition. Salt Lake City: Deseret Book, 2000.

Roberts, B. H. *A Comprehensive History of The Church of Jesus Christ of Latter-day Saints, Century One.* 6 vols. Salt Lake City: The Church of Jesus Christ of Latter-day Saints, 1930.

———. *The Missouri Persecutions.* Salt Lake City: Bookcraft, 1965.

Smith, Joseph. *History of The Church of Jesus Christ of Latter-day Saints.* Edited by B. H. Roberts. 7 vols. 2d ed. rev. Salt Lake City: The Church of Jesus Christ of Latter-day Saints, 1932–51.

———. *Personal Writings of Joseph Smith.* Compiled and edited by Dean C. Jessee. Revised edition. Salt Lake City: Deseret Book, 2002.

Smith, Joseph F., and Richard C. Evans. *Blood Atonement and the Origin of Plural Marriage: A Discussion.* Salt Lake City and Independence, Mo.: Deseret News Press and Zion's Printing and Publishing, 1905.

Smith, Joseph Fielding. *Doctrines of Salvation.* Compiled by Bruce R. McConkie. 3 vols. Salt Lake City: Bookcraft, 1954–56.

———. *Life of Joseph F. Smith, Sixth President of the Church of Jesus Christ of Latter-day Saints.* Salt Lake City: Deseret News Press, 1938.

Smith, Lucy Mack. *History of Joseph Smith by His Mother, Lucy Mack Smith: The Unabridged Original Version.* Compiled by R. Vernon Ingleton. Provo, Utah: Stratford Books, 2005.

———. *History of Joseph Smith by His Mother, Lucy Mack Smith.* Edited by Preston Nibley. Salt Lake City: Bookcraft, 1958.

————. *History of the Prophet Joseph by His Mother, Lucy Smith.* Edited by George A. Smith and Elias Smith. Salt Lake City: Improvement Era, 1902.

————. *The Revised and Enhanced History of Joseph Smith by His Mother.* Edited by Scot Facer Proctor and Maurine Jensen Proctor. Salt Lake City: Bookcraft, 1996.

Snow, Eliza R. *Biography and Family Record of Lorenzo Snow.* Salt Lake City: Deseret News, 1884.

Stocker, Rhamanthus M. *Centennial History of Susquehanna County, Pennsylvania.* Baltimore, Md.: Regional Publishing Company, 1974.

Taylor, John. *The Gospel Kingdom.* Edited by G. Homer Durham. Salt Lake City: Deseret Book, 1943.

Tullidge, Edward W. *The Women of Mormondom.* New York, 1877. Reprint, Salt Lake City, 1997.

Vogel, Dan, comp. and ed. *Early Mormon Documents.* 5 vols. Salt Lake City: Signature Books, 1996–2002.

Von Wymetal, Wilhelm Ritter. *Joseph Smith, the Prophet, His Family and His Friends.* Salt Lake City: Tribune Printing and Publishing Company, 1886.

Walker, Kyle R. *United by Faith.* American Fork, Utah: Covenant Communications, 2005.

Whitney, Orson F. *Life of Heber C. Kimball.* Salt Lake City: Stevens & Wallis, 1945.

Woodruff, Wilford. *Leaves from My Journal.* 1882. Reprint, American Fork, Utah: Covenant Communications, 2005.

————. *Wilford Woodruff's Journal.* Edited by Scott G. Kenney. 9 vols. Midvale, Utah: Signature Books, 1983.

Young, Brigham. *Manuscript History of Brigham Young, 1801–1844.* Compiled by Elden Jay Watson. Salt Lake City: Smith Secretarial Service, 1968.

Youngreen, Buddy. *Reflections of Emma, Joseph Smith's Wife.* 3d ed. Provo, Utah: Maasai, 2001.

Index